Cross-National Public Opi
about Homosexuality

Cross-National Public Opinion about Homosexuality

Examining Attitudes across the Globe

Amy Adamczyk

UNIVERSITY OF CALIFORNIA PRESS

University of California Press, one of the most
distinguished university presses in the United States,
enriches lives around the world by advancing scholarship
in the humanities, social sciences, and natural sciences. Its
activities are supported by the UC Press Foundation and
by philanthropic contributions from individuals and
institutions. For more information, visit www.ucpress.edu.

University of California Press
Oakland, California

Library of Congress Cataloging-in-Publication Data

Names: Adamczyk, Amy, 1974– author.
Title: Cross-national public opinion about homosexuality :
  examining attitudes across the globe / Amy Adamczyk.
Description: Oakland, California : University of
  California Press, [2017] | Includes bibliographical
  references and index.
Identifiers: LCCN 2016033504 (print) | LCCN 2016034743
  (ebook) | ISBN 9780520288751 (cloth : alk. paper) |
  ISBN 9780520288768 (pbk. : alk. paper) |
  ISBN 9780520963597 (ebook)
Subjects: LCSH: Homosexuality—Public opinion—
  Cross-cultural studies. | Homosexuality—Religious
  aspects—Cross-cultural studies.
Classification: LCC HQ76.25 .A33 2017 (print) |
  LCC HQ76.25 (ebook) | DDC 306.76/6—dc23
LC record available at https://lccn.loc.gov/2016033504

Manufactured in the United States of America

26 25 24 23 22 21 20 19 18 17
10 9 8 7 6 5 4 3 2 1

For Donald

Contents

Illustrations

TABLES

Introduction

Patterns across Nations, Mixed Methods,
and the Selection of Countries

In 2010 the Ugandan newspaper *Rolling Stone* printed the names of one hundred gays and lesbians along with their photos, addresses, and a subtitle that read "Hang Them" (Muhame 2010). In Uganda, which is a Christian-majority country, 95% of residents say that religion is very important (Pew-Templeton Global Religious Futures Project 2011). Homosexuality[1] carries a prison sentence, and the publication was devastating for the individuals identified. Violence followed, and several people who were named in the paper were attacked. One of the victims was the outspoken Ugandan gay rights activist David Kato, who was beaten to death in his home with a hammer (Gettleman 2011). Several other Ugandans have reported being brutally attacked and raped by community members and the police once their same-sex relationships were discovered (Day 2011).

In addition to threats of physical abuse, there are many social and mental challenges to living in a nation that is hostile to homosexuality. As one gay Ugandan refugee explains, "It was difficult because you cannot be open [about your sexuality]. You can't socialise like any other person. A lot of the time, you have to keep your distance. You feel you're not yourself. It makes things really hard" (Day 2011). Public-opinion data reveal that 91% of Ugandans say that homosexuality is never justified, and government officials have been supportive of residents' views. James Nsaba Buturo, who was Uganda's well-known minister of ethics and integrity and describes himself as a devout Christian, has said, "Homosexuals can forget about human rights" (Gettleman 2011).

In sharp contrast, in 2001 the Netherlands became the first nation in the world to make it legal for same-sex couples to marry and adopt children (Eccleston 2001). Ever since, same-sex couples from around the globe who want to get married have flocked to the Netherlands. As the Dutch politician Vera Bergkamp explains, "Gay marriage is Holland's best export product because we have shown that it is possible." With only 16 percent of residents reporting that homosexuality is *never* justified, the Netherlands is often portrayed as a very friendly place for gay people, and the government is keen on maintaining its reputation. The Dutch government provides financial support for local lesbian, gay, bisexual, transgender, and queer (LGBTQ) organizations in countries where these individuals are at risk, it offers protection for people who are being threatened because of their sexual behaviors or identity, and it has been lobbying for mutual recognition of same-sex marriages within the European Union (Government of the Netherlands, n.d.). At the same time, the Netherlands, along with other European nations, has been accused of promoting a neocolonial agenda that depicts its people as the saviors of Africa's homosexual community and frames individual rights as more important than other, more basic needs (El-Tayeb 2011; Martina 2013).[2]

The contrast between Uganda and the Netherlands illustrates the massive divide in public opinion about homosexuality across the globe. Figure 1 presents a map of the world using World Values Survey (WVS) for the percentage of residents within each nation who report that homosexuality is never justified. Throughout much of the Global North a minority of people (less than 41%) feel that homosexuality is never justified. The percentage increases in places like Russia, India, and China, going as high as 75%. In Africa, the Middle East, and parts of Southeast Asia attitudes become much more conservative, with over 75% of people disapproving of homosexuality.

Why are there such big differences in public opinion about homosexuality? Part of the answer comes in understanding how national characteristics shape individuals' attitudes. Disapproval of homosexuality is not randomly distributed across the world's countries. Rather, there are patterns in how nations tend to cluster in regard to attitudes. Some of the poorest societies in the world are found in Africa, where residents have some of the least supportive attitudes. Conversely, many nations located in the Americas and Europe not only have some of the friendliest atti-

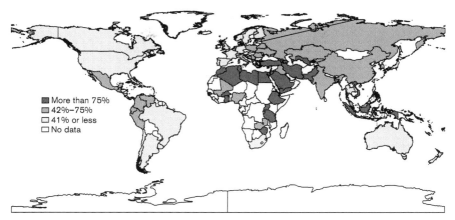

FIGURE I. Map of the percentage of residents in each nation who say homosexuality is *never* justified. (Society N = 87)

SOURCE: WVS, waves 4, 5, and 6.

NOTE: Attitudes have been evenly divided into three groups, with 29 nations in each key category.

tudes, but are particularly wealthy and have long-standing and well-functioning democracies. The relationship between societal characteristics, like a nation's religious culture (i.e., dominant religion and mean level of religious importance) and level of economic development (i.e., GDP), and individuals' attitudes is referred to as the *macro-micro link* (Coleman 1986; Collins 1981; Hazelrigg 1991). Much social science research has been devoted to understanding how a nation's surrounding culture (e.g., a nation's religious climate) and structures (e.g., laws and policies) influence action, and how individuals' actions combine to shape the larger culture. The research that I present follows this previous work in considering the influence of the surrounding culture and structures, as well as the role of individual factors, in shaping attitudes about homosexuality.

While national characteristics can influence individuals' attitudes, when the public feels that a given issue is particularly important their opinions can drive public policy (Burstein 2003). Coleman (1986) describes this as "the process through which individual preferences become collective choices; the process through which dissatisfaction becomes revolution" (1312). It is no coincidence that the vast majority of Ugandans disapprove of homosexuality, and the Ugandan government recently imposed a fourteen-year prison sentence for people caught having same-sex sexual relationships. Similarly, just as Americans' attitudes

TABLE I   PERCENTAGE OF SOCIETIES SUPPORTIVE OF HOMOSEXUALITY, BY THE
LEGAL STATUS OF HOMOSEXUALITY *(SOCIETY* N = *87)*

	National support for homosexuality		
Laws	Unsupportive	Mean level of support	Supportive
Homosexuality illegal	73%	23%	4%[a]
Homosexuality legal (but not union)	27%	51%	22%
Marriage or marriage-like union allowed	0%	17%	83%

SOURCES: WVS, waves 4, 5, and 6; ILGA 2015 (in Carroll and Itaborahy 2015).

NOTE: "Unsupportive" indicates the 30% of countries where the largest proportions of residents said that homosexuality is never justified. "Supportive" indicates the 30% of countries where the smallest proportions of residents said that homosexuality is never justified.

[a]The exception is Singapore, where 41% (average for assailable years) report that homosexuality is not justified, and homosexuality is illegal for men.

have become vastly more liberal in the past twenty-five years, American policies have adjusted accordingly. In 1990 76% of Americans said that sexual relations between two adults of the same sex are always wrong, and up until 1993 gay and lesbian military personnel could be discharged if the government discovered them having a same-sex sexual relationship. In 1993 "Don't ask, don't tell" became law, making it easier for these individuals to remain in the military as long as they did not make public their sexual orientation. By 2011 only 46% of Americans thought that same-sex relations were always wrong (Bowman, Rugg, and Marsico 2013). This same year "Don't ask, don't tell" was repealed, making it possible for gay and lesbian military members to serve openly.

The relationship between attitudes and laws is not always as closely connected as it appears in the United States, but typically there is a strong correlation. In table 1, I present the relationship between residents' support for homosexuality within nations and information on laws and policies regulating homosexuality from ILGA (the International Lesbian, Gay, Bisexual, Trans and Intersex Association). Consistent with the idea that public opinion is associated with and in some cases drives laws and policies, 73% of nations classified as having unsupportive residents have made homosexuality illegal. In contrast, there are no nations where residents are unsupportive *and* same-sex marriage or a marriage-like relationship is allowed. Conversely, 83% of societies that are supportive of homosexuality allow for same-sex marriage or a marriage-like union.

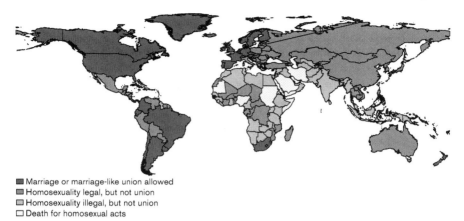

Marriage or marriage-like union allowed
Homosexuality legal, but not union
Homosexuality illegal, but not union
Death for homosexual acts

FIGURE 2. Map of laws regarding homosexuality throughout the world as of 2015. (Society N = 253)
SOURCE: ILGA 2015 (in Carroll and Itaborahy 2015).

Like the variation found in attitudes, nations that have the harshest penalties for homosexuality tend to share some of the same characteristics, such as being located in Africa or the Middle East and having a high proportion of residents who say religion is important. In figure 2, I present a map of the world with four different types of laws related to homosexuality. In countries like Kenya and Morocco, people can be imprisoned for having same-sex relationships. In Yemen, Iran, and Saudi Arabia, homosexuality for some people (e.g., Muslims) is punishable with death (Itaborahy 2012). In contrast, nations located in Europe and the Americans have put forth laws that allow gay and lesbian couples to enter a marriage-like union, which includes many or even all of the same legal benefits as a traditional marriage. Consistent with the laws, these nations also have some of the most approving attitudes about homosexuality. Once polices and laws are in place, they can take on a life of their own, further shaping how residents view homosexuality and interact with lesbian, gay, bisexual, and transgender individuals. Laws related to homosexuality can influence whether people who are attracted to the same sex reveal their sexual orientation to family and friends, and feel comfortable building a life with a gay or lesbian partner. Likewise, the extent to which nations have public opinion and laws that support homosexuality can shape the likelihood that gay subcultures will arise, TV shows will include nontraditional characters, and children with heterosexual parents will meet those from families with homosexual parents.

There has been a lot of research on the history of policies and laws regarding homosexuality within a single country (d'Emilio 2012; Epprecht 2013; Munro 2012), and there have also been comparisons between a few nations (De la Dehesa 2010) on homosexuality-related topics.[3] However, there is a lack of understanding of the major influences that shape differences in how residents across the globe view homosexuality. Factors like economic inequality (Andersen and Fetner 2008b), overall levels of education (Štulhofer and Rimac 2009), and a high number of human rights organizations (Hadler 2012) (e.g., Amnesty international) have been proposed as important reasons why countries vary so much in how residents feel about homosexuality and the laws they enact.

For some nations, characteristics like the number of human rights organizations, or the relationship between political parties and LGBTQ organizations, may be particularly important for changing homosexuality-related policies and public opinion (Hadler 2012). But these factors may be unique to only a few countries rather than a wide variety of nations across the globe. Additionally, a more parsimonious dimension, like democracy, may capture many of the processes (e.g., number of human rights organizations, relationship between LGBTQ and political organizations) that contribute to more acceptance. In the next two chapters I show that the strength of a nation's democratic institutions, its level of economic development, and its religious context can explain a lot of the differences across the world in levels of acceptance.

While these factors are important in explaining cross-national variation, the way that they shape attitudes varies substantially. Each nation has a different story to tell about the processes through which economic development, democracy, and religion shape public opinion. In the United States, for example, democratic principles, including freedom of speech, and a lot of free time and entertainment funds, have led to a cornucopia of gay-friendly television shows, movies, politicians, and celebrities that have connected with people all over this large nation, as well as many other people throughout the world. As a result, even Americans who are unlikely to personally know an openly gay person have connected with popular gay and lesbian media personalities, like Will from the television show *Will & Grace,* contributing to increasing support for homosexuality (Garretson 2009; Loftus 2001). Likewise, for over twenty years American celebrities have been "coming out" to the public on a regular basis. Hence, when Anderson Cooper, a well-known American news commentator, announced in 2012 that he is gay, the public expressed relatively little surprise. As a reporter for the *National Post* explained, "Coming out no longer commands the Ellen Degeneres 'I'm Gay' magazine cover splash. Nor does it stir the kind of shock and surprise that met Hollywood leading man Rock Hudson when his homosexuality became widely known" (Boesveld 2012).

In contrast to the United States, South Africa is less economically developed and only recently became democratic. Nevertheless, almost ten years before the United States, South Africa legalized gay marriage. In both South Africa and the United States democracy has been a key force in shaping laws and policies. However, it has manifested itself differently in these two nations. Because of the brutal history of apartheid, when South Africans first developed their constitution in the 1990s, they included a statement that forbids discrimination on the basis of sexual orientation. This statement was a precursor to the same-sex marriage bill, which was passed in 2006. The logic was that under apartheid the vast majority of South Africans had been denied basic civil rights and liberties. With the new constitution they did not want anyone to be excluded (Botha and Cameron 1997; Croucher 2002), and a similar logic was used in passing the nation's same-sex marriage law. The key point is that democracy and economic development are likely to be underlying forces that shape public opinion within nations, but the processes, institutions, and organizations through which they have an effect are unique to that specific nation's or region's history and cultural context.

With the research presented in this book my aim is to provide insight into the major factors that shape cross-national differences in how residents feel about homosexuality. I give attention to both the general individual and country characteristics that shape public opinion about homosexuality across nations, but also to the way these factors work within specific countries and combine with a nation's unique history and social context to shape attitudes, laws, policies, and enforcement regarding homosexuality.

MIXING METHODS AND CROSS-NATIONAL RESEARCH

Throughout the book I take a mixed-methods approach to examining the factors that shape cross-national public opinion about homosexuality. The different methods include cross-national analysis of quantitative data (i.e., survey and institution data), comparative country case studies, content analysis of newspaper articles, and qualitative interviews. For the cross-national analysis of public opinion, I use the fourth, fifth, and sixth waves of the World Values Survey (WVS),[4] which include almost 85% of the world's population. In the following section I provide more information on how the book's research methods—specifically, the cross-national analysis and case studies—fit together.

With my cross-national analysis of the WVS, I use hierarchical modeling techniques to examine dozens of societies with the goal of isolating relationships that are discernible across many countries. My aim is to confirm or refute broad theoretical explanations. This approach tries to be as parsimonious as possible so that the fewest number of factors are used to explain the biggest patterns, emphasizing generality over complexity (Ragin 2014). Rather than identify the unique individual and historical factors that have shaped attitudes over time within a single country, the goal is to explain general patterns across many nations. Because significance tests tend to favor rejecting rather than accepting theoretical relationships, quantitative analysis techniques tend to be more conservative in making empirical generalizations than other research approaches, like case studies (Ragin 2014).

One weakness of cross-national analyses of quantitative data is that the findings can become overly general and abstract. For example, in the second chapter I explain that economic development is an important factor in explaining differences between many nations in how residents view homosexuality. Insights drawn from the work of Hofstede (2001), Schwartz (1999, 2006) and Inglehart (2006, 1997) provide the theoretical rationale for understanding why economic development shapes attitudes, but it is unclear how these processes play out within individual nations. An alternative to cross-national quantitative analysis is the comparative case-study design, where only a few nations are examined at the same time and the research is focused on finding similarities and differences among select countries (Lor 2011).

Case studies in general tend to provide a lot more detail (i.e., "thick description") and complexity than quantitative cross-national analyses. They also tend to focus on the specific actions of organizations (e.g., Spain's Izquierda Unida) and individuals (e.g., Matthew Shepard, Nelson Mandela's support for gays and lesbians) at particular historical junctures (e.g., the end of Franco's rule) rather than structural influences (e.g., economic development), which tend to dominate explanations derived from cross-national quantitative analyses (Ragin 2014). A case-oriented approach works best when the number of cases is small (Gerring 2007). A comparison of two or three cases is manageable, but with too many additional cases the complexities and comparisons begin to multiply, making it difficult to support claims and not see every country as completely unique (Ragin 2014).

The research presented in this book combines these two approaches. In the first two chapters I use a cross-national analysis of quantitative data to isolate patterns across many nations. These analyses reveal that democracy, economic development, and the religious context of a nation are the most powerful factors for understanding cross-national attitudinal differences. To better understand unique actions and how larger differences identified in the quantitative analysis play out within individual nations, in chapters 3, 4, and 5, I provide comparative case studies.

For combining the cross-national quantitative analysis with the comparative case studies, an explanatory sequential design is employed and proceeds with two successive phases of data collection (Creswell 2004; Creswell et al. 2003). First, the quantitative data are analyzed and findings established. Second, I use a set of nations from the WVS sample for additional comparison. The dimensions of comparison (i.e., democracy, economic development, and a nation's religious context) are drawn from the quantitative findings (Creswell et al. 2003). I use case-study analysis techniques for three nations with a substantial number of mainline and conservative Protestants (i.e., chapter 3), for three Muslim-majority nations (i.e., chapter 4), and for three Catholic-majority countries (chapter 5). Each set of case-study nations focuses on a given dominant religion—in part, to hold it constant so that other macro-level processes (e.g., economic development) can be examined (Lor 2011). Hence, in the analysis of nations with a high proportion of Protestants, all three countries share the same dominant faith (i.e., Protestantism), as well as other characteristics (e.g., English as the official language), but differ in their geographic location as well as their level of economic development, history of democracy, and residents' attitudes toward homosexuality. By holding the dominant religion constant in these chapters, I can show more clearly how other key dimensions are shaping attitudes.

In the three case-study chapters, the discussion about each nation is divided into sections that focus on the influences of religious salience, economic development, and democracy. I also give attention to other factors (e.g., proximity to Europe, the influence of the United Nations, spread of HIV/AIDS) that may be important within a given country or set of nations, but cannot be found across the entire dataset of countries either because the factor is not relevant for all countries or because the data to examine the influence are unavailable for the large sample. When possible I use additional quantitative data in the comparative case-study chapters to assess changes over time or to show how, for example, a given Muslim-majority country compares with other nations that have a substantial proportion of Muslims.

The information used to construct the case studies comes from a close reading of the existing literature, research, and legal documents on homosexuality-related issues in each nation, as well as additional quantitative data (e.g., government favoritism of religion) when they are available. Additionally, in the case studies of nations with substantial proportions of Protestants (chapter 3) and Muslims (chapter 4), my research team and I coded hundreds of articles to compare how the prominent papers in these nations frame homosexuality and whom they use as claimsmakers. (See appendix D for details on the data collection and analysis.) The newspaper analysis also draws on a mixed-methods design, where a close reading of several articles initially led to the categories for the frames (e.g., religion, human rights, Western influences) and claimsmakers (e.g., religious officials, social-movement leaders). Once we quantitatively coded all of the newspapers, the findings were unpacked by reading select articles that could provide additional insight.

Finally, in chapters 6 and 7, I focus on the national-level factors shaping public opinion about homosexuality in Confucian societies (i.e., places with strong Chinese cultural and historical influence). Again, a sequential explanatory design is employed (Creswell 2004). Chapter 6 uses WVS survey data to assess how Confucian cultures shape residents' attitudes. The key quantitative findings then become the basis for directing several semistructured expert interviews (Bogner, Littig, and Menz 2009) in Taiwan.

HOW WERE THE CASE-STUDY NATIONS SELECTED?

Because the scope of this book is so large, a wide range of nations could have been selected for additional case-study analysis. In the end I chose tens nations: Uganda, South Africa, the United States, Indonesia, Malaysia, Turkey, Italy, Spain, Brazil, and Taiwan. The primary criteria for selecting case-study countries were the extent to which each set provided meaningful variation in attitudes, economic development, democracy, and religious salience. In the next two chapters I will show that these are key factors for explaining cross-national attitudes about homosexuality. For some countries the dominant religion also plays a role in shaping views. However, because economic development, democracy, and religious salience are particularly important across multiple nations, the case-study countries all have the same dominant religion, making it possible to hold this factor constant while these other characteristics are examined.

A number of criteria were used to select the case-study countries. Because I employ a sequential research design, all of the case-study nations needed to be included at least once in one of the three previous waves of WVS data collection. In any given WVS wave, which is conducted approximately every four years, only about a quarter of the world's nations are included. Unfortunately, not all countries ask all questions—most importantly the item regarding justification of homosexuality, which was a requirement for case study inclusion.

The case-study countries also include those where I could get a reasonable amount of information on public opinion. Societies where homosexuality is criminalized often have a lot less information on the public's attitudes. Most people in these nations tend to oppose homosexuality, resulting in little variation in attitudes and in some cases (though not all[5]) little discussion in the public press. For example, in Iran there have been reports that between 1980 and 2000 an estimated four thousand individuals accused of homosexuality have been killed (Spencer 2008), and in 2007 Iran's president, Mahmoud Ahmadinejad, made a speech suggesting that there are no homosexuals in Iran[6] (H. Cooper 2007). In part because of the hostile climate in Iran, there are few discussions about or research on homosexuality, much less the public's attitudes on this highly deviant topic and illegal behavior.

Finally, for the comparative case studies I wanted to include nations with medium to large populations from a variety of regions and places where important attention has been given to homosexuality-related issues. Other countries could certainly have been chosen, but, as it is, a meaningful subset of the world's population is represented. Aside from the ten countries included in the case studies, I also present a large cross-national analysis, which includes eighty-seven nations, and an additional quantitative chapter (i.e., chapter 6) is devoted to Asia, which houses approximately 60% of the world's people.

The Protestant case-study nations, which I discuss in the third chapter, include the United States, South Africa, and Uganda and represent a wide array of views about homosexuality. In addition to being a moderately liberal country, the United States is the third-largest country in the world and will likely be of great interest to many readers. I selected

South Africa because it has a unique history of allowing for same-sex marriage but not always having particularly tolerant views. I chose Uganda because it is highly conservative and in recent years has received massive attention for its draconian homosexuality-related legislation. Uganda (with 37 million inhabitants) and South Africa (53 million) are also relatively large (CIA World Factbook 2015). All three of these nations have populations with high levels of religious belief and a mixture of mainline and conservative Protestant adherents, as well as Catholics. In the next chapter I show that nations with a mixture of Christian groups, especially those that include conservative Protestants, tend to have much more conservative views than residents living in countries, like Sweden and Norway, that are dominated by mainline Protestant denominations. The nations chosen also differ in their levels of economic development and democracy.

In chapter 4, Malaysia, Indonesia, and Turkey are used for a comparative case study of Muslim-majority countries. I selected Indonesia because among Muslim nations it has the largest population (255 million) (CIA World Factbook 2015), and it is relatively conservative, with approximately 90% of residents reporting that homosexuality is never justified (see table 3). Turkey is also large (79 million) (CIA World Factbook 2015), but more moderate and located on the border of Europe and Asia, providing insight into how regional European pressure may be shaping attitudes and policies. Malaysia is more liberal, but located in Asia, moderately sized (30 million) (CIA World Factbook 2015), and is much richer than Indonesia, providing useful insight into how economic development across Muslim nations shapes views.

The chapter on Muslim nations does not give a lot of attention to the most conservative Arab countries, where homosexuality is punished with death. There are a couple of reasons for this. When I first started analyzing the data for this study, the sixth wave of the WVS, which includes many more Muslim nations than previous waves, was not finished. For nations that had data, I had concerns about the validity of survey responses in countries, like Iran, Saudi Arabia, and Yemen, where the governments are particularly harsh in condemning homosexuality. While there is some academic literature on homosexuality in these Arab countries, there is very little on more subtle differences in public opinion. Likewise, in part related to the lack of freedom of the press, homosexuality is minimally discussed in very conservative Arab newspapers and on television, limiting my ability to glean information on the public's views from a media analysis.

The comparison of nations with Catholic cultures appears in chapter 5 and focuses on Spain, Italy, and Brazil. These countries represent a range of views regarding homosexuality, with Italy being the most conservative, Brazil being more moderate, and Spain being the most liberal. These nations also vary in their level of economic development and democracy, span two continents, and have relatively large populations. Brazil, for example, is the fifth-largest country in the world, with over 200 million people, and Spain (48 million) and Italy (61 million) both have relatively large populations (CIA World Factbook 2015). Spain was also of interest because it has been a leader in liberal homosexuality-related legislation. Likewise, Italy houses the Vatican and is considered the home of the Roman Catholic Church.

Following a survey analysis of Confucian cultures in chapter 6, chapter 7 provides an in-depth examination of attitudes about homosexuality in Taiwan. I selected Taiwan for a case study, in part, because the country has a strong research infrastructure that is open to international scholars, and there is some acceptance of homosexuality, which makes asking about the public's attitudes much easier. Taiwan was also included in several waves of the WVS, and I was able to spend time there conducting twenty-six interviews with key claimsmakers who either worked for or volunteered with organizations focused on religion, human rights, homosexuality-related issues, academia, politics, or the media.

The next chapter focuses on how religion, along with several key demographical characteristics, shapes differences in attitudes about homosexuality. Cross-national data from the WVS are used to establish global patterns, and in later chapters I use the case studies to better understand the factors shaping attitudes among individuals in key sets of nations.

PART ONE

Public Opinion across the World

CHAPTER 1

The Importance of Religion, and the Role of Individual Differences

In the United States, the majority of residents report that religion is very important (Pew Research Center 2012a). Additionally, many American city and community ordinances do not allow alcohol to be sold on Sundays (Legal Beer, n.d.), several radio and television stations regularly provide religious programming (Hangen 2002; Hilmes 2013), and along major roads throughout the United States there are billboards with religious messages declaring, "Jesus Christ died for the sins of the world" and "Life is nothing without God" (see Meyer 2013). On Sundays many Americans attend worship services and spend time with other religious people in formal or informal activities (Newport 2015).

While people in the most religious regions of America like the Bible Belt are likely to take their faith very seriously, across the nation residents are quite religious, much more so than in western Europe (Holifield 2014; Pew Research Center 2012a). Somewhat similarly, in many Muslim-majority nations like Morocco and Egypt, the call for prayer rings out across communities five times a day, prompting the majority of Muslims to stop what they are doing to pray (Pew Research Center 2012d). In many Muslim-majority countries, most residents attend mosque at least once a week and fast during the holy month of Ramadan (Pew Research Center 2012d). Conversely, in northern Europe, where historically mainline Protestant faiths like Lutheranism have dominated, many residents do not regularly attend church services or find religion to be very important (Manchin 2004).

Across the globe there is wide variation in the extent to which people are religious and live in places with strong religious cultures. The religion to which one adheres, as well as personal religious importance, has a meaningful influence on feelings about homosexuality. Additionally, differences across national religious contexts can affect attitudes, even for people who are not very religious. In this chapter I examine the roles of personal religious beliefs and the national religious context (i.e., dominant religion and mean level of religious importance), as well as individual demographic characteristics, for shaping public opinion about homosexuality.

MAJOR RELIGIONS' AND FOLLOWERS' ATTITUDES ABOUT HOMOSEXUALITY

Religions tend to vary quite substantially in the extent to which their adherents find homosexuality problematic. In figure 3, I present predicted scores for disapproval of homosexuality by different religious affiliations. The two most conservative religious groups appear to be Protestants and Muslims, followed by Hindus. The most liberal groups are Jews, Catholics, and people with no religious affiliation. Buddhists and Eastern Orthodox Christians fall in the middle. A number of other studies have found some of the same religion differences for homosexuality-related attitudes (Adamczyk and Pitt 2009; Ellison, Acevedo, and Ramos-Wada 2011; van den Akker, van der Ploeg, and Scheepers 2013).

Why do affiliates of Muslim and Protestant faiths appear more likely than others to disapprove of homosexuality? A flawed but reasonable explanation would be that their major religious texts differ in what they say about homosexuality. For Judeo-Christian faiths, homosexual behaviors are explicitly mentioned and condemned in the Bible. For example, the Bible's Old Testament, which is used by both Jews and Christians, declares, "If a man lies with a man as one lies with a woman, both of them have done what is detestable. They must be put to death; their blood will be on their own heads" (Lev. 20:13 [Moo 1973]). Like the Bible, the Qur'an is also clear that homosexuality is problematic: "Do you approach males among the worlds. And leave what your Lord has created for you as mates? But you are a people transgressing" (Qur'an 26:165–66 [Aminah Assami 2011]).

Whereas Judeo-Christian and Muslim religious texts make clear proscriptions regarding homosexuality, Buddhism offers less-explicit guidance. In the Vinaya, which provides the regulations for Buddhist monks,

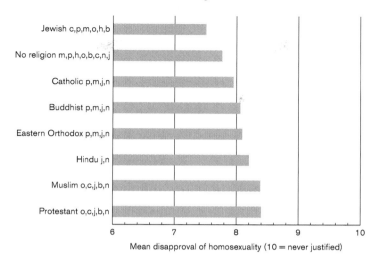

FIGURE 3. Marginal estimates for mean disapproval of homosexuality by religious affiliation. (Society N = 87; individual N = 202,316)

SOURCE: WVS, waves 4, 5, and 6.

NOTE: Whenever multilevel data are used, the range of the dependent variable, which is justification for homosexuality, goes from 0 to 10, where 10 means "never justified." Marginal estimates are presented for a married Protestant man who has completed secondary school and has a mean score on all other individual-level variables in model 2 of table 8 in appendix B. This profile is held constant so religious differences can be assessed. Lowercase letters indicate significant differences (p < .05, two-tail test) between each religious group and the others, where p = Protestant, m = Muslim, h = Hindu, o = Eastern Orthodox, b = Buddhist, c = Catholic, n = no religion, and j = Jewish.

sexual intercourse is prohibited, and this is typically interpreted as including sex with anyone. Hindu texts provide more direction, explicitly stating that homosexual acts require penance. The ancient Hindu code, for example, explains, "A twice-born man who commits an unnatural offence with a male, or has intercourse with a female in a cart drawn by oxen, in water, or in the day-time, shall bathe, dressed in his clothes" (Vinaya 11,174 [Bühler 1886]).

Religions typically have subgroups or denominations that operate under a common name, tradition, or identity. Within Islam, for example, there are Sunni and Shiite Muslims. Finer distinctions could also be made based on the school of Islamic thought (e.g., Hanafi for Sunni Muslims). These narrower categories can be particularly important for understanding differences within the major religions for how adherents view homosexuality. In the WVS, Judeo-Christian faiths are the only ones for which researchers collected more detailed information on subgroups.[1] While all Judeo-Christian faiths use a religious text that explicitly proscribes homosexuality, figure 3 shows that Jews, Catholics, and Eastern Orthodox Christians have not been as successful as Protestants at getting their adherents to form attitudes that are consistent with biblical statements that condemn homosexuality.

The findings about Protestants may seem somewhat surprising because many Protestant adherents in Europe and the United States appear quite liberal, and indeed many are. The reason that Protestants in figure 3 appear to have attitudes that are more similar to those of Muslims rather than of Catholics or Jews likely has to do with the much more traditional views that conservative Protestants have relative to mainline Protestants. Unfortunately, the WVS data do not distinguish between mainline (e.g., Presbyterian Church USA, United Church of Christ, and American Baptist Churches USA) and conservative or Evangelical Protestant denominations (e.g., American Baptist Association, Assemblies of God, Christian Brethren, and American Reformed Presbyterian Church). In a separate analysis I found that, compared with Muslims, Protestants have much greater variation in their attitudes,[2] suggesting that this group is a lot less cohesive. Additionally, research conducted in the United States, which has many diverse Protestant faiths, making it particularly ideal for examining differences, has found that when they are divided into mainline and conservative Protestant groups, the latter are especially likely to disapprove of homosexuality (Finlay and Walther 2003; Fulton, Gorsuch, and Maynard 1999; Hill, Moulton, and Burdette 2004). Conversely, mainline Protestants are more likely to resemble Catholics in their views about homosexuality (Burdette, Ellison, and Hill 2005).

Part of the reason for differences among Protestants is that mainline groups are more likely to interpret the Bible metaphorically and conservative Protestants are more likely to interpret it literally. With a literal interpretation of the Bible, conservative Protestants take a very basic view of the text and are less inclined to update their understanding with a more modern view of the world (Ellison and Musick 1993; Emerson and Hartman 2006; Hunter 1987). Likewise, as I discuss in more detail below, researchers have found that, compared with mainline groups, conservative branches of Protestantism have been growing more rapidly and that in some countries religious decline has been less extreme among conservative Protestants compared with mainline groups (Bibby 1978; D.M. Kelley 1977, 1978). Because conservative Protestants are more likely to interpret the Bible literally, have been more successful at getting their adherents to abide by religious proscriptions, and have been growing faster—and are, therefore, increasing their influence—the entire group of Protestants (conservatives and mainlines) found in figure 3 appears to have attitudes that are more likely to resemble those of Muslims than those of other Judeo-Christian groups.

THE POWER OF RELIGIOUS REWARDS AND COSTS

The less supportive attitudes of Muslims and many Protestants exhibited in figure 3 are consistent with findings from a vast array of empirical studies (Adamczyk and Pitt 2009; Finlay and Walther 2003; Fulton, Gorsuch, and Maynard 1999; van den Akker, van der Ploeg, and Scheepers 2013; Hill, Moulton, and Burdette 2004; Kuyper, Iedema, and Keuzenkamp 2013). Indeed, it is rare to find research showing that Muslims and Protestants, especially those who adhere to more-conservative versions, report friendlier attitudes about homosexuality than other religious groups. The extent to which adherents literally interpret their religious texts can provide some information on differences in attitudes. As I explain below, rational choice perspectives on religion (Finke, Guest, and Stark 1996; Finke and Stark 2005; Iannaccone 1994, 1995; Stark and Finke 2000) are able to offer additional insight into why Muslims and Protestants (likely the more conservative ones) have been so successful at getting their followers to maintain attitudes that are consistent with religious proscriptions.

For much of the twentieth century social scientists generally thought that as nations became more economically developed, religious belief would decline. The idea was that when people began to feel more physically secure (Inglehart and Baker 2000) and were exposed to different religions, they would start questioning their faith, and eventually give up their beliefs for a more "rational" understanding of the world (Berger 2011).[3] Consistent with these ideas, throughout the twentieth century religious belief in Europe—specifically, western Europe—appeared to be declining (Crockett and Voas 2006; Voas 2009; Voas and Crockett 2005). Many early social scientists who thought that religious secularization was occurring (e.g., Durkheim, Weber, Marx, and Freud) resided in Europe. The idea that the world was becoming more secular had a big influence on how they generally viewed religion at that time.

In the latter part of the twentieth century, researchers began to notice that religious belief was not universally declining. In many nations outside of western Europe, religious belief seemed to remain relatively high.

For example, in 1990, 80% of Americans reported that religion is important (WVS 2015). In contrast, in 1990 only 34% of Germany's residents reported that religion was important, in Spain it was 53%, and in Sweden it was 27%. In 2005 the proportion of Americans who found religion important dropped to 70% but was still quite high, especially compared with residents from many western European nations. In addition to relatively high levels of religious belief in many non-European countries, researchers began noticing that many newer religions (Stark and Iannaccone 1997), such as the Jehovah's Witnesses, were expanding (D. M. Kelley 1977, 1978). Likewise, religious fundamentalism seemed to be increasing in places, like Iran, that previously seemed to be secularizing (Almond, Appleby, and Sivan 2003). Finally, in some of the countries from the former Soviet Union (Greeley 1994), which had made great attempts to squelch belief, religious faith appeared to be increasing. The patterns revealed at the end of the twentieth century suggested that religious belief was not universally decreasing. Rather, in some places and for some religions it appeared to be growing.

Researchers working with the "New Paradigm" (C. M. Warner 1993), as it was initially referred to, began to develop alternative thoughts about what contributed to the rise and fall of religious belief. These researchers borrowed ideas from microeconomics to explain why some religions and denominations were much more successful than others at recruiting converts and maintaining their congregations (Finke, Guest, and Stark 1996; Finke and Stark 2005; Iannaccone 1994, 1995; Stark and Finke 2000). Ideas from the New Paradigm can help us understand why people from some religions and denominations are more likely than others to disapprove of homosexuality. The micro basis of these ideas is that people maximize benefits and try to reduce costs, even when they are considering which religion to follow (Iannaccone 1994, 1995; Stark and Finke 2000).

A key reason why people tend to stay in the same religion as their parents is that early religious experiences are likely to shape later religious preferences. For example, people who grew up with traditional organ music may not like religious services where an electric guitar is being played. Likewise, some people may have always felt comfortable with fellow adherents "speaking in tongues" (i.e., glossolalia), which is practiced by some conservative Protestants. However, individuals who are not familiar with it may find it bizarre and unsettling. Because people are typically born into a given faith (Myers 1996), there are high costs, such as disappointing family members and fewer opportunities to socialize with friends, to leaving their religion. Indeed, Ellison and Sherkat (1995) point out that in some places the social and familial obligations to belonging to a given religion may be so strong that regular religious involvement may be perceived as involuntary.

Along with the costs of not belonging to a religion, there are typically a lot of benefits to being involved with a specific faith. By actively participating in a given religion or denomination, many adherents may feel that they will ultimately be rewarded for their devotion with a wonderful afterlife (Iannaccone 1994; Stark and Finke 2000). There are also short-term benefits. In many nations, including Ireland and Poland, religious organizations have been important institutions for organizing citizens around political goals (Bosi 2008; Johnston and Figa 1988). If residents are interested in political or economic change, it can be very useful to be involved with the local religious community. In the United States, for example, the Black church has historically been a key organizer for social and political concerns related to the African-American community (Lincoln and Mamiya 1990).

Additionally, some places of worship offer a warm and friendly group of congregants (Iannaccone 1994), free babysitting during religious activities, language classes, after-school activities for teens (Adamczyk 2012a, 2012b; Adamczyk and Felson 2012), and social, financial, and physical- and mental-health services (Cnaan, Sinha, and McGrew 2004; Twombly 2002). If adherents are encouraged to primarily interact with other religious followers, the religious organization typically provides opportunities to socialize. These occasions may include ice-cream socials, bowling nights, and Sunday-morning breakfasts.

Religions and denominations differ in the extent to which they make demands on their followers and their ability to get their adherents to abide by religious proscriptions (Iannaccone 1994). These demands may include restrictions on food (e.g., not eating pork, beef, or onions), dress (e.g., wearing the hijab), and interactions (e.g., not spending time with unrelated people of the opposite sex). It may seem that having many restrictions would make a religion less desirable. Certainly, there are some religious groups that are particularly strict, and the heavy obligations cause some people to leave. But, as Stark (1996b) and Iannaccone (1994) point out, under the right circumstances the exact opposite may occur. Some people may feel that because they make sacrifices that other people are unwilling to make, they have a particularly special relationship with God.

How do these ideas shed light on differences between religions in how adherents think about homosexuality? Differences in attitudes about homosexuality can partially be explained by the success of different religions and denominations in getting their adherents to abide by religious proscriptions and develop feelings and opinions that are consistent with more-literal interpretations of homosexuality in religious texts. Muslims and conservative Protestants are some of the fastest-growing religious groups (Almond, Appleby, and Sivan 2003; Bibby 1978; D. M. Kelley 1977, 1978). They also appear more successful than others at getting their followers to abide by their demands. A number of studies have found that relative to other major religions, conservative Protestants and Muslims are better able to shape a range of attitudes and behaviors, including those regarding premarital and extramarital sex (Adamczyk and Hayes 2012), alcohol consumption (Adamczyk 2011; Ghandour, Karam, and Maalouf 2009), prostitution (Stack, Adamczyk, and Cao 2010), pornography (Sherkat and Ellison 1997), and abortion (Adamczyk 2008; Evans 2002).

CATHOLICISM, VATICAN II, AND LIBERAL ATTITUDES ABOUT HOMOSEXUALITY

Before discussing the role of religious importance, differences in the views of Catholics and Protestants warrant some attention. In certain parts of the world (e.g., North America and Europe) Catholicism and Protestantism share a lot of similarities and to some extent have competed with each other for adherents. It may seem like Catholics should be more conservative in their attitudes than Protestants—in part because they have some sex-related proscriptions, like birth control and divorce, that many Protestant groups do not share. However, as shown in figure 3, Catholics are significantly more liberal than Protestants in their views about homosexuality. Why are Catholics on average more tolerant than Protestants? There are a couple of reasons for these differences.

Because several nations in the WVS did not make finer distinctions between conservative and mainline Protestants, both groups are combined in figure 3. Protestants appear more conservative, in part, because a substantial proportion of them are likely to take the Bible literally and, as discussed above, their brand of Protestantism generates higher levels of devotion. Catholics and mainline Protestants are more inclined to view the Bible metaphorically. Additionally, in the 1960s the Catholic Church enacted Vatican II, which revised many Catholic rituals and softened restrictions. The church's goal was to provide a more individual-ized and less institutionalized version of Catholicism (Pope 2012; Vati-can II—Voice of the Church, n.d.). However, by making the faith more accessible, Vatican II may have inadvertently reduced the extent to which adherents felt that they were giving a lot to a demanding God who was going to allow only the most ardent believers into his kingdom. Since Vatican II Catholic religious engagement has declined (Ignazi and Well-hofer 2013; Stark and Finke 2000; Stark and Iannaccone 1996), even as many people still claim a Catholic religious and cultural identity.

Since the Catholic Church is clear in its condemnation of homosexu-ality, Catholics who are actively engaged in their faith and take it very seriously are going to be less likely to approve of homosexuality. How-ever, the proportion of Catholics who say their religion is very impor-tant is only 48%, which is much lower than it is for Muslims (78%) and Protestants (60%).[4] If people are born Catholic or in a nation, like Italy or Spain, where the Catholic Church has a long history, many may con-tinue to claim a Catholic identity, even if they do not actively attend religious services or use their faith to inform their attitudes and behav-iors. (See chapter 5.)

THE KEY ROLE OF RELIGIOUS IMPORTANCE IN SHAPING ATTITUDES

So far I have been focused on explaining how adherents of the various major religions differ in their attitudes about homosexuality. As noted above, all major religions have proscriptions regarding homosexuality. Within any of the major religions, people who are highly committed to their faith, regardless of what it is, are going to be more likely to disap-prove of homosexuality (Ellison, Acevedo, and Ramos-Wada 2011; van den Akker, van der Ploeg, and Scheepers 2013; Hill, Moulton, and Bur-dette 2004). Indeed, as I illustrate in figure 4, the extent to which people say religion is important in their lives has a greater influence on their attitudes than the specific religion to which they adhere. As I explain below, there are several processes through which religious importance may shape attitudes (Olson, Cadge, and Harrison 2006; Sherkat et al. 2011; Whitley 2001).

One of the major ways through which religious importance is likely to shape views is through individuals' engagement with a community of other religious believers. Individuals who say that religion is important in their lives are more likely to be physically involved in their faith (Pew

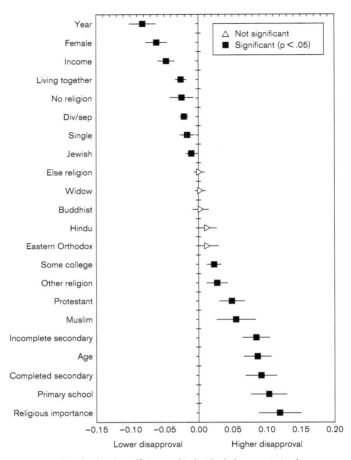

FIGURE 4. Standardized coefficients of individual characteristics for explaining disapproval of homosexuality. (Society N = 87; individual N = 202,316)

SOURCE: WVS, waves 4, 5, and 6.

NOTE: It can be difficult to compare standardized variables for both dummies and interval-level variables from the same model. The standard formula, which is used here, is: Beta = unstandardized coefficient * (standard deviation of the dependent variable / standard deviation of the predictor) (Beta = β (Sx/Sy). One problem with standardizing interval and dummy variables this way is that, although a standard deviation is applicable to interval-level variables, it does not intuitively make sense for dummy variables. To assess relative influence among dummy variables, their untransformed coefficients can be compared with each other. The coefficients used to create this figure were taken from model 1, table 8 in appendix B. The reference category for religious affiliation is "Catholic," for marital affiliation it is "married," and for education it is "completed college."

Research Center 2008). All religions have opportunities for people to engage other adherents through religious classes, services, rituals, and study groups. With these activities religious followers are likely to get formal exposure to how their religion views homosexuality, and all religions have some proscriptions regarding homosexuality. In sermons and speeches some religious leaders may describe homosexuality as a sin or social evil (Adamczyk, Kim, and Paradis 2015). Many religious organizations are also likely to informally disseminate information about issues such as homosexuality through fliers and word-of-mouth, and help organize people from within and outside their congregations to attend public talks and protests related to the morality of homosexuality or the legalization of same-sex relationships (Agadjanian and Menjívar 2008; Miceli 2005; Scheitle and Hahn 2011).

A lot of research has found that, along with formally engaging their faith, individuals who take their religion seriously are likely to develop relationships with other religious followers who may influence their feelings and behaviors (Adamczyk and Felson 2012; Adamczyk and Palmer 2008; Regnerus 2002, 2003). Through social interactions (Akers 2009; Sutherland 1947) with other religious people, adherents learn how to think about and address a given issue. As a result of exposure, observation, and interaction with other religious followers, adherents may come to disapprove of homosexuality. Additionally, when people feel attached to others they are less likely to exhibit attitudes and participate in behaviors about which they think others would disapprove (Hirschi 2009). Finally, a number of studies have found that the more formally and informally religious people are involved with other religious adherents, the less time and energy they have to develop relationships with individuals who may have alternative views (Scheitle and Adamczyk 2009; Schwadel 2005).

Through social learning (Akers 2009; Sutherland 1947) and control processes (Hirschi 2009), religious adherents may develop attitudes that are consistent with religious proscriptions regarding homosexuality. But even if they do not initially support the views of their religion, Kelman's (2006) work suggests that over time they may adopt dominant perspectives to maintain their sense of self and increase the likelihood of a desirable relationship with others whom they value (see also Adamczyk and Hayes 2012). As a result, adherents who belong to a religion that disapproves of homosexuality may adopt the more negative views of the larger group to preserve relationships with other congregants and maintain a self-image based on the expectations of their religious reference group.

SPURIOUS RELATIONSHIPS, RELIGIOUS SWITCHING, AND CHANGES TO RELIGION

Up until this point, religious beliefs and affiliation have been described as *influencing* attitudes, and there is good reason to think that they precede feelings about homosexuality. Most people develop their initial beliefs when they are children. Parents have one of the most important effects on their children's religious faith (Myers 1996; Ozorak 1989), in part, because they control the religion to which their children have access and the extent of their children's involvement, since they will likely bring them to the house of worship. In general, people's level of religious involvement tends to change at least some over their life course, decreasing during young adulthood as they leave home and encounter new experiences, and increasing again as they settle down and begin to have children of their own. Nevertheless, religious affiliation tends to remain stable. Research has found that a relatively small proportion of people switch faiths, especially from stricter denominations to more liberal ones or from one major religion, like Islam, to another, such as Christianity (Barro and Hwang 2008; Scheitle and Adamczyk 2010). Likewise, a key predictor of the strength of people's religious faith is their parents' level of religious belief and engagement (Ruiter and Van Tubergen 2009). Even before children have much understanding of the differences between homosexuality, bisexuality, and heterosexuality, if their parents are religious, they will have been exposed to religion, and initial beliefs are likely to have begun developing (Myers 1996).

While there is good reason to think that religious beliefs precede views about homosexuality, personal experiences, including relationships with openly gay men and lesbians, can affect attitudes about homosexuality, even among religious people. When more-religious individuals encounter ideas or have experiences that make them rethink their views on a given issue, like homosexuality, how do they negotiate the potential discord between their religion and feelings about homosexuality? If religious believers have experiences that suggest that homosexuality is not as morally problematic as their religion argues, they may try to downplay how their faith views homosexuality, focusing instead on their faith's other valuable characteristics.

Additionally, within the same religion and even denomination, there is a range of different perspectives on the morality of homosexuality, depending, in part, on how literally leaders encourage adherents to view religious proscriptions. Religious believers who struggle with inconsistencies between their religion's view and personal feelings about homosexuality may switch to a more accepting or tolerant denomination or house of worship (e.g., church or mosque) within the same religion (e.g., moving from Missouri Synod Lutheran to Evangelical Lutheran). If individuals cannot find a more appealing "brand" of religion that better matches their feelings, they may ultimately leave their faith.

Religions and denominations can also change their stance on homosexuality, which can affect the way adherents feel about homosexuality. For example, over the past thirty years American Evangelical Christians' views on homosexuality have become a little more liberal (J. N. Thomas and Olson 2012), though they are still a lot less tolerant than mainline Protestants and Catholics. This change in the church's perspective appears to be moving very slowly, though in step with society-wide adjustments that have occurred within the United States (Andersen and Fetner 2008a; Loftus 2001). As church leaders, religious publishers, and Christian media outlets put forth more-liberal interpretations on the morality of homosexuality, they may influence how religious believers view homosexuality. There is a dynamic interaction between larger societal perspectives on homosexuality, adherents' feelings about same-sex relationships, and the views put forth by religious organizations, leaders, and publishers.

WHY CONSERVATIVE RELIGIOUS ENVIRONMENTS REDUCE SUPPORT FOR HOMOSEXUALITY

When people think about the influence of religion, they may consider the role that personal religious beliefs play in shaping attitudes. However, the religious beliefs of others can also have a powerful effect on one's own attitudes and behaviors (Adamczyk 2009; Adamczyk and Felson 2006; Adamczyk and Palmer 2008) and how they see the world (Finke and Adamczyk 2008; van den Akker, van der Ploeg, and Scheepers 2013). For understanding cross-national attitudes about homosexuality, the overall strength of religious belief within a nation is particularly important. In appendix B, table 8, model 3, I provide insight into how a nation's overall levels of religious importance shape attitudes. Even after accounting for a range of personal characteristics including personal religious beliefs, as the overall level of religious importance increases, all residents become less accepting of homosexuality.

What is the process through which the national religious context shapes residents' attitudes?[5] The macro religious climate will include some of the power of more-intimate and local religious influences. Hence, when a high proportion of people within a nation find religion important, friendship groups are more likely to be infused with religious people whose views on issues like homosexuality are likely known or assumed. To preserve relationships with other religious people they value and to maintain a self-image based on reference-group expectations, even residents with little religious faith may adopt majority views on moral issues like homosexuality.

Additionally, in more-religious nations both local and national media outlets are likely to reflect dominant religious views, and businesses, schools, and other institutions will be more likely to support religiously inspired preferences, including those that disapprove of homosexuality. In more-religious countries, religious organizations may assume more functions, including organizing social events and coordinating residents to take civic and political action. In some religious nations like Saudi Arabia, religious leaders provide direct input into government decisions, making laws and creating policies that support religious precepts that are likely to condemn homosexuality. Likewise, the more highly religious and conservative people are, the less likely residents will be to encounter ideas and individuals who challenge religion-inspired perspectives regarding homosexuality. The government in more-religious countries may censor newspapers, magazines, and television so that they do not violate religious sensibilities. They may also restrict nonprofit organizations and human rights groups that promote views that are inconsistent with conservative religious precepts. Finally, there may not be any gay bars or other social places for LGBTQ individuals to meet other people who have friendlier attitudes, and there may be limited access to Internet sites where one could get more information about gay and lesbian people.

Even if the macro religious climate is not giving a direct message about the unacceptability of homosexuality, norms and policies related to other "moral" issues such as premarital sex may remind residents that religious precepts are generally supported. For example, Islam discourages the free mixing of the sexes (Muslim Women's League 1999), and many Muslim leaders and adherents support this religious precept. Nations like Saudi Arabia have formally implemented laws and policies that limit the mixing of the sexes, and religious police monitor public interactions (Raphael 2009). As a result, all residents are less likely to see men and women who are unrelated to each other informally interacting in public. But even in nations that do not have such laws, if they have a high proportion of religiously engaged Muslims, religious precepts regarding interactions between the sexes may be informally supported (Adamczyk and Hayes 2012). These religiously inspired restrictions serve to remind both religious and secular residents that they are living in a country where religious precepts related to a range of issues, including homosexuality, are generally upheld.

Differences in the macro religious climate can explain, in part, why there are such big differences in cross-national attitudes about homosexuality. Additionally, because the macro religious context has an effect on attitudes beyond the influence of personal religious beliefs, it may be particularly difficult to change the way a nation's people view homosexuality. Not only would people's understanding of religious precepts regarding homosexuality have to change, but so would the larger culture (e.g., informal norms and values) and structure (e.g., laws, policies, and religious police) so that even less-religious people would come to see homosexuality in a new light.

THE ROLE OF THE DOMINANT RELIGION

In addition to the strength of religious belief within a country, the majority religion is likely to shape attitudes. Most nations are dominated by a single world religion, and only Christianity and Islam are prominent in a large number of nations. In countries like Azerbaijan, Niger, and Senegal, over 95% of people affiliate with Islam. Conversely, in nations such as Namibia, Haiti, and the Democratic Republic of the Congo, less than 1% of people affiliate with Islam and over 90% of people affiliate with Christianity (i.e., Catholicism or Protestantism). While Hinduism and Buddhism have large followings, these faiths dominate a minority of nations, and only in Israel does Judaism dominate.

As discussed above, conservative Protestants and Muslims are more likely than other religious adherents to disapprove of homosexuality, in part, because these faiths are particularly successful at generating high levels of religious belief and commitment. Additionally, their leaders are more likely to encourage a literal interpretation of religious proscriptions. In figure 5, I present the mean disapproval level of homosexuality by the dominant faith of the nation. Nations that are dominated by Islam have the highest mean level of disapproval. Nations with a mixture of conservative Protestantism and other types of Christianity also have populations that are highly disapproving. I noted above that many European nations have Protestant-majority populations and are supportive of homosexuality, but their more conservative counterparts in other parts of the world

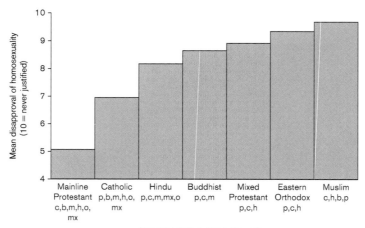

FIGURE 5. Marginal estimates for individual disapproval of homosexuality by the majority religious faith in the nation. (Society N = 87; individual N = 202,316)

SOURCE: WVS, waves 4, 5, and 6.

NOTE: Marginal estimates are presented for a married Protestant man who has completed secondary school and has a mean score on all other individual-level variables in model 2 of table 8 in appendix B. Lowercase letters indicate significant differences (p < .05, two-tail test) between each religious group and the others, where p = Mainline Protestant, mx = Mixed Christian, m = Muslim, o = Eastern Orthodox, c = Catholic, b = Buddhist, and h = Hindu. In a separate analysis I found that controlling for whether the respondent lived in Africa had no significant effect on the results.

lower the overall mean for Protestant nations in general. This distinction is well illustrated in figure 5, where, unlike in the individual-level analysis, I am able to differentiate between mainline Protestant countries and nations that include a mixture of Christian faiths, including conservative Protestants. The nations categorized as mainline Protestant are Finland, Great Britain, New Zealand, Norway, and Sweden. (See appendix A.) As a whole, these nations have the most liberal views. Additionally, while these nations have Protestant histories, they have some of the lowest proportions of residents who are activity engaged in their faith.

Another distinction that is important in figure 5 is that nations dominated by the Eastern Orthodox faith (e.g., Russia, Romania, Ukraine, etc.) also appear to have highly disapproving views. Indeed, there is no statistical difference in the level of disapproval between residents living in mixed Protestant, Muslim, and Eastern Orthodox nations. The individual-level data found in figure 3 show that Muslims and Protestants have the least-approving views, and these findings are consistent with those found in figure 5. Conversely, figure 3 shows that, relative to others, Eastern Orthodox adherents fall in the middle. They are more liberal than Muslims and Protestants, and less supportive than Jews and people with no religion. They do not differ significantly from Buddhists or Catholics.

So why do people living in nations dominated by the Eastern Orthodox faith appear so conservative when Eastern Orthodox adherents appear relatively moderate? I think that part of the answer comes from some of the other dynamics surrounding homosexuality in nations dominated by the Eastern Orthodox faith. Many Eastern Orthodox nations have Communist pasts and only recently became democratic. In the next chapter I will explain the important role that democracy has in shaping attitudes. Additionally, over the last twenty years many Western nations have increasingly supported homosexuality and related rights. Some Eastern Orthodox nations, like Russia, have pushed back against this pressure, which seems related, in part, to historical conflicts (i.e., the Cold War) between these countries and concerns related to Western imperialism (Stan and Turcescu 2000; Wilkinson 2014). Likewise, there has been a movement in some Eastern Orthodox nations to embrace "traditional values," which are being promoted as a key part of national identity (Turcescu and Stan 2005; Wilkinson 2014). The differences presented in figure 5 may be more illustrative of historical, cultural, and institutional dynamics than the influence of Eastern Orthodox adherents, who on average have attitudes that fall at the mean for religious followers across the world.

MORAL COMMUNITIES AND PUBLIC OPINION ABOUT HOMOSEXUALITY

In addition to a direct influence of the religious climate on all residents, social scientists have investigated whether some religious contexts, such as schools and friendship groups, have a greater effect on the attitudes and behaviors of more-religious people than secular individuals. Sociologists of religion refer to this relationship as the *moral communities hypothesis,* which posits that when religious adherents are around other religious people, religious followers' own beliefs are more likely to influence their own behaviors (Finke and Adamczyk 2008; Regnerus 2003; Stark 1996a; Stark, Kent, and Doyle 1982). Rodney Stark (1996a), who initially laid the groundwork for the moral communities hypothesis, explains that when individuals are around other religious people, "religion enters freely into everyday interactions and becomes a valid part of the normative system" strengthening the relation between personal religiosity and behavior (164). Conversely, when more-religious individuals are in the minority, religion becomes a compartmentalized part of their life and is less likely to shape attitudes and behaviors.

Researchers have tested the moral communities hypothesis by looking at whether a high proportion of people within friendship groups (Adamczyk and Felson 2006; Adamczyk and Palmer 2008), schools (Regnerus 2003; Stark, Kent, and Doyle 1982), regions (Stark 1996a), and nations (Finke and Adamczyk 2008; Scheepers, Te Grotenhuis, and Van Der Slik 2002) strengthen the relationship between personal religious beliefs and attitudes and behaviors related to premarital sex, delinquency, and crime. The greatest support for the moral communities hypothesis has been found at more-micro levels like friendship groups (Adamczyk 2012c) and schools (Regnerus 2003; Stark, Kent, and Doyle 1982). Very few studies have found support for the moral communities hypothesis at the national level, and there have not been any studies finding that the country religious context moderates the effect of personal religious beliefs on attitudes about homosexuality. I, too, tested for a moral communities effect on attitudes about homosexuality and did not find a statistically significant influence. (See appendix B, table 9, model 5.)

It would make sense that the moral communities effect is more likely to be found in more-micro contexts. Stark, Kent, and Doyle (1982) point out that it is in more-intimate groups and places where people really get to know each other that religious norms become salient. Some of the religious influence emanating from smaller contexts emerges at the national level, but this force is more likely to affect all people rather than just more-religious individuals. For understanding the influence of the national religious context on attitudes about homosexuality, it is important to keep in mind that the proportion of residents who find religion important influences the attitudes of secular *and* religious residents.

OTHER DEMOGRAPHIC CHARACTERISTICS THAT SHAPE ATTITUDES

Aside from the importance of religion and religious affiliation, there are several other demographic characteristics, such as age, gender, and education, that are associated with attitudes about homosexuality. In the next chapter I am going to take a closer look at the macro factors, aside from religion, that shape public opinion. The remainder of this chapter focuses on the other personal characteristics that are likely to shape disapproval of homosexuality across a range of different nations.

In figure 4, I presented the relationship between seven substantively meaningful and statistically significant demographic characteristics (i.e., religious importance, education, age, religious affiliation, marital status, income, and gender) for explaining disapproval of homosexuality in a sample of eighty-seven nations across the world. Beyond the characteristics presented in figure 4, there are a host of other factors that may explain why some people are more likely to approve of homosexuality than others. For example, seeing two men being physically beaten by police for holding hands may increase sympathy for homosexuality-related issues. Conversely, being propositioned as a youth by someone of the same sex may lead to less tolerance for homosexuality. There are likely to be some additional factors that could explain attitudes but cannot be as easily measured. Figure 4 presents the major demographic factors that researchers, including me, have found to be consistently related to feelings about homosexuality and are relatively easy to measure

Across the world, women tend to have more liberal attitudes about homosexuality than men (Hinrichs and Rosenberg 2002; Kerns and Fine 1994; V. K. G. Lim 2002; Meaney and Rye 2010; Winter, Webster, and Cheung 2008). Research has found that one of the most common explanations for why men and women differ relates to variation in gender-role values (Butler 1990). Men are more likely than women to have attitudes that are consistent with traditional gender roles (Brown and Henriquez 2008). People who have more-traditional views of gender are more likely than others to think that women should be feminine and nurturing and be their family's primary caretaker. Likewise, from a more-traditional perspective, men should appear strong, masculine, and stoic, and be the family's primary breadwinner.

Because they are not exclusively attracted to the opposite sex, people who engage in same-sex behaviors do not follow traditional gender roles. Additionally, they may dress or act in ways that do not conform to traditional gender stereotypes. Some research has suggested that gender differences in tolerance for homosexuality can be completely explained by gender differences in traditional gender-role attitudes (Kerns and Fine 1994). Hence, rather than biology explaining differences between men and women, people who strongly value traditional gender roles may be less likely to be supportive, regardless of their gender.

The majority of scholarly work on attitudes about homosexuality does not distinguish between feelings toward various LGBTQ individuals. For researchers interested in understanding how gender and sexual identity intersect, as well as the ways race and economic status may complicate this relationship, this lack of data is a big limitation (Worthen 2013). Unless one asks how people feel about different groups (e.g., bisexual vs. gay, or black queer men vs. white queer women), it is difficult to assess the extent to which the public's views may change depending on individual characteristics. Some of the research (Herek 2000; Hinrichs and Rosenberg 2002; Kerns and Fine 1994) that has tried to disaggregate attitudes related to various LGBTQ individuals has found that men and women tend to differ more in their attitudes toward gay men than toward lesbians. Studies by Eliason (1997) and Herek (1988), for example, find that heterosexual men are more likely to feel coldly toward gay men but have warmer feelings towards lesbians, perhaps because lesbians are seen as less of a threat to their masculine identities. Likewise, research by Herek and McLemore (2013) shows that some people tend to express less-favorable views toward bisexual individuals than toward those who are exclusively homosexual, possibly reflecting negative stereotypes that bisexuals are less likely to be monogamous and more likely to spread sexually transmitted diseases like HIV.

As I show in figure 4, education also has an important role to play in explaining why people differ in their attitudes. People with higher levels of education on average tend to have more supportive views. Some research has argued that education can increase cognitive sophistication, leading to more tolerance and support for homosexuality (Ohlander, Batalova, and Treas 2005). People with higher levels of education are more likely to have nuanced understandings of the world and are more likely to be accepting of ambiguities and inconsistencies (Jackman and Muha 1984). Some research has also found that while less-educated people are more likely to rigidly classify others, more-educated people are less likely to make judgments that are mediated by irrational anxieties (e.g., feelings of threat) (Sniderman et al. 1991). They may also be better at expressing their feelings about other out-groups (Chong 1993), drawing a distinction between their personal views about specific behaviors (i.e., the morality of homosexuality) and whether a group that they may not personally like should be given civil liberties and rights.

In appendix B, table 8, model 1, I present the coefficients for individual-level influences, including education. As I was putting this analysis together, I found that education did not have a linear effect on attitudes whereby peoples' attitudes became incrementally more tolerant as individuals gained education. There were some differences between respondents who, for example, attended primary school as opposed to secondary school. However, for different educational levels the biggest increases in tolerance were found for individuals who attended college versus those who only completed high school. The importance of this distinction emerges again in the next chapter when I discuss the macro influence of education on shaping attitudes.

Along with education, I show in figure 4 that income also has a liberating influence on attitudes about homosexuality. While more-educated people also tend to have higher incomes, the influence of income remains even after accounting for education. (See also Andersen and Fetner 2008a, 2008b; and Kuyper, Iedema, and Keuzenkamp 2013.) Why do people with higher incomes tend to be more supportive of homosexuality? Some work has found that people with higher incomes tend to be more tolerant (Andersen and Fetner 2008b), in part, because they tend to enjoy a greater sense of security. People with lower incomes are more likely to be particularly concerned about having enough money to support themselves and their families. Conversely, research has suggested that individuals with more economic resources are less likely to feel competition from others and, hence, are more likely to be comfortable in their social position, leading to greater trust and limiting prejudice (Kunovich 2004).

In addition to gender, education, and income, a number of studies, including my findings presented in figure 4, show that marital status appears to have a role in shaping attitudes (Sherkat et al. 2011; Sherkat, De Vries, and Creek 2010). People who are more conservative and value a more traditional family structure are more likely to get married. Once married, they are likely to develop relationships with other people who hold more-conservative values and have a traditional family, further influencing their attitudes about homosexuality.

A final demographic factor that a number of previous studies, and my findings presented in appendix B, have found to be associated with attitudes is age. The influence of age tends to be confounded with cohort differences where the same age group (e.g., baby boomers, generation X) tends to have many of the same experiences and, therefore, develop similar attitudes. Younger people and those from later cohorts tend to have more-permissive attitudes about sex-related issues in general (Finke and Adamczyk 2008) and about homosexuality in particular

(Kuyper, Iedema, and Keuzenkamp 2013). One possible reason for this relationship is that younger people often have more time and energy than older individuals. People tend to invest in important social problems and movements that are pushing for change when they are not overly committed to their occupations, families, or a specific geographical location (Ryder 1965)—any of which may limit the time, energy, and interest they have in new social issues.

Major historical events can also have an important influence on young minds, shaping the way an entire cohort thinks about a given issue. For example, beginning in the 1980s the HIV/AIDS crisis in the United States became a major news issue. For some Americans the media attention given to HIV/AIDS and the government's initially inadequate response may have had a role in shaping their views. Research has found that, once people begin to adhere to a given set of values, they tend to become more cognitively and structurally constrained so that the views they develop in their youth are likely to maintain themselves as they get older (Alwin and Krosnick 1991).

TRADITIONAL VALUES, AN AUTHORITARIAN PERSONALITY, AND CONTACT

Aside from the five demographic characteristics I discussed above (i.e., gender, education, income, marital status, and age), there are three additional factors that previous research has found are fairly consistently related to attitudes about homosexuality. These are traditional values, an authoritarian personality, and the extent of contact with openly gay and lesbian individuals. These factors tend to overlap with some of the other demographic characteristics mentioned above. Men and married individuals, for example, are more likely to value traditional gender roles, which can explain why they tend to have cooler feelings about homosexuality than others. But, irrespective of their gender, people with more-traditional values about sex and gender issues are also more likely to view homosexuality as problematic (Brewer 2003; Hicks and Lee 2006; Lottes and Alkula 2011), in part, because LGBTQ individuals do not conform to traditional gender roles (Kerns and Fine 1994; Whitley 2001).

People who value extreme gender-role rigidity may also have stronger authoritarian leanings (Adorno et al. 1950; Altemeyer 1998). The characteristics associated with an authoritarian personality include a strong desire for order, power, security, status, structured authority, and obedience. Research has found that because people with these traits tend to have a stronger attachment to the status quo, they are more likely to oppose ideas that are new or different from what they already know, including views that may be seen as challenging traditional establishments (Haddock and Zanna 1998). They may also be more likely to react punitively toward people whose behavior seems unconventional (Abrams and Della Fave 1976). Consistent with these ideas, a number of studies have found that individuals with authoritarian personality characteristics tend to be less supportive of homosexuality (Detenber et al. 2013; K. Kelley et al. 1997; Vicario, Liddle, and Luzzo 2005; Whitley and Lee 2000).

Finally, there is a lot of research showing that people who are friends with someone who is openly gay or lesbian are likely to have friendlier feelings toward homosexuality (Detenber et al. 2013; Herek and Capitanio 1996; Hinrichs and Rosenberg 2002). Indeed, across a range of studies, personally knowing someone who identifies as gay or lesbian is an important predictor of people's feelings about homosexuality (Detenber et al. 2013; Herek and Capitanio 1996; Hinrichs and Rosenberg 2002). Familiarity, especially if it is related to likability, tends to breed empathy, trust, and compassion. Of course, the relationship can also work in the opposite direction. Openly gay and lesbian individuals are going to be hesitant about coming out to someone who does not seem supportive of homosexuality. Conversely, if they feel that someone is accepting, they may be more inclined to reveal their identity and develop a relationship.

THE POWERFUL INFLUENCE OF OVERLAPPING INDIVIDUAL CHARACTERISTICS

The way that social scientists tend to measure and present the influence of individual characteristics may make it seem like these factors operate in isolation. All of the individual factors discussed above and presented in figure 4 do indeed have independent influences on attitudes. Hence, irrespective of their gender, married couples are more likely than single individuals to disapprove of homosexuality. Likewise, even though income and education are correlated, they have unique effects on attitudes. However, these factors also tend to have reciprocal relationships with each other, strengthening their overall influence. Hence, someone who has more-traditional values *and* a more authoritarian personality is more likely to be interested in getting married. Getting married is likely to lead to more interactions with other people who have conservative values, further enforcing an individual's own disapproving views about homosexuality and limiting the likelihood of their interacting with someone who is openly gay.

While each individual characteristic can influence the extent to which people disapprove of homosexuality, their collective effect is powerful. Hence, young single women who are childless, graduate from college, have high incomes, and are moderately religious have a mean disapproval score of 6.20 on a scale ranging from 1 (i.e., homosexuality is always justified) to 10 (i.e., homosexuality is never justified). In contrast, older, married, highly religious men with a primary school education and low incomes have an average score of 9.36.

CONCLUSION

This chapter has provided insight into the influence of religion and several demographic characteristics for understanding why people differ in how they feel about homosexuality. Gender, education, income, marital status, age, and religion are important factors. Regardless of where they live, my analysis presented in figure 4 and appendix B shows that on average people who have the same demographic profile tend to have attitudes that vary in a similar way. Hence, in both Uganda and the United States older people tend to have more-disapproving attitudes than younger individuals. In terms of how demographics shape attitudes, residents across the world are not that different from each other. Among the demographics examined, religious importance has the greatest influence on attitudes about homosexuality.

Not only do personal religious beliefs shape attitudes, but so does the religious context of a nation. Overall levels of religious importance within a nation, as well as the dominant religious faith, can shape attitudes about homosexuality, even for people who do not think religion is very important or do not affiliate with a given faith. Additionally, as I showed with the contrast between religious adherents and the dominant faith, differences between individual religious adherents (e.g., Eastern Orthodox, Protestant) are not always mirrored at the national level. Factors like the cultural history and regional dynamics may be at least partially responsible for cross-national differences in attitudes that appear to be related to the dominant religion.

CHAPTER 2

The Importance of Democracy and Economic Development

Nigeria's civil war ended in 1970, but the country has continued to experience ethnic and religious violence. Most recently, the militant Islamist group Boko Haram has been terrorizing northern parts of Nigeria. Since 2009 they have killed more than five thousand people. In April 2014 Boko Haram garnered national attention by kidnapping over two hundred girls from a secondary school (Chothia 2014). In addition to Nigeria's being a politically unstable and violent country, poverty is widespread there, especially in rural areas, where 80% of residents live below the poverty level (Rural Poverty Portal 2014). The *Vanguard,* a Nigerian-based paper, describes the impoverished situation of many residents when quoting Sulaiman Afose, a twenty-year-old male living in Lagos: "We have lots of people who are poor and they live in houses made with planks, they don't know what will be the next thing for them. You will see a situation where 10 people are living in a room. It is difficult for their children to have access to quality education. There is no good health care and all the[y] get is nothing to write home about. Many of these people are not educated and so, they don't know what it is and what to do to make a living" (Balogun and Sessou 2012).

In addition to poverty and political instability, Nigeria has a very poor human rights record, which includes bombings, vigilante killings, torture, rape, and beatings (U.S. Department of State, Bureau of Democracy, Human Rights and Labor 2013). Homosexuality is illegal, and in December 2013 the Nigerian Senate passed the "Same Sex Marriage

(Prohibition) Bill," which makes supporting LGBTQ organizations punishable with up to ten years in prison (U.S. Department of State, Bureau of Democracy, Human Rights and Labor 2013). Consistent with this new law, public-opinion data show that just 1% of Nigerians feel that society should support homosexuality (Pew Research Center 2013). Below I argue that the devastation, poverty, and political instability in Nigeria cannot help but shape how many Nigerians feel about homosexuality, which is largely seen as a Western import that challenges the traditional family structure and grossly violates religious proscriptions.

This chapter explores the important roles that democracy and economic development play in shaping cross-national attitudes about homosexuality. Below I explain that when a society is regularly faced with economic and political uncertainty, residents are likely to have strong in-group loyalty and to support the values and behaviors, like a traditional family structure, that are similar to what they have always known. However, as economic development increases, a nation's cultural values shift and residents increasingly begin to value self-expression, creativity, and the pursuit of happiness. This move in value orientations can help explain why residents living in nations with higher levels of economic development are more likely than others to find homosexuality justifiable. Democracy also contributes to friendlier attitudes, by exposing people to diverse groups and teaching them to respect people's rights, even if they do not personally like those people. After accounting for democracy, economic development, and the religious context of a nation, other characteristics—like economic inequality, the number of nongovernment organizations, and overall levels of education—are less important in shaping attitudes, though they may work as mediators, or play a more important role within a smaller group of countries.

ECONOMIC DEVELOPMENT AND ATTITUDES ABOUT HOMOSEXUALITY

While most nations either have completed or are currently passing through major stages of economic development, they go through these processes at different paces and time periods. Toward the end of this chapter I will discuss some of the complications with positing a linear relationship between increasing development and tolerance across the world. Nevertheless, many nations experience somewhat similar processes, making it possible to anticipate certain changes in cultural values. As I explain, this adjustment in cultural values can provide a lot of

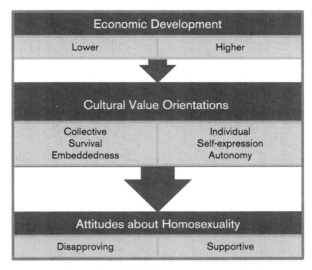

FIGURE 6. Illustration of the influence of economic development on value orientations, which shape attitudes about homosexuality.

insight into the relationships between economic development and attitudes about homosexuality.

While there has been ongoing debate about what forces give rise to economic development, regardless of the specific factors and historical influences, social scientists generally agree that as modernization and economic development increase, a nation's cultural values change in predictable ways (Inglehart and Baker 2000; Marx 1867; Schwartz 2006). Several researchers have developed schemes to explain how economic development influences cultural value orientations. Schwartz (1999, 2006, 2014) posits that higher levels of economic development are likely to lead to a shift in cultural value orientations from those oriented toward embeddedness within the group to autonomy. Similarly, Inglehart and colleagues (Inglehart 2006; Inglehart and Baker 2000; Inglehart and Oyserman 2004) argue that economic development is likely to lead to a shift in values from those based on survival to those oriented toward self-expression. And Hofstede (2001) explains that as nations become richer, values increasingly focus on the individual rather than the collective.

There is a lot of overlap between these ideas (Inglehart and Oyserman 2004; Schwartz 2006). As I illustrate in figure 6, for all three schemes, economic development is related to a change in cultural value orientations whereby people living in poorer nations are more likely to have values oriented toward survival, the collective, and embeddedness. Conversely, people from richer countries are more likely to have values that focus on self-expression, autonomy, and the individual. The shift from one end of the spectrum to the other has important implications for theorizing about how economic development shapes attitudes about homosexuality.

In nations with lower levels of economic development, residents will generally have fewer material resources, which is likely to make them more concerned about survival-related issues (Bell 1976; Inglehart and Baker 2000). Each day they may need to think about whether they will have enough food to eat and water to use. They are likely to worry about getting sick or injured and losing family members to illness and death. By pooling their resources, individuals can increase their chances of survival. As a result, residents in poorer nations are more likely to rely on the larger group, and dependency is likely to breed strong loyalty and commitment. In these societies cultural values are likely to reflect this focus on survival (Schwartz 2006).

As nations become more developed, the resources available for all residents increase, which reduces dependency on the extended family and larger group. With less dependency, people have more opportunities to make choices for themselves and obtain autonomy. Likewise, as societies become more advanced, diverse skills, knowledge, and innovation are needed to meet new societal challenges. As a result, people in these more secure places begin to specialize in a given occupation, such as banker or plumber (Durkheim 2014). It becomes increasingly easy for individuals to stand apart from the group, and unique values, ideas, and preferences are less likely to be seen as problematic. With less focus on their own and their group's survival, people's orientation to the world begins to change (Schwartz 2006). The unknown feels less frightening, and residents become more comfortable with new and different ideas, behaviors, and perspectives.

As a substantial portion of a nation becomes economically secure, more resources become available to help everyone maintain at least a minimal level of economic security. As a result, in richer nations, most residents are able to attend primary and secondary school, get health care, and drive on well-maintained roads. As resources become available to improve the lives of everyone, some people will advocate for laws that require all residents to partake of collective resources, such as compulsory education. A number of residents are likely to feel that everyone benefits when all people have resources such as health care, education, and access to the police and fire departments.

This interest in improving the lives of all residents applies not only to physical, educational, and safety-related needs, but also to the likelihood that people feel content and able to express their individual uniqueness. Not surprisingly, economic development is associated with an increase in people's interest in democratic practices (Inglehart and Oyserman 2004; Welzel, Inglehart, and Kligemann 2003). But even after accounting for the strength of democratic institutions, national levels of economic development are likely to shift cultural value orientations from those focused on survival to those oriented toward self-expression. Likewise, in more economically developed countries people are more likely to focus on individual needs, uniqueness, and creativity, and less likely to emphasize group solidarity and loyalty. With more security, residents become more willing to tolerate and even embrace different ideas (e.g., homosexuality) and unconventional individuals (e.g., same-sex couples) and groups (e.g., LGBTQ organizations) that once would have been seen as nonnormative and potentially threatening.

Conversely, when a society is regularly faced with economic uncertainty, residents are more likely to support values and norms that are similar to what they have always known (Inglehart, Norris, and Welzel 2002). As a result, people living in poorer nations are less likely to find a homosexual lifestyle acceptable, approve of same-sex couples adopting children, or be willing to live next to a gay person. In these more uncertain and insecure places individuals may feel that even if you are attracted to someone of the same sex, a heterosexual, normative, and traditional relationship is best for the individual, family, and society. Additionally, residents may feel that focusing on issues such as civil liberties and the pursuit of happiness may be a little silly when more basic needs related to food, shelter, and safety are in danger of not being met.

These theoretical ideas suggest that there should be an empirical association between economic development and friendlier views about homosexuality. In table 2, I present the relationship between differences in laws regarding homosexuality across nations at various levels of economic development,[1] which is measured here as 2008 per person gross domestic product (GDP) in U.S. dollars. Whereas 52% of low-GDP nations have laws where homosexuality is illegal, only 16% of high-GDP countries have these laws. In contrast, none of the low-GDP nations allow for marriage or marriage-like relationships for same-sex couples, but 47% of high-GDP nations do.

TABLE 2   PERCENTAGE OF COUNTRIES IN EACH INCOME BRACKET (GDP PER
CAPITA IN 2008 U.S. DOLLARS), BY LEGAL STATUS OF HOMOSEXUALITY
(*COUNTRY* N = *174*[a])

	Mean national income per capita			
	Low (less than $1,850)	Medium ($1,851-$8,209)	High (more than $8,209)	Total
Homosexuality illegal	52%	46%	16%	38%
Homosexuality legal (but not union)	48%	46%	37%	44%
Marriage or marriage-like relationship allowed	0%	9%	47%	18%

SOURCES: Association of Religious Data Archives' *Cross-National Socio-Economic and Religion Data,*
2011; ILGA 2015 (in Carroll and Itaborahy 2015).
[a]Because this table focuses on laws, many more countries are included. Because poorer nations are
especially unlikely to have public-opinion data, when we focus on laws the GDP ranges are lower than
they would be if we were looking at GDP for societies that have attitudinal measures.

A similar association can be found for attitudes. In figure 7, I show
that in nations with a low GDP, the proportion of people within each
country who say homosexuality is never justified is particularly high.
Whereas Germany's 2008 GDP was about $45,000, only about 16% of
Germans think that homosexuality is *never* justifiable. In sharp contrast, the 2008 GDP in Uganda was $453, and 91% of Ugandans think
that homosexuality is *never* justifiable.

The survey question that the WVS regularly uses to ask residents
about homosexuality focuses on whether it can ever be justified.[2] This
wording may not fully capture residents' feelings about homosexuality,
since some people may think that homosexuality is morally wrong or
not justifiable but still believe that gay and lesbian individuals should
have the same civil rights and liberties as other people (G. B. Lewis
2003; G. B. Lewis and Gossett 2008; Olson, Cadge, and Harrison
2006). Some nations in the WVS have asked respondents whether they
would be willing to live next door to neighbors who are homosexual—
offering an alternative perspective on feelings about homosexuality. As
I show in figure 8, even if the question focuses on feelings about having
same-sex neighbors, GDP moves in tandem with more-accepting attitudes. In nations with GDPs below $8,000, the regression line shows
that on average approximately 60% of residents report that they would

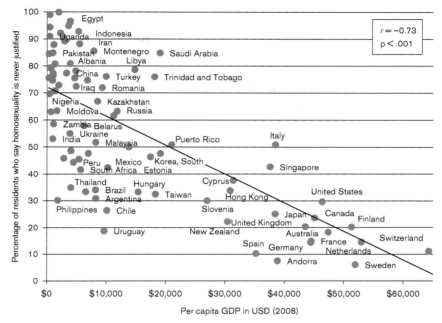

FIGURE 7. Scatter plot of the relationship between GDP per capita and the proportion of residents who report that homosexuality is *never* justified. (Society N = 86)

SOURCES: ARDA's Cross-National Socio-Economic and Religion Data, 2011; WVS, waves 4, 5, and 6.

NOTE: The WVS includes three societies (Andorra, Puerto Rico, and Taiwan) that are not technically countries. Norway (2008 GDP = $94,759; 6.4% never justified) is excluded because it makes the trend line particularly steep. To improve visualization, some labels have been removed.

not want homosexual neighbors. Conversely, in nations with GDPs above $45,000, less than 30% of residents feel this way.

Several other studies have also found a robust correlation between higher levels of economic development and more-accepting attitudes. The association remains even if researchers employ a different measure of feelings about homosexuality (Hadler 2012; van den Akker, van der Ploeg, and Scheepers 2013; Štulhofer and Rimac 2009), use a different sample of nations (Gerhards 2010; van den Akker, van der Ploeg, and Scheepers 2013; Pew Research Center 2013), or vary the analysis technique (Lottes and Alkula 2011; Štulhofer and Rimac 2009).

Do all residents in nations with high levels of economic development experience this shift in values, or do only richer people experience it? The theoretical ideas presented by Inglehart and Baker (2000), Schwartz

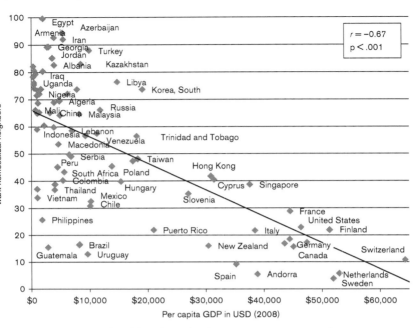

FIGURE 8. Scatter plot of the relationship between GDP per capita and proportion of residents who report that they do not want homosexual neighbors. (Society N = 84)

SOURCES: ARDA's Cross-National Socio-Economic and Religion Data, 2011; WVS, waves 4, 5, and 6.

NOTE: Norway (2008 GDP = $94,759; 5.66% do not want homosexual neighbors) is excluded because it makes the trend line even steeper. To improve visualization, some labels have been removed.

(2006), and Hofstede (2001) suggest that because these forces are occurring at a societal level, everyone's attitudes should adjust. Statistical analysis techniques (i.e., hierarchical linear models) make it possible to examine how country characteristics (e.g., economic development) *and* individual factors (e.g., personal income) shape individuals' attitudes. In appendix B, table 8, model 4, I empirically show that in more-developed nations, all residents, both rich and poor, are more likely to have tolerant attitudes than their counterparts in less economically developed societies.[3]

Figure 9 provides the average value for feelings about homosexuality for people living in nations at three different levels of economic development. Whereas residents of rich countries have a mean score of 7.8, people in societies with an average GDP (i.e., $15,000) have a score of

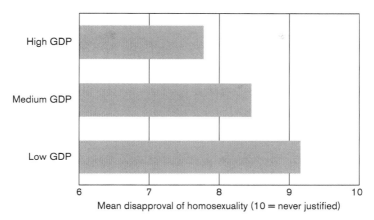

FIGURE 9. Marginal estimates of individual disapproval of homosexuality, by GDP (per capita). (Society N = 87; individual N = 202,316)

SOURCES: ARDA's Cross-National Socio-Economic and Religion Data, 2011; WVS, waves 4, 5, and 6.

NOTE: Marginal values are presented for a Protestant man living in a mixed Christian society with a mean score on all other variables in model 4 of table 8 in appendix B. The three measures of GDP are based on the sample mean ($15,000 per capita) and approximately one standard deviation above and below the mean.

8.5, and residents from poorer nations have a score of 9.2. Across all of the models presented in appendix B, economic development, which is being measured with GDP, remains a robust indicator of individuals' attitudes about homosexuality. Several other studies (Hadler 2012; Hooghe and Meeusen 2013; Lottes and Alkula 2011; Štulhofer and Rimac 2009) have reached a similar conclusion regarding the positive and significant relationship between economic development and attitudes even after a host of other factors are considered.

There is strong theoretical and empirical support for the idea that as nations become more economically developed, cultural value orientations shift in a somewhat predictable way, leading to friendlier attitudes. Other studies have found that. in addition to homosexuality, residents from richer nations are also more likely to be tolerant of prostitution, premarital sex, and divorce, and there is an increase in the importance of friends and leisure, gender equality, and acceptance of foreigners (Adamczyk 2013; Inglehart 2006; Inglehart and Baker 2000; Inglehart, Norris, and Welzel 2002; Stack, Adamczyk, and Cao 2010). Tolerance of homosexuality is just one example of how residents' feelings toward a wide array of issues may change as nations win their battles against economic insecurity. Having provided the rationale and empirical tests for why residents in richer nations are more likely to be tolerant, in the next section I address the influence of democracy.

DEMOCRACY AND TOLERANCE

Along with economic development, the extent of democracy within a nation can also promote tolerance. A number of studies have found that democracy can contribute to more-tolerant attitudes, in part, by increasing awareness and knowledge of behaviors or ideas that may be considered new or different (Peffley and Rohrschneider 2003). In functioning democracies, the government not only represents the interests of the majority, but within reason tries to protect the interests of the minority (e.g., Mormons, Amish, Native Americans, etc.). Residents from democratic nations should be able to present new and different ideas with limited concern about government censorship. Because freedom of speech is protected, the number of opportunities to present alternative ideas unencumbered increases. As a result, residents living in long-standing and well-functioning democracies tend to get more exposure to a range of different perspectives (Thompson 1970), which research has shown can increase tolerance (Hadler 2012).

Along with more awareness and knowledge of new ideas, social scientists have found that democracies promote tolerance by encouraging exposure to and active participation in democratic processes (Guérin, Petry, and Crête 2004). Embedded within the concept of democracy are ideals or standards of governmental behavior that are thought to be essential for a well-run democracy. These ideals include fairness, impartiality, equality, freedom of speech, and the right to demonstrate—all of which have implications for how people view homosexuality and corresponding civil liberties and rights. In well-run and stable democracies, these abstract democratic principles should guide the government's actions, resulting in more-tolerant treatment of individuals who may be seen as different from the norm (Peffley and Rohrschneider 2003).

Based on these ideas, more-democratic nations should have residents who are more tolerant of homosexuality. In appendix B, table 8, model 5, I test this relationship, and figure 10 presents the predicted scores for three different types of government. The mean attitudinal score for people living in nondemocratic nations is 8.8. For residents living in anocracies, which include a mixture of autocratic and democratic traits and tend to be vulnerable to political instability, residents are a little more

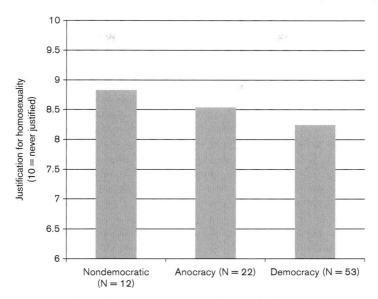

FIGURE 10. Marginal estimate of individual disapproval of homosexuality by three types of government. (Society N = 87; individual N = 202,316)

SOURCES: United Nations polity score; WVS, waves 4, 5, and 6.

NOTE: The United Nations' polity score captures the regime's authority spectrum. Each society was initially given a score ranging from -10 (hereditary monarchy) to +10 (consolidated democracy) on a 21-point scale. The UN then converted the scores into three regime categories: "autocracies" (-10 to -6), "anocracies" (-5 to +5), and "democracies" (+6 to +10). For WVS data, marginal values are presented for a Protestant man living in a mixed Christian society with a mean score on all other variables in model 5 of table 8 in appendix B.

liberal, having a mean score of 8.5. With a score of 8.2, individuals living in democratic nations tend to have the least disapproving attitudes. Several other researchers have found a similar influence of democracy on attitudes about homosexuality and other sex-related issues (Hadler 2012; Hooghe and Meeusen 2013; Scheepers, Te Grotenhuis, and Van Der Slik 2002).

While a more democratic government should contribute to more-tolerant views, a number of studies have noted that the learning of tolerance varies with the duration of democracy (Hadler 2012; Peffley and Rohrschneider 2003), and time of exposure can be critical. In democratic societies, residents learn to become more tolerant toward groups they may not personally like by viewing and participating in democratic elections, hearing about civil-liberty disputes in the news, personally employing democratic methods to oppose the government, and watching the government uphold the civil liberties of unpopular groups (Nelson, Clawson, and Oxley 1997). This process takes time, and people living in nations with longer histories of democracy tend to have more-tolerant views (Hadler 2012).

WHAT OTHER COUNTRY-LEVEL FACTORS SHAPE CROSS-NATIONAL ATTITUDES?

The first chapter showed that a nation's religious culture (i.e., dominant religion and mean level of religious importance) has an important role in shaping public opinion about homosexuality. So far in this chapter I have shown that economic development and democracy are also important factors in explaining cross-national attitudes about homosexuality. Aside from these, are there any other country-level forces that could explain cross-national differences in attitudes about homosexuality? The following section addresses some of these other potential influences, beginning with economic inequality and then considering the effects of overall levels of education, the number of nonprofit organizations, and gender inequality.

Economic Inequality Does Not Shape Attitudes

Some research has suggested that economic inequality could affect support for homosexuality (Andersen and Fetner 2008b). This work is grounded in the idea that when there is a wide gap between the rich and poor, residents may feel that they do not have a lot in common with others, leading to less-generalized trust. Generalized trust is the trust that people have in others they may not have met, and it is typically contrasted against particularized trust, which is the trust that people have in others that they know (Nannestad 2008). High levels of economic inequality could decrease generalized trust and limit the sense of commonality that residents feel with each other (Uslaner and Brown 2005). It seems reasonable that decreased generalized trust, which may result from economic inequality, could lead to less tolerance for out-groups, including homosexual individuals. Does a nation's level of economic inequality lead to less support for homosexuality?

Using data from Europe, North America, and Australia, where the most economically developed and tolerant nations are located, Andersen and Fetner (2008b) found that higher levels of economic inequality within a nation reduced tolerance for homosexuality among all people, but especially those in lower economic classes. In contrast, drawing on a wider range of countries from around the world (i.e., India, China, and Mexico), Hadler (2012) did not find any influence of economic inequality, migration, or unemployment, which could theoretically decrease generalized trust, on residents' attitudes about homosexuality. Consistent with Hadler's research, my analysis of eighty-seven diverse nations from the WVS does not show any significant effect of economic inequality on individuals' attitudes about homosexuality (see appendix B, table 9, model 1).

It is possible that, just as economic inequality may increase perceptions of threat and thereby lower individuals' generalized trust, diversity could have the opposite effect (see Schlueter and Scheepers 2010). When people are exposed to diverse ethnic, religious, and economic groups, they may learn that people who appear different may not be particularly threatening, leading to more tolerance. Cities, for example, typically have high levels of diversity, including a lot of economic inequality, foreigners, a vast array of religious groups, and people of different sexual orientations. People living in more-urban areas tend to be more tolerant than their rural or suburban counterparts on a range of issues, including homosexuality (Hadler 2012). Additionally, as I noted in the first chapter, contact with gay and lesbian individuals does not decrease but rather tends to increase tolerance for homosexuality (see Gelbal and Duyan 2006; Heinze and Horn 2009). As heterosexual individuals come to know LGBTQ individuals, feelings of threat may wane. Any effects that economic inequality may have on threat or decreased generalized trust may be offset by the positive influence of diversity on increasing tolerance.

Rising Levels of Education: Not What You Might Think

Along with economic development and democracy, there is good reason to think that high societal levels of education are likely to lead to friendlier attitudes about homosexuality. Indeed, I noted in the first chapter that more-educated people tend to have more-tolerant attitudes. A number of studies have found that through education, people are exposed to new ideas, and traditional concepts are more likely to be questioned and possibly rejected rather than automatically accepted (Dalton 1984; Inglehart 1990). Clearly education is important for increasing tolerance about seemingly deviant or new ideas. But can a higher proportion of more-educated people within a nation have a liberalizing influence on all residents, even those with low levels of education?

Education and economic development are moderately correlated, and in empirical studies it is not unreasonable to use one as a proxy measure for the other.[4] The United Nations regularly publishes the Human Development Index, which assess overall well-being across nations. It consists of measures of life expectancy, education, and GDP. As GDP increases, educational levels also tend to rise. However, the roles of GDP and overall levels of education in shaping attitudes about homosexuality would seem to follow different theoretical processes. Economic development seems to promote tolerance by increasing people's sense of security, shifting cultural values for all residents within a society from those oriented toward the group to those focused on individual difference. In contrast, the mean level of education would seem to increase tolerance by exposing all residents to diverse perspectives and challenging them to think critically about new issues and ideas. In model 2 in table 9 of appendix B, I assess the statistical relationship between mean levels of education and attitudes. This model shows that even before GDP is considered, there is no statistically significant effect of mean levels of education on attitudes. Other research has found a similar relationship (e.g., Štulhofer and Rimac 2009).

In the first chapter I noted that education seems to have its greatest liberalizing effect on attitudes about homosexuality for individuals who attend college. However, the vast majority of the world has less education (see Barro and Lee 2001), which could minimize any influence that college graduates have on societal attitudes. If education has an effect on attitudes about homosexuality largely at the highest levels, and there are not many people who attend college, this would explain why mean societal levels of education do not have much of an independent influence. Conversely, economic development appears to increase security and limit reliance on the group for everyone, leading to a societal shift in value orientations, resulting in more tolerance among all residents.

Gender Inequality, Nonprofit Organizations, and Other Macro Influences

Before moving to the next section, there are two additional factors that are worth discussing because they seem like such reasonable and logical explanations for cross-national differences in attitudes across nations. These factors are gender inequality and the prevalence of government and nonprofit organizations.

There is some research (Basow and Johnson 2000; Polimeni, Hardie, and Buzwell 2000) showing that people who are more likely to value traditional gender roles are less likely to support homosexuality. By allowing for same-sex relationships, homosexuality can be viewed as challenging conventional gender roles where men and women are seen as having clearly defined social roles and responsibilities (Whitley 2001). As I explained in the first chapter, people who value a clear gender division are more likely to find homosexuality problematic. Researchers McVeigh and Diaz (2009) examined differences between U.S. states that did and did not vote to ban same-sex marriage in the United States. They found that opposition to same-sex marriage was particularly strong in places characterized by a predominance of traditional gender roles and family structures. Their findings suggest that across the United States, in the late 2000s gender inequality was important for understanding differences in attitudes and laws related to homosexuality. Do overall levels of gender inequality shape cross-national attitudes?

If we look only at the correlation between gender inequality and support for homosexuality, there is a significant relationship. However, once GDP, democracy, and the religious context are all considered in the same model, gender inequality no longer has a statistically significant effect on attitudes. (See appendix B, table 9, model 3.) One reason why the relationship seems to disappear is that these other factors also shape gender inequality. A lot of research has shown an effect of democracy, economic development, and the religious context of a nation on gender inequality and related attitudes (B. C. Hayes, McAllister, and Studlar 2000; Inglehart, Norris, and Welzel 2002; Steel and Kabashima 2008; Tommasoli, Cornwall, and Lynch 2013). Homosexuality is often considered a gender-related issue. Hence, once these other factors are considered, gender inequality is no longer related to disapproval. Some of the same macro dimensions that appear to shape attitudes about homosexuality are also likely to shape the level of gender inequality within a nation.

Just as it is reasonable to expect that gender inequality is related to attitudes, theoretically it would be sensible to think that a vibrant nonprofit sector could also shape views about homosexuality. Many nations have a number of national and international organizations working to shape the public's understanding of various issues. Human rights tend to be an important concern for many of these groups, which include Amnesty International, Human Rights Watch, and the United Nations. These organizations try to influence the discourse surrounding various concerns, and they put pressure on state actors to adopt legislation that supports a given issue.

In figure 11, I present the size of standardized coefficients for explaining cross-national attitudes with democracy, GDP, the dominant religion, mean religious importance, and the number of international government and nongovernment organizations. Factors represented by triangles do not have a significant influence on attitudes. The factors with the greatest explanatory power are economic development, democracy, and the religious context.[5] Once these other influences are considered, the number of nonprofit organizations appears unrelated to attitudes.[6]

Just as democracy and economic development are likely to shape attitudes about homosexuality, they are also likely to shape the ability and willingness of nations to house human rights and other nonprofit organizations. Hence, after accounting for democracy and economic development, the number of international government and nongovernment groups does not appear to have any direct and independent influence on attitudes. That said, it is possible that the number of international government and nongovernment groups shape attitudes by mediating the relationship between democracy and attitudes within many nations. However, they do not seem to have an independent influence outside of these other factors.

Aside from the forces already discussed, there are a number of other potential country characteristics that could influence public opinion. In appendix C, I list seventy additional factors that could hypothetically shape attitudes about homosexuality. The appendix shows the correlation between each of these variables and mean levels of disapproval and also how this relationship changes when economic development, democracy, and the religious context of a nation are also considered. There are several indicators that initially appear statistically significant, but their significance disappears when economic development, democracy, and the religious context are also included. Based on these analyses,[7] there is good reason to think that across a large sample of the world's nations, economic development, democracy, and the religious context are the key country-level factors shaping attitudes about homosexuality.

Up until this point I have focused only on trends across a large number of countries. It is possible that within a single nation, factors like high gender or economic inequality could shape how homosexuality is viewed and the likelihood that corresponding legislation is proposed. However, these influences would not appear in a cross-national quantitative analysis because they would apply only to a single country

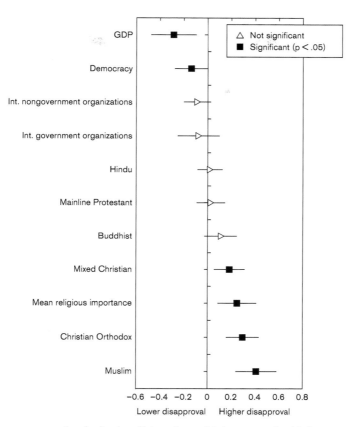

FIGURE 11. Standardized coefficients for explaining country-level influences on the proportion of residents who disapprove of homosexuality. (Society N = 87)

SOURCES: United Nations; The Economist Intelligence Unit's Index of Democracy 2008, Yearbook of International Organizations 2010 (Union of International Associations); WVS, waves 4, 5, and 6.

NOTES: Ordinary least square regression coefficients for examining mean country disapproval of homosexuality were standardized using the following formula: Beta = unstandardized coefficient * (standard deviation of the dependent variable / standard deviation of the predictor) or (Beta = β (S_x / S_y). The comparison category for dominant religious faith is Catholic.

or subset of nations. For a country characteristic to be statistically significant in a cross-national analysis, the factor has to be important in many nations. The next section takes a closer look at some of the limitations with focusing too much on factors that are related only to attitudes across many countries.

So far I have shown that economic development, democracy, and a nation's religious context are key characteristics for shaping cross-national attitudes about homosexuality. Together these macro forces explain the majority (67%) of the variation across nations in how residents view homosexuality. An additional 20% can be explained by differences in the composition of nations. Between the composition and contextual influences, there is only 13% of the variance in attitudes across nations left to explain.

Since researchers can so straightforwardly quantify economic development, democracy, and the religious context of a nation, and since these are clearly powerful within the context of other factors that can be quantitatively measured, it may seem that the theoretical processes underlying these empirical relationships are simple or straightforward. However, there are some issues with these ideas and the cross-national quantitative data available to test them. Below I explain these concerns and offer suggestions for other key factors that may have a role in shaping public opinion about homosexuality but cannot be so easily quantified.

One of the challenges with quantitatively examining the influence of economic development on attitudes is that it is difficult to empirically establish the extent to which attitudes about homosexuality are changing through similar processes across multiple nations. Nations go through industrialization and modernization at different paces. For understanding how economic development shapes attitudes, how quickly or slowly a nation passes through development can influence the extent to which external forces (e.g., Western media) shape exposure to and discussions about homosexuality-related issues, which, in turn, can affect residents' attitudes. While there is evidence (Inglehart 1971, 1997) that many countries have passed or are moving through somewhat similar stages, nations that got started earlier (i.e., the United States and Western Europe) took longer to go through these phases than societies that are going through them now.

When nations are at different stages of development and regularly interact with each other in a globalized world, other, more economically developed and powerful countries may try to influence them through state relationships, nongovernment organizations, media, trade agreements, religious groups, elites (e.g., celebrities, politicians), and so forth. In the last ten years the United Nations, Europe, and the United States have increasingly moved to protect homosexuality-related rights. Homosexuality is much more likely to be a crime in nations with lower GDPs. Some rich countries are trying to influence poorer ones to adopt policies that are consistent with higher tolerance. These more economically developed nations are pressuring others in a way that they themselves did not experience because they were the first to go through processes of modernization and industrialization and passed through them in a less globalized era.

How nations respond to outside pressure is not always clear or predictable. For example, homosexuality has been considered illegal in Uganda since British rule. In 2005 Uganda amended its constitution to explicitly define marriage as an act between a man and a woman. In 2008, the General Assembly of the United Nations proposed a resolution to support gay rights. Shortly thereafter the Obama administration announced that it would provide funding to support civil-society organizations in protecting the human rights of LGBT individuals across the world. Not only did Uganda seem unmoved by these announcements, but in 2014 it decided to make a first-time offense of gay sex punishable with up to fourteen years in prison. In the next chapter I explain that the Ugandan government seems to feel some resentment toward other nations around the issue of homosexuality. While economic development is often an important characteristic for shaping attitudes, it does not influence all nations similarly, and other factors, including pressure from outside the country, can be very important.

Related to the different paces through which nations develop, attitudes within some countries have changed much quicker than in others. Attitudes are typically seen as changing through either cohort replacement or period effects. With cohort replacement, younger and more tolerant generations replace older and more conservative ones, leading to a gradual shift in public opinion over time (Brooks and Bolzendahl 2004). With this process, people's attitudes are seen as changing minimally once they have developed (Alwin and Krosnick 1991). The alternative process is period effects. When there are rapid cultural, legal, and political changes surrounding a particular issue, the attitudes of many residents may change quickly (Andersen and Fetner 2008a; Treas 2002).

The ideas put forth by Inglehart (1971) and Schwartz (1999; 2006) on changes in cultural values suggest that attitudes adjust gradually through cohort replacement. It takes time for economic development to shape cultural values, so corresponding attitudinal change is likely to happen slowly, over generations. However, in some nations, including the United States, attitudes about homosexuality have changed quicker than cohort replacement would suggest. Over the last thirty years in the United States all age cohorts seem to have developed more liberal attitudes toward homosexuality (Brewer 2003; Loftus 2001; Sherkat et al. 2011; Treas 2002). Additionally, lesbian and gay celebrities and characters have gotten more media exposure; homosexual subcultures have expanded, becoming much more visible; and there have been well-publicized changes to same-sex marriage laws and civil rights. In contrast, other countries have not experienced the same rapid cultural, political, or legal changes related to homosexuality. For these nations, changes in attitudes are more likely to result from younger, more liberal generations replacing older, more conservative ones.

Events may also occur within nations that alert residents to a particular issue, which could then change the way they view it. For example, in the early 2000s Taiwan did not require education in schools regarding gender-related issues, but legislators were drafting a law that would require it. On April 20, 2000, a transgender boy, Yong-Chi Yie, who had been taunted by his middle school classmates because of his appearance, was found dead in a pool of his own blood in the school bathroom. The event prompted Taiwanese officials to include education about gay and transgender issues in their bill, changing its title from "Gender Equality" to "Gender Equity" (Hsieh 2012). In this case, a specific event seems to have led to changes in legislation. Of course, the Taiwanese may have already been moving in a more liberal direction, possibly because of democracy and increasing levels of economic development. The event may have simply given more urgency and awareness to a topic that would have inevitably become an important concern.

A key challenge for studies that want to examine change over time is that the data are often limited to nations that already have high levels of economic development. It is incredibly difficult and expensive to gather survey data in many countries, especially those with poor infrastructures and a lack of information on the population, which makes sampling much more challenging. Currently, there are only three surveys that regularly ask about feelings regarding homosexuality across many nations in several different regions of the world. They are the WVS, the International Social Survey Programme, and Pew's Global Attitudes Project. I use the WVS for the bulk of my cross-national analysis because survey administrators made it their goal to gather data in a large number of countries that are at different stages of economic development, even if the quality may be lower because of challenges in gathering a representative sample. (See Kuhar 2013; Szalma and Takács 2013.)

The WVS grew out of the European Values Survey. Started in the 1980s, it initially included only ten western European nations, but shortly thereafter the survey was done in twelve non-European countries (Heath, Fisher, and Smith 2005). While the WVS now has information on over eighty-five countries, the overwhelming majority of them do not have data for most survey waves, which is a major impediment for assessing how changes in economic development and democracy across several nations are related to adjustments in attitudes. At the time I was writing this book there was only one study that had investigated changes over time across many nations, accounting for both individual and country-level factors. In a sample of thirty-two countries, Hadler (2012) found that over a twenty-year period GDP had a tolerance-fostering effect. His findings are consistent with the ideas and analysis presented in this chapter. However, he also encountered some of the same challenges as other researchers. Most of the countries included in his analysis are largely Christian, are located in the Global North, and have moderate to high levels of economic development.

Since some societies did not ask about homosexuality until the last few waves of the WVS, researchers cannot test—across a range of different countries, over a reasonably long period—the extent to which changes in economic development and democracy are associated with increasing tolerance. Indeed, as I mentioned above, nations are likely to move at different rates through the stages of economic development, with some taking decades and others passing through them relatively quickly. Because so many countries are missing data during the WVS's earlier waves, the models presented in appendix B are constant, providing a single snapshot of the factors shaping attitudes across the world during the past fifteen years. However, with the country case studies in the next three chapters I am able to discuss and illustrate changes within individual nations. I am also able to explain how—along with economic development, democracy, and the religious climate—factors like social-movement activity, a culture of "coming out," and media influences have contributed to more tolerance in some countries.

An additional weakness of WVS data and most other cross-national surveys is that all of the available questions are very general, providing little insight into how people may see various LGBTQ individuals and what they view as "homosexual." There is a rich body of work from cultural studies that focuses on intersectionality, which refers to people's multiple interlocking characteristics defined in terms of their relative sociocultural power and privilege (Parent, DeBlaere, and Moradi 2013). Within research on sexuality, *intersectionality* is often used to describe the complexities in studying LGBTQs as a homogenous group when these individuals (e.g., lesbian, bisexual) often have very different identities and experiences that are further complicated by factors like gender, race, and economic status. A lot of work has found that characteristics like race can shape how LGBTQ individuals feel about themselves (J. Allen 2011; Bowleg 2013; Diaz et al. 2001; Smuts 2011), as well as how others perceive and interact with them (Worthen 2013). In many nations located in the Global North, for example, rich white gay men may be seen as more acceptable and less "deviant" or "problematic" than poor transgender Africans or African-American women.

The WVS asks only a few survey questions about homosexuality and does not distinguish between different groups (e.g., bisexual versus Queer) or make it possible to assess how factors like economic status might intersect with these other dimensions. Even in a single nation like the United States, which has a lot of survey research on homosexuality, few studies have examined how people differentially view LGBTQ individuals, much less how attitudes may differ based on factors like race, ethnicity, and gender (Worthen 2013). While it cannot be assessed with WVS survey questions that ask only about homosexuality, intersectionality is likely to play a role in how people view LGBTQ individuals and enter into their assessments about homosexuality.

The earlier part of this chapter focused heavily on the macro forces that are associated with attitudes about homosexuality. There are clearly some problems with putting too much weight on available public-opinion data and economic development, democracy, and the religious context of a nation when we try to understand cross-national attitudes. In trying to explain why there are such big differences in how nations view homosexuality, there is inevitably some tension between broad cross-national macro forces (i.e., democracy and economic development) and the data available to assess these processes on the one hand, and the specific events and historical processes that shape attitudes within particular countries on the other. (See Ragin 2014.) Whereas my cross-national survey analysis provides a more static view of the factors shaping attitudes, the case studies discussed in the next three chapters offer a more dynamic perspective.

RELIGIOUS CONTEXT AND THE ANTI-ASCETIC HYPOTHESIS

In the first chapter I discussed the important role that religion has in shaping residents' attitudes and how a country's religious context can influence feelings even for respondents who are not religious. Before ending this chapter, it is important to consider how religion is related to economic development and how their combined influence may shape public opinion about homosexuality. As I explain below, personal religious beliefs are more likely to shape attitudes about homosexuality in richer rather than poorer societies. This process can help explain why homosexuality remains such a divisive issue in many economically developed nations like the United States.

In the 1960s researchers (e.g., Middleton and Putney 1962) began putting forth the idea that personal religious beliefs tend to have a greater effect on attitudes and behaviors that are characterized by normative ambiguity (e.g., alcohol use), rather than attitudes and behaviors that are universally condemned (e.g., rape) (Burkett and White 1974; Hadaway, Elifson, and Petersen 1984; Tittle and Welch 1983). This is known as the anti-ascetic (i.e., abstinence from self-indulgent behaviors) hypothesis. The basic idea is that when laws are in place, there tend to be strong norms, values, and beliefs about the acceptability of certain behaviors. Since secular norms and laws are already in place, personal religious beliefs are less likely to shape how people view illegal behaviors like stealing or murder. As a result, secular and religious people tend to think, for example, that stranger rape is unacceptable.

When secular norms are more ambiguous and laws are less severe, religion is more likely to serve as a guide for attitudes and behaviors. Personal religious beliefs influence attitudes and behaviors, in part, because more-religious people are more likely to internalize the views of their faith. Religious leaders and organizations are likely to condemn anti-ascetic behaviors, such as alcohol consumption, homosexuality, and premarital sex, in a way that secular authorities in many nations (although not all) typically do not. Hence, for people who are religious,

religious beliefs are more likely to shape religiously proscribed attitudes and behaviors (i.e., premarital sex), even if the larger society does not condemn these acts.

A lot of empirical research has examined which behaviors personal religious beliefs are most likely to affect (Adamczyk 2013; Adamczyk and Pitt 2009; Finke and Adamczyk 2008; Hadaway, Elifson, and Petersen 1984; Reisig, Wolfe, and Pratt 2012; Tittle and Welch 1983). In general, personal religious beliefs appear to have little influence on the acceptability of universally condemned behaviors such as murder, rape, and incest. However, for minor crimes, such as recreational drug use and underage drinking, personal religious beliefs are more likely to act as a deterrent (Adamczyk 2012; Reisig, Wolfe, and Pratt 2012). While all members of a nation are held accountable for actions that are universally sanctioned, personal religious beliefs are more likely to serve as a guide when there are *not* clear social sanctions or universal agreement about a behavior's detrimental social costs.

The logic of the anti-ascetic hypothesis suggests that personal religious beliefs will have a greater influence on attitudes about homosexuality in nations with higher levels of economic development, where there should also be more normative ambiguity about the acceptability of homosexuality. When there is ambiguity in the larger culture about the acceptability of certain behaviors, more-religious people should be more likely to turn to religious institutions, religious officials, and trusted religious friends to make judgments about the acceptability of behaviors like homosexuality. When there is a lack of secular guidance, such as federal laws, and people encounter a range of possible responses, religion should be a more important authority source for making decisions and judgments. Hence, in nations with higher levels of economic development, people who are religious should be more likely to have attitudes that are consistent with religious proscriptions regarding homosexuality. Conversely, while the majority of people in poorer nations may find homosexuality problematic, personal religious beliefs should have less of an influence on attitudes because religion will be one of many authority sources (i.e., government, parents, friends, etc.) disapproving of homosexuality.

In figure 12, I illustrate the relationship between economic development and personal religious beliefs, using information presented in appendix B, table 9, models 4 and 5. In nations with low levels of economic development, residents on average have an attitudinal score of 9.67, which is highly disapproving of homosexuality. In poorer nations, there is a very

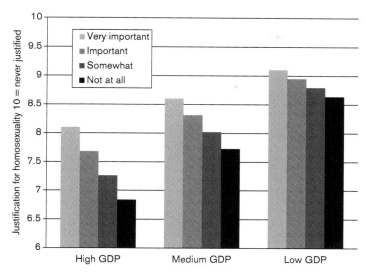

FIGURE 12. Marginal estimates of individual disapproval of homosexuality, by GDP. (Society N = 87; individual N = 202,316)

SOURCES: ARDA's Cross-National Socio-Economic and Religion Data, 2011; WVS, waves 4, 5, and 6.

NOTE: Predicted values are presented for a Protestant man living in a mixed Protestant country with a mean score on all other variables in model 4 of table 9 in appendix B. The three measures of GDP are based on the sample mean (i.e. $15,000 per capita) and approximately one standard deviation above and below the mean.

small attitudinal gap between people who find religion important and those who do not. In contrast, in richer nations, residents on average are more liberal, with an average attitudinal score of 8.41. However, there is also a bigger attitudinal gap between people who find religion to be very important and those who do not. In richer countries, religious belief is more likely to direct attitudes about homosexuality than it is in poorer countries, where everyone, both rich and poor, are likely to disapprove.

This relationship offers some insight into why many social issues, such as homosexuality, have remained salient even as nations become more economically developed. In poorer countries, religious and secular people are likely to agree about the unacceptability of behaviors like homosexuality, abortion, and euthanasia. Conversely, in richer societies, more-religious people are more likely to disagree with secular individuals about the acceptability of these behaviors. This rift can help explain why in relatively rich nations there is so much mobilization around issues like homosexuality (Gaskins, Golder, and Siegel 2013).

CONCLUSION

This chapter has explored the major societal forces, aside from religion, that are likely to shape public opinion. Economic development is associated with more-supportive attitudes. Likewise, democracies tend to have more-supportive residents. There are a wide range of characteristics that at first glance would seem important for explaining public opinion about homosexuality. These factors include economic and gender inequality, the mean level of education in a country, and the number of international and domestic nonprofit organizations. However, these other characteristics do not have any unique explanatory power for understanding why residents differ so dramatically in the extent to which they find homosexuality acceptable. That said, they may have an indirect influence, working through these more distant forces (e.g., democracy), or they may have an effect in a subset of nations (e.g., western Europe).

With the analysis in this chapter I also showed that as economic development increases, personal religious beliefs have a greater influence on attitudes. This relationship suggests that there may need to be a reorientation of thinking about the link between religion and friendlier attitudes. Economic development is likely to make all people within a nation more tolerant. However, economic development is also likely to accompany a shift in cultural values, resulting in fewer directives to orient attitudes. As a result, for people who are religious and live in wealthier nations, personal religious beliefs may be more likely to shape their views about homosexuality.

One of the strengths of a quantitative cross-national analysis is that it can help isolate the key characteristics that shape public opinion across the world. This is powerful. Why are there such vast differences between countries in public opinion and laws regarding homosexuality? Much of it can be explained by differences in the level of economic development, strength of democracy, and a society's religious context. Across a large number of the world's nations these are the key factors for explaining cross-national differences in public opinion about homosexuality. That said, other influences may be important for understanding the dynamics that shape public opinion *within* some countries.

In the next chapter I take a closer look at some of the forces operating within Uganda, South Africa, and the United States that have pushed public opinion and related laws in a given direction. Like the other comparative case studies, this chapter holds the dominant religion constant, making it easier to examine the influences of economic development and democracy, which vary substantially across these nations. Economic development, democracy, and religious salience are used as points of comparison for examining cross-national differences in attitudes. The case-study chapters provide an opportunity to see more clearly influences shaping attitudes that may be specific to a given country or region, and also where democracy, religious salience, and economic development do not have as strong of an influence as might be expected based solely on information from the large cross-national analysis.

PART TWO

Comparative Case Studies for Understanding Attitudes

CHAPTER 3

Shaping Attitudes in Protestant Nations

A Comparison of the United States, Uganda, and South Africa

Across the world many residents living in the Global North have expressed particularly tolerant views about homosexuality, and some of these nations have been forerunners in legalizing same-sex marriage and protecting against discrimination. Most of these countries have Christian histories. It may, therefore, seem that the divide in attitudes is driven by differences between Islam and Christianity. However, variation in attitudes between Muslim- and Christian-dominated nations, as well as among Protestant nations, is complicated by a number of factors. Decades ago Nordic countries like Sweden and Norway, which have majority Protestant populations, began implementing very liberal legislation related to same-sex relationships. Conversely, several African societies (i.e., Uganda, Kenya, Zimbabwe) that also have Protestant majorities have condemned homosexuality and have experienced a lot of police violence and vigilante killings directed at gay, lesbian, and transgender individuals (Cooper 2015; U.S. Department of State, Bureau of Public Affairs 2012; Gettleman 2011). This chapter takes a closer look at how economic development, democracy, and religion shape attitudes about homosexuality in a set of nations (i.e., Uganda, South Africa, and the United States) that include a mixture of Protestant faiths.

Across the world, 32% of the population is Christian, with Protestants accounting for about 37% of them (Pew-Templeton Global Religious Futures Project 2011). North America, Europe, and Africa are home to the highest proportions of Protestants. Both North America and Africa include countries that have a wide range of different Protestant groups, often with a substantial minority of Catholics and relatively high levels of religious belief and engagement (Association of Religious Data Archives, n.d.; CIA World Factbook 2013). Conversely, European Protestant nations like Sweden, Norway, and Great Britain are dominated by mainline groups like Lutherans and Anglicans.

Compared with other Protestant denominations, many mainline faiths have not been as successful at generating high levels of religious belief (Iannaccone 1994), and most European Protestants are not actively engaged in their religion. For the mainline Protestant nations included in the WVS (see appendix A), only 9% of residents attend religious services once a week or more. Conversely, over 60% of people living in mixed Protestant nations attend weekly, and in some Protestant nations like Ghana and Tanzania over 80% do. The United States was initially settled by Europeans and shares many of the same characteristics as these nations, including high levels of economic development and a stable democracy. However, many Americans (many more than northern Europeans) are actively engaged in their religion. (Pew Research Center 2015a). Consistent with their greater valuing of religion, at times Americans have been slower to accept homosexuality than northern Europeans (Pew Research Center 2012a). However, attitudes have been changing, and in 2015 the United States joined several other countries across the world in legalizing same-sex marriage.

The previous two chapters used quantitative data to establish the key factors shaping attitudes across many nations. In this chapter I present a comparative case study of Uganda, South Africa, and the United States to better understand the processes producing these relationships (i.e., sequential exploratory mixed-methods design). These nations offer an ideal comparison for understanding how economic development and democracy shape public opinion. These countries include a mixture of conservative and mainline Protestants, making it possible to hold the dominant religion constant so that other influences can be examined. Great Britain colonized all three nations, and English is their official language, making it easier to conduct additional analyses of documents written in English. These countries differ in their level of economic development and strength of democracy, making it possible to see how these elements shape public opinion in nations that have a somewhat similar religious makeup.

In addition to using survey data and information on the history of and social, political, and economic climate in these nations, my research team and I conducted a content analysis of newspaper articles (i.e., the *New Vision,* the *Daily Monitor,* the *Star,* the *Daily News,* and *USA Today*) for 2008. The newspaper analysis provides additional comparable information on how the average resident may understand homosexuality, and also the frames and claimsmakers that the major news press in each nation uses. (Appendix D presents more-technical information about the newspaper analysis.) I first discuss Uganda, then South Africa, and finally the United States. In the overview of each society, the history and environment related to public opinion and laws are presented. As each new case-study nation is introduced, more comparative information is presented, so that the last case study (i.e., the United States) discusses more fully differences between it and Uganda and South Africa. In the final part of this chapter I discuss some of the differences between nations dominated by mainline Protestant groups, most of which are located in Europe, and those that have a mixture of mainline and conservative Protestant adherents.

PUBLIC OPINION IN UGANDA

Like many African residents, most Ugandans are ardently opposed to homosexuality. In figure 13, I show that 76% of Ugandans do not want a homosexual neighbor, compared with 46% of South Africans and 23% of Americans. In addition to public-opinion data, recent newspaper articles have been clear in their condemnation of homosexuality (Adamczyk, Kim, and Paradis 2015). In 2014, for example, the Ugandan tabloid *Red Pepper* printed the names of two hundred people it claimed were homosexual, including several who had not previously come out (Gander 2014). Additionally, there have been reports of individuals identified as homosexual (e.g., David Kato) being attacked or killed because of their sexual identity or suspected behaviors (Gettleman 2011). Same-sex sexual relationships are illegal in Uganda, and over the last decade the government has tried to increase penalties for them.

Prior to 2000 there do not seem to be any survey data on Ugandans' attitudes about homosexuality, limiting knowledge on how views may have evolved. Although Ugandans may long have had highly disapproving attitudes, before this period, discussions about homosexuality were not appearing in the media and few politicians mentioned anything about same-sex relations (Tamale 2003). Since 2000 the public attention given to homosexuality has increased substantially. In his research Grossman (2013) found that in 2003 there were approximately thirty-five newspaper

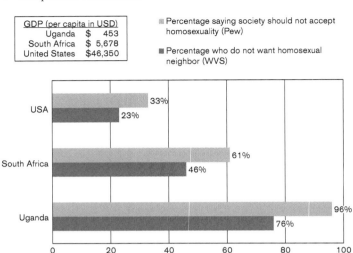

FIGURE 13. Snapshot of GDP and disapproving attitudes in the United States, South Africa, and Uganda.

SOURCES: 2013 Spring Pew Global Attitudes Survey (Pew Research Center 2013); WVS, wave 4; ARDA's Cross-National Socio-Economic and Religion Data, 2011.

articles per year in Uganda that covered homosexuality-related issues. Between 2007 and 2009 the number more than doubled, to about eighty.

There seems to have been an increase in discussions about homosexuality, at least in part, because the Ugandan government has given it more attention. In 2009 a bill, popularly referred to as the "Kill the Gays Bill," was proposed that would have made aggravated homosexuality punishable with death (Bahati 2009). The bill also recommended making it an offense to promote homosexuality, including publishing information related to same-sex sexual practices and providing resources to organizations (e.g., AIDS organizations) working with gay and lesbian individuals (Bahati 2009). Ultimately, the bill's most draconian measures (i.e., death) were removed, and after it was signed into law, the Ugandan judiciary ruled in 2014 that parliament did not have a quorum to pass the legislation (Gettleman 2014).

Because there have been so many passionate and disapproving discussions about homosexuality in Uganda's public domain in the last ten years, some scholars have suggested that the nation has been experiencing a "moral panic" (Awondo, Geschiere, and Reid 2012; Grossman 2013; Sadgrove et al. 2012). Moral panics are often seen as overblown, but potentially useful for people in power or those who want to divert attention away from more pressing and complicated issues. Some researchers have suggested that the high level of attention given to homosexuality may be an attempt to distract the public from more-pressing concerns, like the nation's poor economic conditions (Awondo, Geschiere, and Reid 2012; Grossman 2013). Below I explain the role that Uganda's low level of economic development, relatively weak democracy, and high levels of religious belief are likely to play in shaping attitudes.

THE CULTURE CREATED BY LOW ECONOMIC DEVELOPMENT

With a 2008 GDP of $458, Uganda is considered a relatively poor nation, though in recent years it has begun to undergo processes of economic development. Because of its relatively low GDP and all of the processes that are implied with it (i.e., lower educational attainment, higher fertility, less Internet and media exposure), work by Inglehart (2006), Schwartz (1999; 2006), and Hofstede (2001) would suggest that the culture should be more oriented toward survival, and focused on collective family and community needs rather than individual expression and uniqueness. These cultural orientations should lead to an environment that is highly disapproving of homosexuality.

Industrialization and economic development tend to increase as residents migrate from rural to urban areas, moving from jobs based in the agricultural sector to those in manufacturing and eventually the service industry. With over 85% of residents living in rural areas (Mukwaya et al. 2011) and working in the agriculture sector, Uganda would be considered a rural nation that is just beginning to industrialize. Because homosexuality is illegal and close to 90% disapprove, many Ugandans, especially from rural areas, may not know or meet anyone who is openly gay. As discussed in the first chapter, having contact with openly gay or lesbian individuals can go a long way to increasing empathy (Detenber et al. 2013; Herek and Capitanio 1996; Hinrichs and Rosenberg 2002).

As I will discuss later in this chapter, in other countries like the United States, people who would not necessarily know someone who is gay or lesbian (perhaps because they live in rural areas) have been introduced to them through popular television shows and other media outlets (Schiappa, Gregg, and Hewes 2006). In part related to lower levels of economic development, less than 10% of Ugandans use the Internet (Internet World Stats, n.d.), and only about 25% of households have a

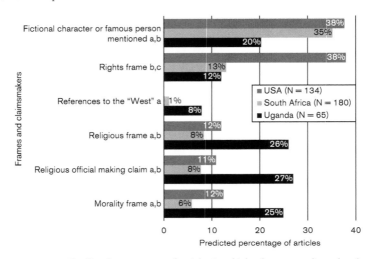

FIGURE 14. Predicted percentages of articles in which a homosexuality-related term is used by key associations and claimsmakers in the United States, South Africa, and Uganda, 2008. (N = 379 total articles with term)

a = Significant difference (p < .05) between Uganda and South Africa

b = Significant difference (p < .05) between Uganda and the United States

c = Significant difference (p < .05) between South Africa and the United States

NOTE: Marginal percentages presented for all newspaper articles in 2008 that mentioned a homosexuality-related term. In producing the percentages, the following variables were held constant: article type, whether the information originated from inside or outside the country, and number of days published each week. See appendix D for more information on the coding and analysis.

television, with the overwhelming majority of these having free-to-air broadcasting (Dataxis 2015). For people who have regular media access, the likelihood of seeing many LGBTQ characters or individuals is small. Figure 14 presents the findings from the newspaper analysis that my research team and I performed for 2008. Relative to those published in the United States and South Africa, the Ugandan newspapers are much less likely to mention LGBTQ individuals or characters. This lack of exposure may contribute to a lack of empathy for these people.

Nations with lower levels of economic development also tend to have high fertility rates, which are likely to have some implications for understanding views about homosexuality. Though it is slowly declining, in 2011 Uganda had one of the highest fertility rates in the world (Uganda Bureau of Statistics 2012). Because a high fertility rate increases the number of people available to work in agriculture, rural residents may be especially likely to value large families (Boserup 1985). In addition to needing family members to farm the land, in rural areas there tend to be fewer costs to having large families. Parents are less likely to have careers, which might otherwise limit family size, and children may be less likely to attend school and college. Large families can also help to secure inheritance and help parents as they get older (Ware 1978). When large families are normative, it may become more difficult for people to embrace life as a single person without children, enter a long-term relationship (whether homosexual or heterosexual) without having biological children, or visualize a same-sex couple raising children. (See Sadgrove et al. 2012.)

With very large families there are also likely to be some concerns about having enough financial support to care for everyone. In Uganda, as in many other countries, men are typically the primary breadwinners. In 2002 there was a 39% wage differential between Ugandan men and women (Sebaggala 2008). Because men make so much more money, women are especially dependent on them to support their families. If daughters do not marry, their families will not receive proceeds from a bride-price or dowry, which is sometimes exchanged in Uganda (Hague and Thiara 2009; Oguli Oumo 2004). Likewise, if sons do not marry, the family will not secure another woman for the household who could help with chores, have children, and take care of elderly parents. By not participating in traditional practices such as getting married, having a large biological family, and accepting duties consistent with traditional gender roles, gay and lesbian Ugandans may be viewed as not submitting their will and preferences to the larger group—which, I explain in chapter 2, is much more likely to be expected in a less economically developed nation.

UGANDA'S WEAKER DEMOCRACY

Along with economic development, Uganda's relatively weak democracy is also likely to play a role in creating an environment that is unsupportive of homosexuality. Like many African nations, Uganda became independent only relatively recently (1962). Before that, beginning in the late 1800s, the British occupied the nation. In 2016 Uganda's president was Yoweri Kaguta Museveni. He came to power in 1986 and initially was lauded as a new generation of African leaders (McKinley 1998). However, his tenure has been marked by problems, including the occupation of the Congo during the Second Congo War, which left millions of people dead. The European Union Election Observation Mission (2011) described the 2011 election, which Museveni won, as "marred by avoidable administrative and logistical failures that led to an unacceptable number of Ugandan citizens being disfranchised."

Embedded within the concept of democracy are ideals or standards of governmental behavior that include fairness, impartiality, equality, freedom of speech, and the right to demonstrate. Seeing the government support and exhibit these principles provides a model for how residents should treat others, even those they personally dislike (Guérin, Petry, and Crête 2004; Peffley and Rohrschneider 2003). Although Uganda is a democracy, it is considered a relatively weak one, with Freedom House classifying the nation's civil liberties as "not free" (Freedom House 2015). There are a number of reports about the government struggling to uphold democratic ideals. For example, in the late 2000s the economic crisis in Uganda started to deepen, and residents began protesting escalating food and fuel costs. In 2011 the nonprofit group Activists for Change urged Ugandans to walk to work in protest, which many did (Gatsiounis 2011) The government responded harshly, approaching the protesters with tear gas and riot gear. Ultimately the government declared Activists for Change unlawful (Human Rights Watch 2012).

In 2009 David Bahati, who was a member of the Ugandan parliament, proposed the Uganda Anti-Homosexual Bill, which would have made aggravated homosexuality punishable with death (Heather 2014; Guardian 2009). The bill sparked massive controversy, with a lot of disapproval coming from other countries. My research team and I analyzed two Ugandan newspapers: the government-owned *New Vision,* which has the highest circulation in Uganda (New Vision 2008); and the *Daily Monitor,* which has the second-highest circulation and is publicly owned. For the one-year period under examination (2008), we found almost no articles that mentioned homosexuality in a positive way. Additionally, as shown in figure 14, compared with the Ugandan papers, articles from *USA Today* were substantially more likely to mention homosexuality in the context of civil rights and liberties. These findings suggest that within the public press Ugandans are getting little exposure to positive portrayals of homosexuality or the idea that it might be seen as a rights-related issue.

As mentioned above, in the late 2000s many Ugandan officials became more vocal in condemning gay and lesbian individuals. Some scholars have suggested that the problematic political and economic conditions in

Uganda may have prompted some government leaders to use the issue of homosexuality as a way to distract from more-pressing economic and political concerns (Sadgrove et al. 2012). The political scientist Guy Grossman makes the point that with higher levels of democratization, incumbent politicians face more pressure to build reputations (Grossman 2013). One way that they can bolster their standing is by focusing on homosexuality-related issues, which can be highly visible, and relevant laws and policies do not require a lot of energy, coordination, or resources to implement. Hence, while a weak democracy may lower tolerance, with increasing levels of democracy politicians are under greater pressure to capture the public's attention. Some may then use homosexuality to garner support, which could further increase disapproval.

While in the mid-2010s the Ugandan government seemed focused on strengthening punishment for same-sex sexual relations and establishments that serve LGBTQ individuals, there are some forces working against it. After the Ugandan newspaper *Rolling Stone* published the names, photographs, and addresses of one hundred homosexuals with the headline "Hang Them," the individuals named sued the paper. The newspaper lost in court, and the court set a precedent for protecting individuals' right to privacy (BBC News 2011). Hence, in Uganda some democratic elements and principals like the independence of the judiciary and support for privacy are somewhat present.

While the Ugandan government is hostile to homosexuality, other nations, including those located in Europe and North America as well as the United Nations, have put a lot of pressure on Uganda to limit its harsh homosexuality-related legislation. In 2012 Uganda received the equivalent of 9.4% of its gross national income as aid (i.e., official development assistance) (Global Humanitarian Assistance, n.d.). After the Uganda Anti-Homosexuality Bill was proposed, several nations cut their funding (Plaut 2014), and the World Bank postponed a $90 million loan (BBC News 2014). At the same time as the bill's proposal, the United Nations General Assembly put forth a resolution to support LGBT rights. Possibly to placate Western donors, the Ugandan government modified its bill to make "aggravated homosexuality" punishable with life in prison instead of death. The bill was ultimately overturned in court. Some legal scholars have suggested that President Museveni may have used the court's ruling as a convenient cover to drop what had turned into a "diplomatic headache" (Gettleman 2014).

Uganda is highly reliant on foreign aid and—in a situation related to being at an earlier stage of economic development—does not seem to have the same political, media, or financial power as other countries. Relatedly, there seems to be some resentment directed at Western nations. As figure 14 shows, my research team and I found that newspaper articles from Uganda that mentioned homosexuality were substantially more likely than those from South Africa, which has a much higher level of economic development—to discuss this issue in the context of Western influences (e.g., United States, Europe). In contrast to the Ugandan papers, only one article from the South African papers mentioned "Western" influences or associations. In part because of pressure from other, more-developed nations, including the United States, homosexuality and the idea of it as a human rights issue seem to be getting framed as something originating from the West and as un-African.

RELIGION'S ROLE IN SHAPING PUBLIC OPINION ABOUT HOMOSEXUALITY IN UGANDA

As I discussed in the first chapter, the religious context of a nation, as well as personal religious beliefs, can influence residents' attitudes. Religion seems to have an important role in shaping public opinion in Uganda. Ugandans have very high levels of religious belief, with 99% believing in God and 94% identifying as a religious person (Association of Religious Data Archives, n.d.). The proportion of Christians in Uganda is about 85%, with the two largest groups being Catholic (about 42%) and Anglican (about 36%). Approximately 5% of Ugandans affiliate with a Pentecostal faith; in other parts of the world such faiths tend to be more conservative than Catholic or Anglican religions. While the Catholic Church is hierarchical and centralized, with the head of the church (i.e., the pope) located in Rome, the Anglican Church is relatively decentralized, and different dioceses have a lot of freedom in the policies they adopt and the views they support.

In many parts of the world the Anglican Church has been one of the few Christian religious denominations to support homosexuality-related issues and individuals early on (Pew Research Center 2012b).[1] In 2003 the Episcopal Church in the United States of America consecrated Gene Robinson as the Anglican Communion's first openly gay bishop. The act was highly controversial, especially for many provinces from the Global South, which responded by declaring "impaired communion," meaning that the baptismal union was not accompanied by orders and sacraments that were fully aligned (Goodstein 2008; Sherwood 2016). At the time Uganda's archbishop of the Anglican Church,

Henry Luke Orombi, joined the revolt in Africa, and along with others boycotted the 2008 Lambeth Conference, which is the decennial assembly of bishops from the Anglican Communion. The analysis of Ugandan newspaper articles that my team and I conducted showed that in 2008 Orombi was regularly quoted in *New Vision* as making negative comments about homosexuality.

In addition to Uganda's Anglican Church being vocally opposed to homosexuality, some American Evangelicals have had a role in shaping discourse about and legal actions related to homosexuality. In March 2009 Scott Lively and two other American Evangelicals (Don Schmierer and Caleb Lee Brundidge) traveled to Kampala to give a series of talks. According to Stephen Langa, the Ugandan organizer, the theme of the event was "'the gay agenda—the whole hidden and dark agenda'—and the threat homosexuals posed to Bible-based values and the traditional African family" (Gettleman 2010). One of the attendees was David Bahati, who ultimately proposed the Uganda Anti-Homosexuality Bill. Some researchers have argued that American Evangelists have had a major role in shaping how Ugandans view homosexuality (Kaoma 2009; Oliver 2012). No doubt they have had some influence, likely over proposed homosexuality-related legislation. However, the WVS data that I presented in figure 13, which documents Ugandans' very high levels of disapproval, were collected between 1999 and 2004, long before Scott Lively and his affiliates held their 2009 conference. Hence, many Ugandans have been opposed to homosexuality at least since the 1990s, even if they have not necessarily been very vocal about it.

While religion is unlikely to be the single factor shaping public opinion in Uganda, along with morality it has proven to be a popular media frame. The United States, South Africa, and Uganda all have relatively high levels of religious belief and large Protestant populations. Yet the extent to which religion is used in newspaper discussions varies substantially. During 2008, 26% of the Ugandan newspaper articles that referenced homosexuality also brought up religion, and 27% of them mentioned a religious official. Conversely, less than 12% of the newspaper articles from the United States and South Africa mentioned religion or included references to religious officials. (See figure 14.)

As noted above, in addition to drawing on more-religious themes, my research team and I found that almost all of the references to religion in the Ugandan papers that mentioned homosexuality were negative. Conversely, in South Africa and the United States, my research team and I did not find any articles that used religion in a negative way. Rather, the majority of articles in *USA Today* either downplayed the importance of homosexuality as a key religious issue or attempted to reconcile Christian beliefs with acceptance. In contrast to Uganda, South Africa and the United States seem to have found some space within at least one national paper where homosexuality-related issues are largely discussed without reference to religion or a lot of negativity, even though all three countries have relatively high levels of religious belief.

PUBLIC OPINION IN SOUTH AFRICA

In sharp contrast to Uganda, South Africa is one of the richest nations in Africa, and it is the first country in the world to have a constitution that guarantees civil liberties for gay and lesbian individuals. Additionally, gay couples can marry and adopt children, and their partners are entitled to spousal benefits and government protections. While South Africans are more supportive than Ugandans, they are not as tolerant and accepting as might be expected given their liberal laws and policies. For example, in 2001 the Netherlands became the first nation in the world to legalize same-sex marriage, and in the 2000s only 13% of the Dutch felt that homosexuality was never justified. Likewise, Spain legalized gay marriage in 2005, and in the early 2000s only 12% of Spaniards felt that it was never justified. Conversely, as I show in figure 15, in the mid-2000s when same-sex marriage was legalized in South Africa, less than half of the residents felt that homosexuality is never justified.

Like Uganda and many other sub-Saharan African nations, South Africa has seen many reports of LGBTQ individuals being victimized (Hunter-Gault 2012; Nel and Judge 2008; Reid and Dirsuweit 2002). Harassment for being or acting "gay" seems to be particularly high among lesbians and poor Black Africans[2] (Wells and Polders 2006). While strangers may direct some violence toward LGBTQ individuals, a lot of victims' stories and reports suggest that physical attacks are also perpetrated by people the victim knows (Reid and Dirsuweit 2002), and rape in general in South Africa (Rape Crisis Cape Town Trust, n.d.), as well as elsewhere, is more likely to be committed by someone familiar. Additionally, because of the history of apartheid in the country, South Africa has some of the highest rates of economic inequality in the world (World Bank 2013b). Its high level of inequality has ramifications for how white and black LGBTQs are treated. In discussing the gay rights clause that was included in the constitution, Sharon Cooper, who is the former editor of *Womyn,* explains that it "has had no impact on the

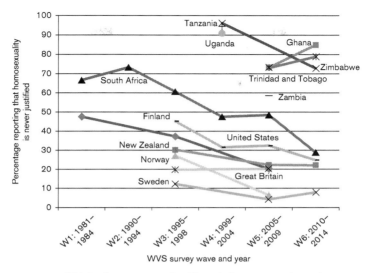

FIGURE 15. Weighted percentages of residents in Protestant nations who report that homosexuality is never justified over time.

masses. It's brilliant legislation but meaningless to people without jobs. The law is a luxury, it only works for rich, white people" (quoted in Cock 2003).

The experiences of many LGBTQ South Africans and the public's view of homosexuality are going to be complicated by how sexuality intersects with race, class, and gender (Lewis and Marshall 2012; Puar 2007; Worthen 2013). Because of the history of apartheid and ongoing racism, sexism, and very high levels of inequality, a number of cultural researchers have found that South Africa offers a particularly vivid lens through which to view the different intersections of race, gender, and class for LGBTQ individuals (Moolman 2013; Smuts 2011; Swarr and Nagar 2004). Unfortunately, assessment of the public's attitudes toward various LGBTQ individuals (e.g., a white, rich gay man versus a poor, black transgender youth) is more limited because the vast majority of public-opinion data ask only about "homosexuality." Nevertheless, I am able to provide some insight into the factors shaping general attitudes about homosexuality in South Africa.

Why did South Africa implement liberal homosexuality-related legislation when residents were not that supportive? As I discuss below, the history of apartheid in South Africa has had a major role in shaping legislation regarding the rights of sexual minorities. Slowly, this legislation, along with other forces, seems to have contributed to more-tolerant views.

INTERCONNECTION BETWEEN GAY RIGHTS AND THE DEVELOPMENT OF DEMOCRACY

Ever since the Dutch and the British began colonizing the nation in the 1600s, racial segregation has been present in South Africa. In 1948 the National Party, which largely represented Afrikaners (i.e., people of Dutch decent), won office in a nondemocratic election in which blacks could not vote. As promised, they set up a system of racial segregation whereby the rights, associations, and movements of most black residents were curtailed to help maintain white minority rule. They enacted many laws, including ones limiting where different racial groups could live and travel, and made it illegal for South Africans to marry or have sexual relations with someone of a different race (Kurtz 2016).

Not surprisingly, throughout the latter part of the twentieth century South Africa encountered a lot of domestic and international pressure to end apartheid, especially given the decolonialization that was happening on other parts of the continent and the diverse racial groups gaining civil rights elsewhere (Barnes 2008). Free elections were finally held in 1994, when Nelson Mandela was elected and the first constitution was developed. In the 1970s some homosexuality rights groups began to form. One of the nation's largest organizations was the Gay Association of South Africa (GASA), which consisted mostly of white males (Cameron and Gevisser 2013). The group was apolitical during a time when the suppression of blacks in South Africa was receiving growing international attention (Conway 2009). In 1984, Simon Tseko Nkoli, who was one of the first South African gay rights activists and one of the few black members of GASA, was imprisoned for three years for speaking out against the policies of the ruling apartheid government (Croucher 2002). Nkoli was imprisoned with members of the United Democratic Front (UDF), which was fighting within South Africa to end apartheid and included future leaders of Nelson Mandela's African National Congress (ANC).

While in prison Nkoli revealed that he was gay, and awareness of his situation seemed to have a positive influence on how many UDF and ANC members viewed homosexuality (Massoud 2003). After being released from prison in 1988, Nkoli formed the Gay and Lesbian Organization of the Witwatersrand (GLOW). GLOW has had a major role in helping pass legislation supporting gay and lesbian individuals and in helping black Africans from impoverished communities understand their rights under the new government (Massoud 2003). In a speech at the first South African pride parade, Nkoli declared: "I'm fighting for the abolition of apartheid, and I fight for the right of freedom of sexual orientation. These are inextricably linked with each other. I cannot be free as a black man if I am not free as a gay man" (Luirink 2000, 5). Important leaders in the fight for democracy (e.g., Nelson Mandela and Desmond Tutu) seemed to draw a similar connection between the two groups (Massoud 2003).

Activities happening outside of South Africa to end apartheid also seemed to play a role in shaping how the new government ultimately felt about homosexuality-related rights. In 1987 Ruth Mompati, who was a member of the executive committee of the ANC (i.e., Mandela's political party), gave an interview in which she described homosexual individuals as "not normal. If everyone was like that, the human race would come to an end" (Tatchell 1987). In an attempt to make clear existing homophobia within the ANC, Peter Tatchell, who was a London-based anti-apartheid and homosexuality rights activist and journalist, published his views (Tatchell 2005). As a result, there was a small backlash against the ANC, which was then petitioned to recognize gay and lesbian rights, and at a 1992 conference it did (Cock 2003).

The relationship between the anti-apartheid movement and the fight for homosexuality-related rights was further solidified by the support of two prominent South African Nobel Prize winners: Desmond Tutu, who was a well-known archbishop; and Nelson Mandela, who was the first democratically elected South African president. Researchers have argued that because activists framed gay rights as part of the anti-apartheid struggle, with figures like Mandela and Tutu supporting the movement it was very difficult for any countermovement to gain much ground (Massoud 2003). As one gay activist explained in Thoreson's (2008) work on South Africa's movement, "[W]hen you have people like Mandela and Tutu affirming gay rights, you've got this huge, huge moral weight against which you have to fight" (688).

The turn to democracy in South Africa ushered in legal protections for gay and lesbian individuals, which at the time resulted in some of the most liberal legislation in the world. However, at least initially the legislation did not have as big an impact on attitudes as might be expected. As shown in figure 15, in 1980 67% of South Africans felt that homosexuality was never justified. This number decreased to 61%

in 1995, further decreased to 48% in 2005, and finally fell to 29% during the sixth wave of the WVS. In contrast, the United States legalized gay marriage only in 2015, and during the early 2010s only 25% of residents felt that homosexuality was never justified.

Why haven't South Africans been more accepting of homosexuality? South Africa is located in a region of the world where nearby nations have been vehement in their condemnation of homosexuality (see also Currier 2012). As I show in figure 15, when the sixth wave of the WVS was collected between 2010 and 2014, more than 70% of Ghanaians, Zimbabweans, and Tanzanians said they felt that homosexuality is never justified. Compared with its neighbors, South Africa appears quite liberal. Additionally, the anti-Western discourse that seems to have pervaded discussions about homosexuality in Uganda is more limited in South Africa, at least as indicated by the major newspapers (see figure 14) and statements by some key officials like Nelson Mandela and Desmond Tutu.

As noted above and shown in figure 14, there was only one South African newspaper article in 2008 that mentioned Western influences in conjunction with homosexuality. Part of the reason for this may be related to the movement's success in framing homosexuality as something South Africans needed to address due to the nation's repressive history of apartheid. Table 12 in appendix D also shows that newspapers in South Africa are less likely than those from the United States to discuss homosexuality in the context of rights and liberties. I suspect that this may have to do with South Africans already having these rights, causing the rights frame to be less relevant for contemporary discussions about same-sex relations.

ECONOMIC DEVELOPMENT AND INEQUALITY IN SHAPING ATTITUDES

While there may be some discrepancy between rights and public opinion about homosexuality in South Africa, given its GDP, attitudes are more tolerant than the nation's level of economic development alone would suggest. The country has a higher level of economic development than Uganda and almost all of its sub-Saharan African neighbors. In a country with a 2008 GDP of about $5,600 (see figure 17), 41% of South Africans across the last three waves of the WVS reported that homosexuality was never acceptable. For this GDP, the regression line in figure 7 shows that about 65% should say it is never justified.

Consistent with its higher level of economic development, South Africa has a fertility rate that is much lower than Uganda's, even in very rural areas where less than 40% of South Africans live (United Nations 2015), compared with over 85% of Ugandans. Because of factors like a very large rural population, high fertility rates, and, of course, homosexuality being illegal, I argued earlier in this chapter that Ugandans are unlikely to meet many openly gay or lesbian individuals. The situation seems different in South Africa, which has a vibrant gay community and many bars, clubs, and organizations that cater to the LGBTQ population. Likewise, South Africa's media is much more likely to show and discuss LGBTQ characters. Table 12 in appendix D presents the likelihood that newspaper articles that mention homosexuality will also discuss fictional characters or famous people. Figure 14 presents the predicted percentages. In South Africa the predicted percentage (i.e., 35%) of newspaper articles that mentioned homosexuality and were also discussing fictional or famous people is very similar to that in the United States (i.e., 38%) and much higher than in Uganda (i.e., 20%). Even if they do not personally know anyone who is gay or lesbian, there is more of a chance in South Africa than in Uganda that residents will get some exposure to LGBTQ individuals through the media.

In addition to having a high level of economic development for its region, South Africa is known for having one of the highest levels of economic inequality in the world, which is likely to lead to very difference experiences for LGBTQ individuals. A common way to measure economic inequality is with the GINI index, which ranges from zero, which means that everyone has the same income, to one, which indicates complete inequality. Few countries go above 0.5, and with a score of 0.58 between 2000 and 2010 South Africa has one of the highest (World Bank 2013b). A primary reason for very high economic inequality is the nation's relatively recent history of apartheid, where whites, which in 2011 constituted 8.9% of the population, had on average much higher incomes than blacks, which constituted 79.2% of the nation (Lehohla 2012). The intersection between economic status, sexuality, and race are likely to exacerbate differences in the social worlds that white and black South African LGBTQs inhabit (Moolman 2013; Swarr and Nagar 2004). While it cannot be assessed with the WVS, intersecting characteristics like gender and race are likely to complicate how different segments of the public feel about various LGBTQ individuals (Worthen 2013).

RELIGION'S ROLE IN SHAPING ATTITUDES
IN SOUTH AFRICA

In Uganda religious ideas seem to be taking the lead in shaping anti-homosexual media discussions and legislation. The situation is different in South Africa. Like Uganda and the United States, a substantial proportion of South Africans (i.e., 80%) consider themselves Christian. Among Christians, 32% would be considered mainline Protestant and 9% would be classified as Catholic (Statistics South Africa 2004). Pentecostals contribute about 26%, African Independent Churches adherents make up approximately 24%, and the remaining Christians belong to other groups.

In contrast to Uganda's Anglican Church, many of South Africa's mainline churches have tended to embrace liberation theology, interpreting Christian teachings in relation to freedom from unjust political, social, and economic conditions (Burchardt 2013). Consistent with this orientation, many mainline South African Protestant churches have a long history of supporting the anti-apartheid movement and, like many ANC party leaders and government officials, have connected the struggle of the two movements. In his research on rights in South Africa, Thoreson (2008) explains, "The churches that are respected are considered worthy because of their historic role in the liberation movement—and these are not necessarily the conservative churches that oppose GLB (gay, lesbian, and bisexual) rights, which may be viewed with skepticism where democratic rights and responsibilities are concerned" (687).

While mainline Protestants are more likely to view the Bible metaphorically, some Christian South Africans, especially Pentecostals, are likely to interpret it literally. However, as Burchardt (2013) notes, there is a limit to the usefulness of a literalist perspective for arguing against homosexuality-related rights in South Africa because some biblical passages can also be understood as proscribing marriage between the races (i.e., Deut. 7:1–6). Mixed marriages were not allowed under apartheid, which the white-dominated Dutch Reformed Church supported. If South African religious groups literally interpret biblical passages about same-sex relations, they could be perceived as suggesting that the apartheid policy criminalizing interracial marriage was consistent with Christian precepts (Thoreson 2008). Yet some Christian South Africans still invoke a literalist interpretation to protest homosexuality-related rights (Reid 2010). There is also an anti-homosexual movement that largely consists of Christians (Croucher 2002). However, given the long anti-

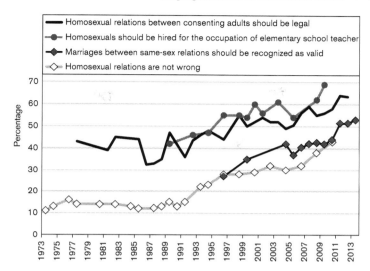

FIGURE 16. Increases in Americans' support for homosexuality-related issues and individuals.

SOURCES: National Opinion Research Center's General Social Survey; Gallup and CNN's Opinion Research Corporation surveys; Gallup and Newsweek's Princeton Survey Research Associates surveys; ABC, Washington Post, and CBS surveys (all sources in Bowman, Rugg, and Marsico 2013).

apartheid struggle, relatively few South African leaders seem willing to draw on a literalist biblical reading of same-sex relations to publicly oppose homosexuality-related rights (Thoreson 2008).

QUICKLY CHANGING ATTITUDES ABOUT HOMOSEXUALITY IN THE UNITED STATES

Compared with Uganda and South Africa, the United States has the most accepting attitudes about homosexuality.[3] The WVS's data collection from the early 2000s, which is the only survey period that includes all three countries, shows that 32% of Americans felt that homosexuality was never justified, compared with 48% of South Africans and 91% of Ugandans. (See figure 15.) As I show in figure 16, the percentage of Americans who feel that homosexual relations are not wrong went from 11% in 1973 to 43% in 2010. Likewise, in 1996 27% of Americans thought that marriage between same-sex couples should be recognized as valid, but by 2013 53% of residents thought that it should be.

As mentioned previously, there are primarily two processes (i.e., cohort succession and intracohort change) through which public opinion tends to change over time. A lot of research has assessed which process is primarily responsible for Americans' liberalizing opinions. Among researchers there seems to be a clear consensus that much of the recent change in attitudes is the result of adjustments within cohorts (Brewer 2003; Loftus 2001; Sherkat et al. 2011; Treas 2002). There simply was not enough time between the 1980s and today for cohorts to fully turn over and account for Americans' vastly more liberal views.

If attitudes regarding same-sex relationships became more supportive for many Americans, what caused the change? Greater visibility of homosexual individuals and their organizing activities can, in part, explain the uptick in tolerance. Through the 1950s LGBTQ individuals were largely unseen, in part, because there were harsh legal and social ramifications for exhibiting any indication of same-sex appearance. Although LGBTQ organizations have long existed, during the 1960s they became more effective organizers (see D'Emilio 2012). At the same time, the civil rights and antiwar movements were in full swing, creating a climate conducive to change, especially through organized protest.

Throughout the 1970s the American public became increasingly aware of homosexuality through movement activity, including the first gay pride parade, and well-publicized incidents like the murder of Harvey Milk. The 1980s brought with it the AIDS crisis, and at first the virus was viewed as something that affected only gay men, initially being called "gay-related immune deficiency." Because of the crisis LGBTQ individuals received a lot of negative publicity. Additionally, as Fetner (2008) points out, at this time the Republic Party actively began to focus on family values, which, among other things, problematized sex outside of heterosexual marriage, including same-sex relationships.

By the middle of the 1990s LGBTQ organizations had begun to gain a lot of positive attention (Brewer 2007), in part, because of their support for HIV-positive individuals and fighting for better medical treatment and civil rights and liberties. Likewise, in 1998 Matthew Shepherd, who was a gay student at the University of Wyoming, was kidnapped, beaten, and tied to a fence for eighteen hours; he ultimately died (Brooke 1998). The incident was heavily publicized and, as Brewer (2003) notes, may have presented a "critical moment" whereby Americans began to seriously reconsider their beliefs and the irrational emotional and violent response that some people had toward LGBTQ individuals.

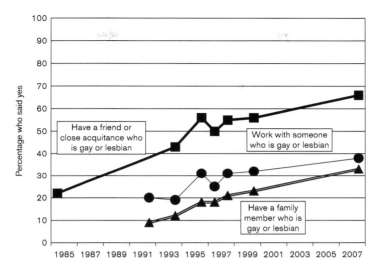

FIGURE 17. Percentage of Americans who over time reported knowing someone who is gay or lesbian and type of relationship.

SOURCE: Newsweek's Princeton Survey Research Associates survey (in Bowman, Rugg, and Marsico 2013).

By the middle of the 2010s not only had public opinion become vastly more accepting, but laws and policies were a lot more supportive. At the same time, many more Americans now knew someone who was gay or lesbian. As I show in figure 17, in 1985 22% of Americans said they had a friend or close acquaintance who was gay, but by 2008 66% did. Below I discuss the contributions of economic development, democracy, and religion in shaping Americans' attitudes.

ECONOMIC DEVELOPMENT, EDUCATION, AND CHANGING GENDER ROLES

Compared with Uganda and South Africa, the United States has a very high level of economic development. It would be considered a fully industrialized nation that beginning in the post-1950s era developed a large service-based economy. The prevailing culture in America could rightfully be described as focusing on individual pursuits and supporting self-expression. However, compared with nations that have similar levels of economic development such as Germany and Sweden, the United States is not as supportive of homosexuality as we might otherwise reason. As shown in figure 7, with a GDP of approximately $46,000 we would expect that about 22% of people would disapprove of homosexuality. With approximately 30% of Americans feeling that homosexuality is never justified, Americans have cooler feelings than their GDP would suggest. Likewise, many European countries with similar levels of economic development, such as United Kingdom and France, began to recognize same-sex civil unions in the 2000s. Only in 2015 did the U.S. Supreme Court legalize same-sex marriage. As discussed later in the chapter, religion, which is more important to many Americans than it is for Europeans, shares a lot of responsibility for why residents are not more liberal.

Compared with attitudes about other sexuality issues (e.g., premarital and extramarital sex), Americans' views about homosexuality have become rapidly more supportive in a relatively short period. Loftus (2001) and Treas (2002) note that part of this change is related to increases in education, which tend to accompany higher levels of economic development. In the early part of the twentieth century the U.S. government made attending primary and secondary school a priority. This led to an increase in the proportion of Americans who completed high school. Beginning in the 1970s the percentage of Americans attending college also began to rise. Of people aged twenty-one in 1970, 32% were enrolled in higher education (Statista, n.d.). By 2012 that figure had increased to 54% (Lumina 2014), which is much higher than in South Africa or Uganda.

As I discussed in the first chapter, education can increase cognitive sophistication, leading to more nuanced understandings of and tolerance for seemingly nonnormative issues and individuals (Jackman and Muha 1984; Ohlander, Batalova, and Treas 2005). Additionally, when residents attend college they are more likely to meet new people and engage alternative ideas that are different from what they have always known. The cross-national analysis presented in chapter 2 showed that a nation's level of economic development has an influence on both rich and poor residents. Conversely, while more-educated individuals tend to have friendlier attitudes, a nation's mean level of education does not seem to have an independent influence on public opinion. (See also appendix B, table 9, model 2.) Part of the reason for the lack of a relationship is that education seems to have its greatest effect on attitudes about homosexuality at the highest level (i.e., college). Across the world a relatively small proportion of people attend college. However, consistent with being a fully economically developed society, the United States has relatively high levels of college attendance, with rates increasing rapidly over the last fifty years (Statista, n.d.).

In the last fifty years, views about marriage and traditional gender roles have also changed. As the gay rights movement moved into full swing in the 1970s, so, too, did America's women's movement. Consistent with changing views of gender, the proportion of women who work outside of the home has substantially increased (Rindfuss, Brewster, and Kavee 1996). There have also been increases in gender equality, which is higher in the United States than in either Uganda or South Africa (Hausmann, Tyson, and Zahidi 2012). As I noted in the first chapter, people who place a lot of value on a strict division of labor tend to be less tolerant of homosexuality (Kerns and Fine 1994). Societal-wide changes in how people view traditional gender roles may have also contributed to how many Americans view homosexuality.

As mentioned above, economic development also brings with it shifts in the population whereby people from rural areas migrate to urban ones. An important difference between the United States, South Africa, and Uganda is the proportion of residents who live in urban areas. Whereas 13% of Ugandans and 62% of South Africans live in urban areas, the vast majority of Americans (83%) do (GeoHive, n.d.). One way this may affect attitudes is by increasing the likelihood of exposure to LGBTQ individuals. Urban areas are more likely to host vibrant LGBTQ subcultures and more people who are "out" (Chauncey 1994). Research has found that compared with rural residents, people from urban areas tend to be more tolerant about a range of things, including homosexuality (T. C. Wilson 1985). The proportion of Americans who live in urban areas has been increasing, going from 74% in 1970 to 83% in 2015 (United Nations 2012).

The United States has experienced a lot of changes since the 1960s, when the homosexuality movement was first becoming visible. Some of the changes in attitudes seem to be associated with developments in the nation's economy, such as a higher proportion of people attending college and changes in gender roles and family structure. As discussed below, democracy and the values embedded in it—values like fairness, impartiality, equality, freedom of speech, and the right to demonstrate—seem to also have had a role.

DEMOCRACY AND POLITICS IN SHAPING AMERICANS' ATTITUDES

The United States is considered one of the oldest modern democracies, having gained independence from the United Kingdom in 1776. On multiple measures of democracy, the United States scores better than Uganda and South Africa. As mentioned above, before the 1970s and even into the 1980s LGBTQ individuals were not particularly visible. Research has found that one factor in gaining the public's approval appears to have been the movement's success in framing their concerns as a matter of civil rights and fair treatment (Loftus 2001).

Additionally, democratic principles related to freedom of the press, along with high levels of economic development that allow for leisure time and access to computers, televisions, and movies, may have contributed to an environment in America where a lot more is known about homosexuality than in places like Uganda. In the 1990s the Internet became widely available, and as of 2011 71% of American households had Internet access (File 2013), making it possible for residents to easily learn more about LGBTQ individuals and subcultures. The 1990s also brought with it some highly likable gay and lesbian television characters. Studies have noted that up until this time there were relatively few positive representations of LGBTQ individuals on mainstream television (Kielwasser and Wolf 1992; Steiner, Fejes, and Petrich 1993). In 1994 Ellen DeGeneres began starring in the sitcom *Ellen*. In 1997 she and her character came out as gay. Shortly thereafter, the television sitcom *Will & Grace*, which focused on a gay man and a straight woman who was his best friend, began to air. For eight seasons the show had a successful run.

In their research on college students, Schiappa, Gregg, and Hewes (2006) found that increased viewing of *Will & Grace* and parasocial interaction (i.e., forming beliefs and attitudes about people through the media) with the characters were correlated with lower levels of sexual prejudice. The relationship was even more pronounced for study subjects who had the least amount of in-person contact with gay or lesbian individuals (Schiappa, Gregg, and Hewes 2006). The United States has the third largest land mass in the world, and potential in-person exposure to minority groups, including openly gay or lesbian individuals, varies substantially across the nation. With television shows like *Ellen* and *Will & Grace*, even people who would not necessarily know an "out" individual could "virtually" know an LGBTQ person. For the media to have an impact on residents' attitudes, programs that include LGBTQ characters have to be allowed to air, and the media in the United States is freer than it is in many other countries (Freedom House 2015).

The Republican Party, which 25% of Americans were affiliated with in 2013 (J.M. Jones 2014), may have had a role in limiting more-positive views, at least for a while. Up until the 1980s neither Republicans nor Democrats—the two main American political parties—seemed to have much interest in homosexuality. However, in the 1980s Americans began to develop more-conservative sex-related attitudes (Loftus 2001). At the same time, as Peters and Woolley (1984, 1988) point out, the Republican Party began to focus on family values, which involved, among other things, support for heterosexual marriage and abstinence education, as well as limiting gratuitous sex and violence in the media. By 1992, the Republican platform also included opposition to same-sex marriage and same-sex couples being allowed to adopt or provide foster care to children (Peters and Woolley 1992).

By the 2010s many Americans were becoming supportive of same-sex marriage, and thirty-eight of the fifty U.S. states had legalized it to some degree. Increasingly, the Republican Party seemed less interested in homosexuality (Rhodebeck 2015). Between 2005 and 2015 the proportion of Republicans who were supportive of same-sex marriage went from 19% to 34% (Pew Research Center 2015c). The increase for Democrats was higher, going from 45% to 65%. With the support of close to 60% of Americans, on June 26, 2015, the U.S. Supreme Court ruled in *Obergefell v. Hodges* that same-sex married couples were to be constitutionally accorded the same recognition as opposite-sex couples, making same-sex marriage legal across the entire nation.

RELIGION AND ITS INFLUENCE IN THE UNITED STATES

Like South Africa and Uganda, the United States has a high proportion of Protestants who are actively engaged in their faith. As I discussed in the first chapter, religion has a major role in shaping public opinion about homosexuality (see also Adamczyk, Boyd, and Hayes 2016; Sherkat et al. 2011; Whitley and Lee 2000). Unlike many of its European counterparts, the United States has relatively high levels of religious belief, even though it also has a high level of economic development and a strong democracy. Whereas in 2005 49% of Americans attended religious services at least once a month, only 19% of Germans and 8% of Swedes (both countries have substantial Protestant populations) did (Association of Religious Data Archives, n.d.). While levels of religious belief have been historically high in the United States, recent research has indicated that they may be declining (Voas and Chaves 2016).

In the United States, Protestants are the largest Christian subgroup (i.e., 51%), followed by Catholics (i.e., 24%) (Pew Research Center

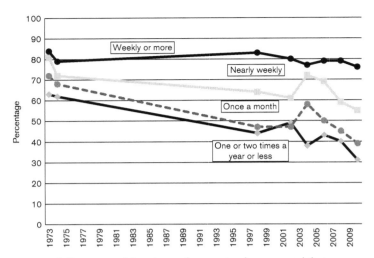

FIGURE 18. Percentage of Americans who over time have reported that homosexual relations are always wrong by frequency of religious attendance.
SOURCE: National Opinion Research Center's General Social Survey (in Bowman, Rugg, and Marsico 2013)

2015a). In American-based studies, researchers typically distinguish between conservative or Evangelical (e.g., Southern Baptist, Assemblies of God) and mainline Protestant denominations (e.g., Episcopal Church, United Methodist Church). Although there is a lot of variation in attitudes among these groups, in the last few decades mainline Protestants and Catholics have followed national trends in becoming increasingly tolerant. In contrast, conservative Protestants and people who frequently attend religious services have been less likely to change their attitudes (Schnabel 2016; Sherkat et al. 2011; Treas 2002). In figure 18, I present the proportion of Americans who report that homosexual relations are always wrong by frequency of religious attendance. In 1973 63% of Americans who attended religious services a few times a year or less felt that homosexual relations are always wrong. By 2010 the percentage had fallen to 32%. Conversely, in 1973 84% of Americans who attended religious services weekly or more felt this way, and by 2010 it was 76%, resulting in a comparatively small drop of 8% over thirty-seven years.

Research has found that a substantial proportion of conservative Protestants view the Bible literally, and tend to be very active in their faith (Steensland et al. 2000). As a result, there are a disproportionate number of conservative Protestant adherents with high levels of religious involvement who disapprove of gay or lesbian individuals (Burdette, Ellison, and Hill 2005). Additionally, many American conservative Protestant leaders, such as James Dobson, have been vocal in their disapproval. However, unlike the more recent explosion of religiously-inspired commentary about same-sex relations and issues in Uganda, religion's connection to public opinion and legislation in the United States is not new. Rather, as Fetner (2008) notes in his research, beginning in the 1980s religion began shaping views about homosexuality. Motivated by a strong orientation toward family values in the 1980s, conservative Christians began to connect with the Republican Party. At the same time mainline Protestants began to align themselves with Democrats.

While many conservative religious groups have had some success in limiting more-liberal legislation, their influence has not been strong enough to overcome the tidal wave of change. Combined, there are many more mainline Protestants and Catholics than there are conservative Protestants, even though the latter have been an impactful minority. Compared with Uganda's news press, my research team and I found that in the United States there is a lot less coupling of homosexuality with religion. In figure 14, I show that the United States is significantly less likely than Uganda to draw on religious themes and claimsmakers, and it is no different from South Africa in its likelihood of discussing LGBTQ issues in the context of religion.

Although it does so less than the Ugandan papers, *USA Today* still published several articles that mentioned homosexuality and religion, suggesting the importance of religion for many Americans. However, over a one-year period (i.e., 2008), my research team and I did not find a single article that used religion to support disapproval of homosexuality. Rather, when religion was mentioned in *USA Today*, it was always placed in a neutral or positive Christian framework. As one editorial from the paper explains: "The truth is that many religious voters probably care more about a candidate's judgment and character than where he or she lines up on the myriad issues facing America. Issues matter, for sure. Religious voters care about a candidate's views on abortion, the war, the environment and gay marriage, for example. But more important is the kind of person we are electing" (O. Thomas 2008). The viewpoint being offered here is that for religious voters, a politician's stance on same-sex marriage is not the most important issue.

LIBERAL PROTESTANT NATIONS

Until now this chapter has focused on nations with relatively high levels of religious belief and a mixture of different Christian groups—mainline and conservative Protestants, as well as Catholics. In the first chapter I distinguished between nations that are dominated by mainline Protestant religions and those that house a mixture of mainline and conservative Protestant denominations. Three of the mainline Protestant nations (i.e., Finland, Sweden, and Norway) included in the WVS are located in Scandinavia, where most residents are Lutheran. The two other countries, Great Britain and New Zealand, have a greater variety of mainline denominations, including Anglicans, Presbyterians, and Methodists, as well as a substantial minority of Catholics (Association of Religious Data Archives, n.d.; CIA World Factbook 2013). These five nations are distinctly more liberal than those that include a mixture of mainline and conservative Protestant groups. In figure 5, I showed that the predicted attitudinal score for residents of nations with largely mainline Protestant faiths is 5, compared with 8.92 (i.e., a higher level of disapproval of homosexuality) for people living in countries that have a mixture of different types of Protestantism. The influence of the dominant faith remains, even after accounting for residents' personal characteristics like economic status and religious salience.

Why are nations that are dominated by mainline Protestant faiths so much more liberal than the others? Part of the answer is related to how the overall level of religious importance shapes attitudes. Nations with a mixture of different Protestant groups tend to have higher overall levels of religious belief. Hence, across the last three waves of the WVS 13% of respondents from nations dominated by mainline Protestant faiths say that religion is very important. Conversely, in nations with a mixture of different types of Protestants, 70% report that religion is very important.

A number of researchers have argued that a plurality of different religions and denominations can increase religious belief (Finke, Guest, and Stark 1996; Iannaccone 1991; Ruiter and Van Tubergen 2009; Stark and Finke 2000). When most residents belong to the dominant religion (e.g., Evangelical Lutheran Church) or religious denominations that are very similar to each other (e.g., mostly mainline Protestant), potential followers have a smaller range of religious options from which to choose, leading some to opt out of religion altogether (Iannaccone 1991). Conversely, when there is a wider variety of religions and denominations available, residents are more likely to find one that matches their religious preferences, increasing the likelihood that they will remain active in the faith (Finke, Guest, and Stark 1996). Additionally, in nations that have been historically dominated by a single faith (e.g., Norway, Finland), the government has at times subsidized that religion (e.g., Lutheran). Stark and Finke (2000) point out that when this happens, religious officials may not have to work as hard to recruit adherents and keep their religious initiatives interesting and innovative, since their salary and church buildings are supported by the state. Likewise, state subsidies can make it harder for other religions and denominations to succeed, ultimately contributing to overall declines in religious belief by limiting exciting and new religious options.

In the first chapter I explained that all religions have proscriptions regarding homosexuality, and when people feel that religion is important, they are more likely to abide by religious precepts, regardless of their religion. But even if someone is not very religious, living in a country with a high proportion of religious residents can influence the attitudes of everyone, secular and religious people alike. While figure 5 accounts for respondents' personal religious affiliations and importance, it does not yet include country levels of religious importance. When I include them, the coefficients for the dominant religion decrease substantially. (See appendix B, table 8, model 3.) Additionally, more-conservative and Evangelical religions are more likely to promote a literalist interpretation of the Bible. A higher proportion of people who take a literalist view, which is more likely in mixed Protestant environments, may contribute to overall feelings about homosexuality within a country, especially when there are high overall levels of religious belief.

Finally, nations that are dominated by mainline Protestant faiths tend to be richer and have stronger democracies. With a 2008 GDP of $94,759, Norway is the richest country in the WVS, and the other four mainline Protestant nations are not far behind it (Association of Religious Data Archives 2011). Conversely, except for the United States, all of the WVS nations that have a mixture of Protestant groups are located in Africa, where economic development is much lower and democracy tends to be weaker than in northern Europe. In appendix B, table 8, model 5, I present the coefficients for the dominant religion, after accounting for GDP, democracy, and religious importance.[4] The coefficient for the dominant religion decreases substantially when these other country characteristics are considered. Indeed, in a separate analysis I found that when all three of them are added, the level of significance (i.e., p-value) for differences between the two sets of Protestant nations is 0.056 (i.e., two-tailed test), indicating that the level of disapproval of homosexuality in these different types of countries is no longer statistically significant.[5] These findings strongly suggest that attitudinal differences between nations with a high proportion of mainline Protestants versus a mixture of different types of Protestantism can largely be explained with democracy, economic development, and overall levels of religious importance.

In the previous section I explained how higher levels of economic development contributed to a more tolerant environment in the United States. Like the United States, European Protestant nations share many of the same attributes related to economic development. Hence, all of these countries are fully industrialized, and, based on ideas from Hofstede (2001), Inglehart (2006) and Schwartz (2006), these countries could be described as focused on individual pursuits and self-expression, much more so than the African nations. Additionally, all of these societies have highly educated residents, with a substantial minority attending college (Barro and Lee 2013). In addition to homosexuality, residents of these nations have very liberal views on marriage, abortion, and other sex-related behaviors (Wike 2014). The higher level of economic development is likely to have contributed to more-tolerant attitudes on a wide range of issues.

Like the United States, all of the northern European countries also have stable democracies. This is going to lead to environments where more social-movement activity is allowed and the press is free. Indeed, Freedom House characterizes all of the northern European nations, as well as the United States, as having a free media (Freedom House 2015). With more freedom of the press, residents should have media access to a wider range of LGBTQ characters, commentators, and personalities. Exposure to these minority groups is going to contribute to more awareness of the challenges that these individuals encounter, increasing empathy. In more-liberal environments, people who identify as LGBTQ may also feel more comfortable with revealing their orientation and identity to friends and family members (Heatherington and Lavner 2008; Kahn 1991), further adding to more-tolerant perspectives.

A key difference between the United States and European Protestant nations is that the latter have very low levels of religious salience. Because many do not feel that religion is important, residents may be unlikely to view homosexuality as a religious issue. As a result, religion is less likely to be an important frame in informal and public discussions about homosexuality, as well as related policy decisions. Indeed, cultural scholars like Fatima El-Tayeb (2011) have argued that in some of the most liberal European nations a key part of many residents' identity is support for homosexuality—much more so than religion, especially affiliation with a conservative one. As she explains, this has complicated how many Europeans see the settlement and assimilation of Muslims, who tend to be visibly religious and have very conservative views about homosexuality (Gerhards 2010). Since the levels of democracy and economic development are somewhat similar for the United States and these other European nations, it seems that higher levels of religious belief in the United States can help explain why the latter has been slower to embrace homosexuality-related rights and liberties and develop more-accepting views.

While higher levels of economic development, stronger democracies, and low levels of religious belief can help explain why European Protestant nations have had such liberal views, I want to emphasize that many of the processes through which these factors shape attitudes may be unique to these specific nations. For example, the Nordic countries have long been categorized as having strong welfare states, and high levels of economic development, as well as strong democracies, seem to have contributed to their creation (Kangas and Palme 2009). Some academics (e.g., Rydström 2000; Rydström and Mustola 2007) have argued that important changes to the legalization of homosexuality in Scandinavian societies coincided with the creation of key elements of the welfare state. Although the United States is a highly democratic and economically developed nation, its government has been much more hesitant to embrace a more progressive income-tax structure and take a larger role in redistributing funds, leading to a smaller welfare sector than in the Scandinavian countries.

Though factors like economic development and democracy can help explain general trends, a lot more information and data would be needed to unpack the specific processes flowing from these country-level factors that have contributed to attitudinal and policy-related changes in, and differences between, the Nordic countries and the United States. Additionally, while economic development, democracy, and religious belief account for a substantial proportion of cross-national differences, some (i.e., 13%) country-level variance in attitudes remains unexplained, leaving room for additional processes. Finally, within individual countries or regions there may be specific processes, cultural elements, and historical incidences that have contributed to residents' views about homosexuality. A large-scale cross-national quantitative analysis cannot account for these factors.

This chapter has focused on three countries where many residents find religion important and where Christianity—specifically, a mixture of different types of Protestantism—is prevalent. Following Christianity, the second-largest religion in the world is Islam. The next chapter looks at how economic development and democracy affect feelings about homosexuality in three key Muslim nations with high levels of religious belief.

CHAPTER 4

Understanding Views in Muslim Countries

An Analysis of Malaysia, Indonesia, and Turkey

While nations like Uganda have received some publicity for their draconian laws and policies related to homosexuality, Muslim-majority countries are often singled out as having exceptionally unfriendly views. Of the seven nations (i.e., Iran, Saudi Arabia, Yemen, Mauritania, Sudan, Nigeria, and Somalia) where homosexuality can be punished with death either across the entire country or in a substantial region, in 2015 (Carroll and Itaborahy 2015) all of them had Muslim-majority populations. There have also been some highly publicized examples of individuals accused of same-sex behaviors being punished with death in these countries. For example, Afghanistan's Taliban are infamous for forcing accused homosexuals to stand next to a tall brick wall while a tank pushes the wall over onto them, crushing them to death (New York Times 1999). Likewise, in 2007 Iranian President Mahmoud Ahmadinejad made a now famous speech at Columbia University in which he stated that there are no homosexuals in Iran (H. Cooper 2007). Between 1980 and 2000 it is estimated that four thousand individuals accused of same-sex acts were executed there (Spencer 2008). While countries like Iran are hostile to homosexuality, there are some Muslim-majority nations where homosexuality is not illegal and where public opinion is more tolerant, though not particularly friendly.

In this chapter I explore how economic development, democracy, and religion shape public opinion about homosexuality in three Muslim-majority countries: Malaysia, Indonesia, and Turkey.[1] These nations were selected, in part, because they include relatively large Muslim populations. Indonesia, for example, has the largest number of Muslims in the world, and Malaysia and Turkey have substantially large populations. Additionally, these countries have an infrastructure that is somewhat conducive to research on homosexuality. Likewise, within these nations researchers have given some social science attention to homosexuality-related issues, even though only a small minority of it focuses on public opinion. Finally, there are some active public discussions about homosexuality, making a newspaper analysis of how homosexuality is framed in the public press possible.

Ideally, in this case-study comparison of Muslim-majority countries I would include some large but less tolerant nations such as Iran, where same-sex behaviors are criminalized and regularly punished. However, because homosexuality is so heavily condemned in societies like these, there is little variation in attitudes (i.e., almost everyone reports being opposed) and almost no academic research on factors shaping public opinion. Additionally, these countries have high levels of media censorship (Freedom House 2015), and as a result, relatively little information can be gleaned from newspapers. Compared with some Muslim-majority countries like Iran and Saudi Arabia, researchers can typically obtain more information on attitudes about homosexuality in Malaysia, Indonesia, and Turkey.

In addition to drawing on open-source information, existing research, and surveys, my research team and I also conducted a systematic content analysis of three daily newspapers—the *New Straits Times,* the *Jakarta Post,* and the *Turkish Daily News*—from these nations during 2008, which is the same year in which the newspaper analysis of mixed Protestant nations was done. (See appendix D for methodological information about the content analysis.) Whereas the quantitative analysis I conducted in the first two chapters established the primary factors shaping public opinion across many nations, this comparative case study is used to better understand the processes producing these relationships, as well as to provide additional information on the other elements shaping attitudes that may be more specific to these nations' unique culture, history, and geographical location.

I begin this chapter with an assessment of Malaysia and then move into an analysis of Indonesia and then Turkey. After providing a brief overview of the historical and social context of homosexuality-related issues, I explain the role of democracy and politics, religion, and economic development in shaping public opinion within each of these

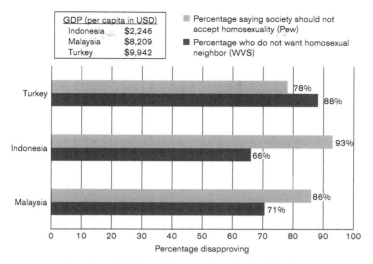

FIGURE 19. Snapshot of GDP and disapproving attitudes in Indonesia, Malaysia, and Turkey.

SOURCES: Spring Pew Global Attitudes Survey (Pew Research Center 2013); WVS, wave 5; ARDA's Cross-National Socio-Economic and Religion Data, 2011.

countries. As each new nation is introduced, additional comparisons are made. I end the chapter with a brief discussion about Muslim countries more generally.

PUBLIC OPINION IN MALAYSIA

Of the three countries discussed in this chapter, Malaysia has the least-tolerant laws and policies regarding same-sex behaviors. In the eighteenth century Malaysia became part of the British Empire, and, as in many of the other nations that the British colonized (Asal, Sommer, and Harwood 2013), sodomy was made illegal (Gerber 2014). In 1957, when Malaysia became independent, the country kept its sodomy legislation (Sodomy Laws, n.d.), which also proscribes oral sex and applies to same-sex and opposite-sex relations. In addition to fines and flogging, the punishment can carry up to a twenty-year prison sentence. Public opinion is consistent with this harsh legislation. In figure 19, I show that in 2013 86% of residents felt that society should not accept homosexuality.

Government officials have also been vocal in their condemnation of same-sex relations. For example, in an interview from *Time* magazine in 2000 Abdul Kadir, who was head of education and research at Malaysia's Islamic Affairs Department, was quoted as saying, "[Homosexuality] is a crime worse than murder. Homosexuals are shameless people" (Ramakrishnan 2000). When asked if individuals have the right to choose whom they want to be with, Kadir responded, "What right are you talking about? This is a sin, end of story" (Ramakrishnan 2000). More recently, this sentiment was expressed by the minister of religion, Jamil Khir Baharom, who explained that "LGBTs" had "'no rights' in Malaysia, given that their 'behavior is against Islam'" (Shah 2013, 270).

While there have been some arrests for sodomy (111 were reported in 1999 [Ramakrishnan 2000]), in 2011 the *New York Times* reported that Malaysian officials rarely prosecute sodomy cases (Goodman 2011). There is an important exception, though. As I discuss below, Malaysia's sodomy law was recently used to prosecute Anwar Ibrahim, who was the nation's deputy prime minister from 1993 to 1998. There is widespread speculation that his conviction was politically motivated. Most Malaysians view sex as a very private issue, and before Ibrahim's arrest there does not seem to have been much public attention given to homosexuality-related issues (Vivian 1998).

In spite of the sodomy law, a disapproving public, and a vocally critical government, a homosexuality subculture with nongovernment organizations (e.g., the Pink Triangle Foundation), bars, discos, and cruising areas has emerged in Kuala Lumpur and other large Malaysian cities. Additionally, women tend to not be subject to the same legal restrictions as men.[2] Hence, Kadir noted in the same 2000 *Time* magazine article, Malaysia has "never arrested lesbian women. There are no complaints, maybe because it is difficult to gauge" (Ramakrishnan 2000). Below I explain the role that a more limited democracy seems to have played in shaping attitudes and discourse in Malaysia.

GOVERNMENT AND DEMOCRACY IN MALAYSIA

In the second chapter, I explained that democracy contributes to tolerance by increasing awareness of things considered new and different. Additionally, when residents witness the government upholding individuals' rights, their trust in the political system tends to increase, and they are more likely to mirror some of the government's actions and support others' civil liberties and rights, even those they may not like. Compared with many Muslim-majority nations, Malaysia is quite democratic, but its democracy is not as strong as it is in several other countries, which seems to have implications for how residents and the government view homosexuality and related rights.

When Malaysia gained independence in 1957, the constitution allowed for both a monarchy and a democratically elected prime minister. With a democracy score of 6.4 (scores range from 1 to 10, where higher numbers indicate a stronger democracy), the nation is seen as having a slightly stronger democracy than Turkey (5.69) and about the same as Indonesia (6.34) (Economist 2008). Because it is racially, ethnically, and religiously diverse, government officials have strongly supported the idea that relations between various groups are somewhat fragile, and therefore everyone has to do their part to limit dissonance. Technically, the constitution allows for free speech, but when it became independent Malaysia held on to the British Empire's preexisting sedition act, which has become increasingly far-reaching and has implications for the amount of exposure the public is likely to get regarding controversial issues, including same-sex relations.

The law criminalizes speech with "seditious tendency," which includes, among other things, bringing hatred or contempt toward or exciting disaffection against the government or engendering feelings of ill will and hostility between different races (Pak 2014). The government has not hesitated in using its power to restrict freedom of speech. In the 2000s Malaysia issued a policy that does not allow any known homosexual individuals to appear on radio or TV (Mackey 2012; Williams 2009). In the newspaper articles that my team and I analyzed we found support for the government's orientation. As shown in figure 20, only 11% of articles mentioned an LGBTQ character or famous person. In contrast, Turkey has a significantly higher percentage (i.e., 23%), and in the previous chapter I showed that the amount for South Africa is 35%, with 38% in the United States.[3] The government's mandate alone may have limited mention of LGBTQ individuals. But the majority of Malaysian newspapers also tend to be owned by either the government or top government officials (Alagappar and Kaur 2009; Zaharom 2014).

Not surprisingly, discussions about homosexuality in the public press tend to be disapproving. In their analysis of Malaysia's *New Straits Times* from 1998 to 2006, Alagappar and Kaur (2009) found that 73% of the articles that mentioned same-sex behaviors and originated from

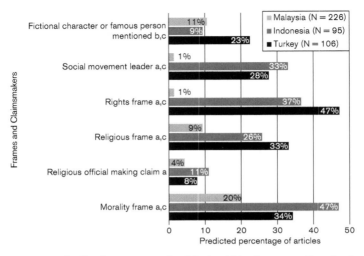

FIGURE 20. Predicted percentages of articles in which a homosexuality-related term is used by key associations and claimsmakers in Indonesia, Malaysia, and Turkey, 2008. (N = 427 total articles with term)

a = Significant difference (p < .05) between Indonesia and Malaysia news articles.

b = Significant difference (p < .05) between Indonesia and Turkey news articles.

c = Significant difference (p < .05) between Malaysia and Turkey news articles.

NOTE: Marginal percentages presented for all newspaper articles in 2008 that mentioned a homosexuality-related term. In producing the percentages, the following variables were held constant: article type, whether the information originated from inside or outside the country, and day of the week it was published. See appendix D for more information on the coding and analysis.

within the country were negative. Other groups that might be inclined to speak on behalf of gay and lesbian individuals are encouraged to remain quiet. For example, there have been suggestions that because academic researchers are heavily dependent upon government appointments and funding, they are unlikely to challenge the government (Williams 2009). If residents rarely hear about or see LGBTQ individuals in the media or discussed by others who might correct misinformation, it becomes less likely that residents will develop a more positive view of homosexuality.

Although LGBTQ fictional characters or celebrities are not regularly seen in Malaysian media and there have been few sodomy convictions, there is a well-known exception. Anwar Ibrahim, who was Malaysia's deputy prime minister from 1993 to 1998, has twice been convicted of sodomy. In 1998 Ibrahim made a major break with the prime minister at the time, Mahathir Mohamad, over economic policies and Ibrahim's preference to institute democratic reforms (Williams 2009). Ibrahim was then accused of sodomy and found guilty. After serving six years in prison, his sentence was overturned in 2004. In 2008, as Ibrahim and an opposition alliance began experiencing a political resurgence, the government charged him with sodomy for a second time. In 2015 he was convicted and sentenced to five years in prison (Hookway 2015). In both of his cases there has been strong speculation that the sodomy charges were not credible and accusations against him politically motivated (Amnesty International 2015; Hookway 2015).

Although sexuality is not regularly discussed in public and certainly not with much detail, Malaysian news officials have given a great deal of attention to Ibrahim's sodomy charges. From the three newspapers from Muslim-majority countries, the Malaysian paper had the highest number of homosexuality-related articles (226). However, a relatively small proportion included mention of religion, morality, rights, LGBTQ individuals, or any other frames. Our analysis was conducted on articles from 2008 when Ibrahim was arrested for the second time. The overwhelming majority of articles (78%) from this period mentioned homosexuality in the context of discussions about the government, with the vast majority focused on Ibrahim's case.

As I noted in the second chapter, it takes time for democracy to shape how residents view unfamiliar issues and ideas. For people to develop trust in democracy, they have to witness the government upholding individuals' rights. There seem to be some limits to this in Malaysia, especially given that these seemingly trumped-up sodomy charges have surfaced twice in the past thirteen years. After Ibrahim was convicted of sodomy in 2015, there was a great deal of criticism within and outside of Malaysia. Amnesty International, for example, said the judgment was "deplorable," and "[j]ust the latest chapter in the Malaysian authorities' relentless attempts to silence government critics" (Amnesty International 2015). The same day the verdict was delivered, the Malaysian political-satire cartoonist Zulkifli Anwar Ulhaque (i.e., Zunar) suggested in a Twitter post that the judiciary had bowed to the country's authoritarian regime in convicting Ibrahi (Guardian 2015). A few hours later Zunar was arrested under Malaysia's sedition act.

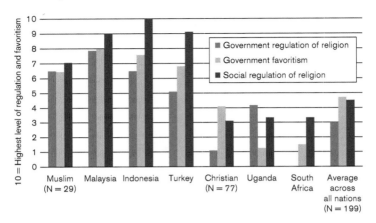

FIGURE 21. Government regulation and favoritism of religion and social regulation of religion (five-year average) in Muslim- and Christian-majority countries.

SOURCES: ARDA's International Religious Freedom Data, Aggregate File (2003–2008) (Association of Religious Data Archives n.d.); U.S. State Department's International Religious Freedom Reports.

NOTE: Data for the United States were unavailable. The measures did not classify Christian nations as either Protestant or Catholic. For this reason, they are combined into a single category: Christian. The estimate of government regulation of religion for South Africa is zero.

RELIGION AND SAME-SEX RELATIONS IN MALAYSIA

In addition to its middling level of democracy, the country's high level of religious belief and adherence to Islam seem to also play a role in shaping attitudes about homosexuality. Fifty-seven percent of Malaysians are Muslim, with the vast majority being Sunni (Association of Religious Data Archives, n.d.). The federal constitution establishes Islam as "the religion of the Federation," with the provision that other religions may be practiced in peace and harmony. While the constitution is meant to uphold the fundamental liberties of all Malaysians, it also allows for a set of Sharia civil and criminal laws that apply only to Muslims. The Association of Religious Data Archives has compiled several cross-national measures of religious freedom, which can provide some insight into the extent of separation between religion and government. In general, Muslim nations do not score well on these measures (Grim and Finke 2010). Across the world the mean is about 3, but with a score of almost 8 (see figure 21), Malaysia is above average in restricting religious freedoms and has a higher score than any of the case-study nations discussed thus far.

What does relatively little religious freedom mean for understanding public opinion about same-sex behaviors? In the first chapter I explained that all of the world's major religions have some objections to same-sex relations, but some religions—namely, Islam and conservative Protestantism—have been particularly vocal in their condemnation. Governments typically have a lot of power and resources. When they are closely aligned with the dominant faith, they can better infuse discussions about same-sex relations with religious sentiment, limiting alternative perspectives and encouraging religion-inspired views that find homosexuality problematic.

Additionally, like many religions, Islam finds both sex outside of marriage and same-sex sexual relations problematic. However, unlike many Christian-majority nations, Malaysian residents and others from Muslim-majority societies tend to be more consistent in upholding religious proscriptions regarding a variety of sex-related behaviors and officially policing an array of sex-related acts. In figure 22, I show that a high percentage of Malaysians view same-sex relations (i.e., 88%), along with premarital (i.e., 87%) and extramarital sex (i.e., 90%), as problematic. Likewise, in Malaysia anyone who appears interested in engaging in same-sex behaviors could be subject to secular or moral policing. Under Sharia law extramarital and premarital sex for Muslims is also illegal (Malaysia 1997), and the secular police are known to arrest people who seem likely to engage in these behaviors (Shah 2013).

In contrast to Malaysia, in Uganda homosexuality seems to be singled out for special attention. Whereas 93% of Ugandans feel that homosexuality is morally problematic, only 77% of residents find sex between unmarried adults morally problematic, and 80% feel that married people having an affair is unacceptable. Additionally, while Uganda does not have any laws prohibiting premarital sex, it has been clear in establishing and more recently enforcing sodomy laws. When people's attitudes are consistent across a range of sex-related issues, as they are in many Muslim-majority societies, their objection to same-sex behaviors may be stemming from a single dominant force—in this case, Islamic-inspired beliefs. Because it is affecting their perspective on a range of behaviors, it may be more difficult to change feelings about same-sex relations, especially when the government is also consistent in policing all behaviors that violate these deep-seated sentiments.

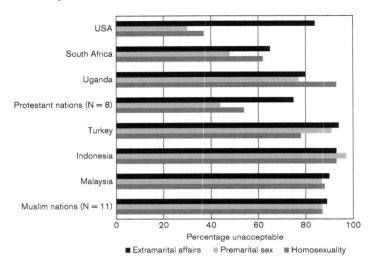

FIGURE 22. Percentage of Protestant and Muslim nations who report that sex-related behaviors are morally unacceptable.

SOURCE: 2013 Pew Research Center's Global Attitudes survey.

NOTE: For each issue, respondents were asked whether sex-related behaviors are morally acceptable, morally unacceptable, or not a moral issue. This figure presents data that refer to a different homosexuality question (i.e. "morally unacceptable") than the one presented in figure 19 (i.e., "should not be accepted by society"). The Muslim estimate includes the following nations: Senegal, Turkey, Lebanon, Nigeria, Pakistan, Malaysia, Tunisia, Indonesia, Palestinian territory, Egypt, and Jordan. The Protestant estimate includes the following: United States, Kenya, Germany, Britain, Australia, South Africa, Uganda, and Ghana. similar to the Protestant estimates, for the fourteen available Catholic countries the percentage for homosexuality is 35%; for premarital sex, 28%; and for extramarital sex, 73%.

ECONOMIC DEVELOPMENT AND PUBLIC OPINION IN MALAYSIA

Whereas religion and the government seem to have a role in shaping public opinion and discourse about homosexuality in Malaysia, economic development seems to have had less of an influence. In the last forty years Malaysia has undergone very high levels of economic growth, which typically would contribute to a more tolerant environment (World Resources Institute, n.d.). The population has also become more urban. In 1990 50% of Malaysians lived in urban areas, but by 2010 72% were urbanites (Trading Economics, n.d.). With higher levels of economic development, women have increasingly begun to work outside of the home, there are fewer arranged marriages, there has been an increase in the age at first marriage, and major declines in fertility, with the fertility rate going from 5 in 1970 to about 2 in 2010 (Jones 1981; Mahari 2011).

All of these factors should contribute to a society that is increasingly shifting from one oriented toward the collective to one that is focused on self-expression, individual pursuits, the right to personal freedom, and more-tolerant views of same-sex relations (Inglehart and Baker 2000). However, because there are harsh penalties for sodomy, the government has been vocal in condemning gay and lesbian individuals, and democratic ideals like freedom of speech are less likely to be upheld; the otherwise liberalizing influence of economic development seems to have had a more limited effect in cultivating friendlier views about same-sex behaviors.

PUBLIC OPINION IN INDONESIA

Also located in Southeast Asia, Indonesia has the largest Muslim population in the world (over 240 million in 2010). When directly asked whether homosexuality is morally acceptable, the overwhelming majority of Indonesians say that it is not acceptable. However, I show in figure 19 that only 66% report that they would not want a homosexual neighbor, which may reflect some ambiguity. The way many Indonesians view homosexuality may be complicated by the preponderance of local rituals and performances that have historically included cross-dressing, mostly of men dressed as women. These performers, who may be referred to as *waria,* also appear in television and print media, and are considered professionals (Boellstorff 2006; Laurent 2005). Like other Indonesians who may be viewed as sexually or romantically desirable (see E.-B. Lim 2013), *waria* would not necessarily be described as gay, lesbian, or bisexual, nor would the person who desires them.

In contrast to Malaysia, homosexuality is legal in Indonesia. The only restriction relates to sexual relations with minors. For heterosexual acts it is a crime to have relations with anyone under the age of seventeen, but for same-sex acts the person must be at least eighteen. Beginning in 1983 Indonesia's official medical guidelines stopped classifying homosexuality as abnormal (Offord 2003). In 1982 Indonesia's first gay rights interest group was established (Offord and Cantrell 2001), and since then many other organizations have arisen, including Gaya Nusantara and Arus Pelangi (Offord 2011). Along with those in Thailand and the Philippines, the LGBTQ movement in Indonesia has been one of the most visible in Southeast Asia.

Indonesia may seem like a relatively tolerant nation, and compared with other Muslim-majority countries like Pakistan and Saudi Arabia, it certainly is. However, a very high percentage of people still say that society should not accept homosexuality. While same-sex behaviors are legal, there are no protections against harassment and discrimination, nor are there benefits for same-sex couples. In 2003 some government officials unsuccessfully tried to enact a bill that would have criminalized homosexuality (365Gay.com Newscenter Staff 2003). Additionally, there have been reports of violence and discrimination against people because of their sexual orientation. In 2011 the Human Rights Commission noted that in Indonesia even the "perception of homosexuality or transgender identity puts people at risk. Violations include—but are not limited to—killings, rape and physical attacks, torture, arbitrary detention" (United Nations 2011, 3). Below I explain how economic development, democracy, and religion seem to have contributed to an environment where many residents feel that homosexuality is not morally acceptable, even as some may feel comfortable having homosexual neighbors (e.g., *waria*).

ECONOMIC DEVELOPMENT AND ATTITUDES ABOUT SAME-SEX RELATIONS

Of the three Muslim nations discussed in this chapter, Indonesia has the lowest level of economic development. Its GDP is only a quarter of that found in Turkey or Malaysia. Since we know that there is a relationship between economic development and tolerance, Indonesia's more accepting attitudes about having homosexual neighbors is somewhat surprising, as is its lack of a sodomy law. However, the very high proportion of people who say that society should not accept homosexuality is consistent with what we would expect. Some of the same economic factors that contribute to residents in other less economically developed nations (e.g., Uganda) having less tolerant attitudes also appear in Indonesia.

Currently, Indonesia is undergoing processes of urbanization, industrialization, and economic development. The share of the population living on less than two U.S. dollars a day has fallen from 91% in 1987 to 51% in 2009. Likewise, between 1967 and 2009 the manufacturing share of GDP has increased by 19%, while the agricultural share has shrunk by 35% (Elias and Noone 2011). While the basis of the economy is moving toward manufacturing, agriculture remains important, accounting for more than 40% of employment, which is similar to the situation in China, and well above that found in Malaysia (Elias and Noone 2011). Consistent with these larger economic changes, the proportion of Indonesians living in urban areas has increased substantially, going from 30% in 1990 to 54% in 2010 (Trading Economics, n.d.). Nevertheless, almost half of Indonesia's population currently resides in rural areas, and this is a much higher proportion of rural residents than in Malaysia, where it is 28% (Trading Economics, n.d.).

Because a substantial part of Indonesia's population still lives in rural areas, a smaller proportion of residents are likely to come into contact with homosexual individuals. However, as mentioned above, even people living far from cities may become acquainted with transsexuals through television or even through direct exposure with *waria* while attending rituals and performances. The greater media attention given to transsexuals in Indonesia is a sharp departure from the situation in Malaysia, where LGBTQ characters cannot be shown on television. Nevertheless, as Blackwood (2007) points out, transsexuals or *waria* are not often portrayed as deserving rights and freedoms, and in television comedies and other forms of media LGBTQ individuals are often seen as the butt of jokes or as part of sensationalized news.

In contrast to other nations that have a high proportion of people still living in rural areas and working in the agriculture sector, Indonesia has a relatively low fertility rate of about 2.4. Since the 1960s it has been decreasing, in part, because of the government's family-planning program, as well as the rising age of marriage, women's higher educational attainment, and increases in family income (Niehof and Lubis 2003). Research has suggested that, along with economic changes and rising levels of education, an increasing focus on the importance of an intimate and romantic relationship may be changing how many Indonesians view marriage (Heaton, Cammack, and Young 2001), which may also have implications for attitudes about same-sex relations and the obligation to enter a heterosexual marriage.

DEMOCRACY, GOVERNMENT, AND ATTITUDES

Like Malaysia, Indonesia is an ethnically diverse country where over seven hundred languages are spoken (Gordon 2005). At times the Indonesian government, much like that in Malaysia, has seized on these differences to argue that the nation needs to maintain harmony, even if individual rights and freedoms are sometimes violated. Its democracy score is about the same as Malaysia's, and in the early 1990s it had a poor human rights record, which has been improving (Humana 1992). Up until 1949 Indonesia was a Dutch colony. After a drawn-out struggle, its colonizers reluctantly agreed to independence. The first president was Sukaron, followed by Suharto, who ruled for thirty-one years, from 1967 to 1998, under a centralized, military-dominated anti-Communist government. In 2004 Indonesians were finally allowed to directly vote for their leader.

For being a new democracy that spent many years under authoritarian rule, Indonesia has a moderate level of press freedom. Every year Freedom House publishes national measures of press freedom in which a rating of 0 means the best and 100 indicates the worst (Freedom House 2015). In 2014 Indonesia had a press freedom score of 49, which is better than both Malaysia (64) and Turkey (62). While there is a lot of room for improvement, Freedom House has described Indonesia as having one of the most open and vibrant media environments in the region (Freedom House, n.d., "Indonesia: Freedom of the Press, 2014"). This portrayal is reflected in figure 20, where I show that the articles mentioning homosexuality in Indonesia's *Jakarta Post* drew on a wide range of frames, including references to rights and claimsmakers, such as social-movement leaders, as well as religion and morality. Additionally, in our qualitative reading of the articles, my research team and I found that when LGBTQ individuals and issues were discussed, the articles tended to include both unsupportive and supportive views.

Indonesia appears to have been publishing information about homosexuality since the 1980s, when the nation was still under authoritarian rule (Blackwood 2007). In addition to the mainstream press discussing homosexuality, Indonesia also has magazines devoted to this issue, has several LGBTQ organizations, and every year holds the largest gay film festival in Asia (Laurent 2005).

Because Indonesia was a Dutch colony, many Indonesians do not speak English. Likewise, lower levels of economic development are likely to limit the ability of residents to travel to other countries. As a result, some scholars have suggested that the idea that one could be homosexual has formed in isolation of Western influences (Boellstorff 2006). Indeed, in the social science research that has been conducted in Indonesia, I found relatively little mention of Western influences, especially when compared with the research done on attitudes about homosexuality in Uganda.

If the media is somewhat open to presenting homosexuality-related issues, if there is a vibrant gay subculture, and if homosexuality is not necessarily seen as a Western import, why don't Indonesians express more-accepting views? As I discussed above, Indonesia's GDP is still quite low, and even though the nation is undergoing processes of economic development, there is evidence that cultural values remain somewhat oriented toward harmony and the larger group.

ISLAM AND ATTITUDES ABOUT HOMOSEXUALITY IN INDONESIA

As they do in Turkey and Malaysia, religious beliefs in Indonesia seem to have a role in shaping the way many residents feel about homosexuality. Whereas only 57% of Malaysians are Muslim, the overwhelming majority of Indonesians (79%) are Muslim, mostly Sunni (Association of Religious Data Archives, n.d.). Despite having a larger Muslim majority than Malaysia, Indonesia has less government regulation (i.e., 6.5) and favoritism of religion (i.e., 7.6). Across the world, the average level of government regulation of religion is 3 and for favoritism of religion it is 4.6. Hence, Indonesia's scores are higher than average. But, as I mentioned previously, the average for Muslim-majority nations in general is high, in part, because religious freedom is related to strength of democracy,[4] which also tends to be lower in Muslim countries.

Indonesia's score for social regulation of religion, which captures the government's feelings toward nontraditional religions, is very high (i.e., 9.7), and higher than in Malaysia (i.e., 8.7), indicating that proselytizing and the development of new religions are highly discouraged. Indeed, Indonesia's constitution acknowledges only six faiths (i.e., Islam, Catholicism, Protestantism, Buddhism, Hinduism, and Confucianism) (U.S. Department of State 2011). Additionally, the Indonesian province of Aceh has adopted Islamic law, which includes a punishment of one hundred lashings for same-sex behaviors (Suroyo and Greenfield 2014).

As mentioned above, when government and religion are closely aligned, each can use the other to reinforce its stance. In her research on the way sexuality has been regulated in Indonesia, Blackwood (2007) notes that beginning in the 1990s Indonesian state officials and Islamic clerics began to directly and publicly address the issue of homosexuality. In 1994 President Suharto instructed the Indonesian delegation at the International Conference on Population and Development not to support the United Nations proposal to adopt a statement supporting same-sex marriage, calling it "such an odd thing" (Oetomo 2001). Around the same time, Blackwood (2007) and Oetomo (2001) note, Muslim leaders were making similar comments and arguing, for example, that discussions of homosexuality and casual sex should not be shown on television.

With such a high proportion of Muslims who also have high levels of religious belief and strongly disapprove of same-sex relations, it may not be that surprising that some of the violence directed at LGBTQ individuals has come from conservative Muslims. However, Indonesia includes a range of Islamic-inspired perspectives, and as Boellstorff (2004) points out, many LGBTQ Indonesians are themselves Muslim. Some Muslim leaders and organizations have been quite vocal in expressing their tolerance. My research team and I discovered that unlike Malaysia's *New Straits Times,* Indonesia's *Jakarta Post* had several articles that mentioned homosexuality in the context of religion and made reference to religious officials. In results similar to what we found in our analysis of *USA Today,* many of the Indonesian articles that mentioned homosexuality and religion were quite positive about same-sex relations, though several also drew on religious discourse to criticize same-sex sexual behaviors.

Like other Muslim nations, Indonesia seems to place same-sex behaviors within a sexual moral domain that includes premarital and extramarital sex. As shown in figure 22, in 2013 93% of Indonesians felt that homosexuality should not be accepted by society, 93% felt the same way about extramarital sex, and an even greater proportion (i.e., 97%) felt this way about premarital sex. Additionally, figure 20 shows that 47% of the Indonesian newspaper articles that mention homosexuality also include references to morality and other moral issues, most of them concerning sex outside of marriage. Public-opinion data and the analysis of newspaper articles suggest that, like many Malaysians, Indonesians tend to view same-sex sexual behaviors as similar to other sex-related acts that are a part of an Islamic-inspired moral framework.

ATTITUDES ABOUT SAME-SEX BEHAVIORS IN TURKEY

Like Malaysia and Indonesia, Turkey is a Muslim-majority nation that is also considered relatively tolerant. It would be classified as a secular state where Sharia law has no role in the judicial system and homosexuality is technically legal. However, like those of Indonesians and Malaysians, Turks' attitudes towards homosexuality are not very supportive. In 2011 and 2013 the Pew Research Center asked Turks whether homosexuality is a way of life that should be accepted by society. In 2011 72% of Turks reported that it should not be, and this number increased a little, to 78%, in 2013. As I show in figure 19, during the fifth wave of the WVS, 88% of Turks reported that they did not want a homosexual neighbor, which is higher than in Indonesia and Malaysia.

As in other nations including Indonesia, attitudes in Turkey regarding homosexuality may be complicated by what "homosexuality" means there. The nation is highly sex segregated: in Turkey, as Cardoso (2009) points out, men and women could be described as occupying two different social worlds. Sex outside of marriage is heavily condemned, with 91% of Turks reporting that premarital sex is unacceptable. Many Turkish men spend a lot of their time with other men, and scholars have noted that in Turkey being "gay" or "homosexual" has to do with the role one plays in same-sex behaviors rather than with simply engaging in sexual acts with a same-sex partner (Oksal 2008; Tapinc 1992)

Because of cross-national differences in how people distinguish between homosexual and heterosexual behaviors, survey questions that simply ask about homosexuality are unlikely to capture all of the same-sex behaviors (e.g., mutual masturbation) that residents of various nations might include. Additionally, when thinking about homosexuality, many Turks may be more likely to focus on men's behaviors. In her research on Turkish college students Sakalh (2003), for example, found that when asked what they associated "homosexuals" with, 59% reported "gay men," and just 3% noted that they perceived homosexuals as lesbians.

As another indicator of the public's feelings, both transsexuals and openly gay men are likely to encounter a lot of challenges in Turkey. A report issued by Transgender Europe found that nearly half of all reported cases of transgender murder in Europe, including Russia, between January 2008 and December 2011 occurred in Turkey (Balzer and Hutta 2012). In their work on Turkey, Bereket and Adam (2008) note that being openly gay can bring a lot of shame and disgrace to one's family. There are reports of both strangers and also people the victim knows attacking them (see Arat and Nuñez 2014). Despite high levels of disapproval, Turkey has an active gay rights movement and several advocacy organizations, as well as gay subcultures in larger cities like Istanbul (Cardoso 2009; Gorkemli 2012). Likewise, in 2003 Turkey became the first Muslim-majority nation to hold a gay pride parade (Peterson and Panfil 2013).

In figure 20, I show that, similar to Indonesia, discussions related to homosexuality in Turkey include a wide range of claims, including rights and morality, as well as claimsmakers, such as religious officials and social-movement leaders. My team and I also found that, in contrast to those from Malaysia and Indonesia, the articles from Turkey include mention of fictional characters and famous people. Consistent with these newspaper frames, private television channels also include shows, such as *Melrose Place,* that have gay and lesbian characters (Gorkemli 2012). In the next section I take a closer look at how economic development, democracy, and religion seem to have shaped public opinion about homosexuality within Turkey.

ECONOMIC DEVELOPMENT AND ATTITUDES IN TURKEY

Much like Malaysia and Indonesia, Turkey has undergone major economic changes in the last fifty years that have led to increases in GDP. In 2013 Turkey's per capita GDP was just under $11,000 (World Bank, n.d.), which is similar to that of Malaysia and much higher than Indonesia's. As the economy has developed, residents have been moving into urban areas, especially large cities like Istanbul. In 1980 44% of Turks lived in urban areas, and by 2010 the proportion had shifted to 71% (IndexMundi, n.d.). Today, the percentage of Turks who live in urban areas is similar to that of Malaysia and greater than it is in Indonesia. Education has also increased in Turkey (World Bank 2013a). The 2010 secondary school enrollment rate is higher in Turkey (i.e., 79%) than in Indonesia (i.e., 67%) and Malaysia (i.e., 69%) (UNESCO Institute for Statistics, n.d.).

Increases in GDP, urbanicity, and education, as well as declining fertility rates, should contribute to a culture that is increasingly shifting from one oriented toward survival and the larger group to one focused on individual concerns and interests, and self-expression (Hofstede 2001; Inglehart and Baker 2000; Schwartz 2006). Consistent with these changes, some research has found that public opinion about homosexuality has gotten a little more liberal (Esmer 2011). However, with a GDP of $9,949 in the mid-2000s, 76% of Turks felt that homosexuality was never acceptable, which is a higher percentage than would be expected given the regression line presented in figure 7.

Despite economic changes, Kagitçibasi and Sunar (1992) point out that Turkey remains a highly patriarchal society with a clear division of labor, which may have some implications for attitudes about homosexuality. Turkey has a higher level of gender inequality (i.e., 0.360 on a scale of 0 to 1, where higher numbers indicate more inequality) than Malaysia (i.e., 0.210), which has a similar level of economic development (United

Nations Development Programme n.d). Some scholars have described the patriarchal system in Turkey as similar to that found in Latin America and other Mediterranean nations (Murray 1992), where the father's role is seen as maintaining the family and the mother's role is viewed as caring for family members and supporting her husband.

Along with clearly specified gender roles, as mentioned above, Turkey has strong norms that often keep the sexes, especially those who are not related to each other, segregated in public. Additionally, premarital sex is so strongly condemned that some researchers have suggested that Turkey has a "cult of virginity" (Necef 1999). Several scholars have pointed out that young people are unlikely to have a lot of heterosexual outlets to experiment with sex. Sex is seen as a very private issue, and discussions about it tend to be reserved for very close same-sex friends (Aral and Fransen 1995; Tapinc 1992). These factors may contribute to gay and lesbian individuals being unlikely to reveal their sexual orientation to family members and people who are not very close friends (Bereket and Adam 2008). As a result, many Turks may not personally know anyone who claims a homosexual identity, which could limit empathy with the challenges these individuals are likely to encounter.

GOVERNMENT, DEMOCRACY, AND ATTITUDES

Along with Malaysia and Indonesia, Turkey is considered a democratic Muslim society. It is seen as more democratic than Libya, Algeria, Egypt, Morocco, and Saudi Arabia. Conversely, Turkey's democracy score (5.69) is slightly lower than Malaysia's (6.36) and Indonesia's (6.34). In the 1920s Turkey became a secular nation, removing its constitutional clause that had made Islam a state religion, and in the mid-1940s Turkey ended its single-party political system. Today, it is considered a democratic republic whereby the elected prime minister is head of government and there is a multiparty system. In 1945 Turkey also became a founding member of the United Nations and has maintained close political ties to other European nations. In 2005 Turkey began to formally negotiate full membership in the European Union (EU) (European Commission, n.d.).

Because of its proximity to other parts of Europe and interest in being part of the EU, Turkey, more so than Indonesia or Malaysia, is under political pressure from Western nations to make policy changes in support of homosexuality. Beginning in the 1980s Turkey's treaty-ratification rate in human rights began to increase, and it improved even more in the

1990s and 2000s, when the country was trying to meet EU membership criteria. However, in 2013 international organizations, including Human Rights Watch, suggested that some of Turkey's advances related to human rights were slipping (Human Rights Watch, n.d.).

Consistent with assessments made by international organizations like Human Rights Watch, some Turkish government officials have been vocal in their disapproval of homosexuality. For example, in a 2010 newspaper interview Selma Aliye Kavaf, who was minister of state responsible for women and families, called homosexuality a "disease" that "needs to be treated" (Commission on Security and Cooperation in Europe 2012). The Turkish government has also played a major role in limiting information on homosexuality in the media. Turkey's criminal code includes prohibitions regarding "public exhibitionism" and "offenses against public morality," which have been used to discriminate against homosexuals and limit access to information about homosexuality (European Commission 2012). Freedom House (2015) categorizes Turkey's press as "not free." Malaysia's press is also considered "not free," but Indonesia's press is seen as "partially free."

Like research done elsewhere, studies conducted in Turkey have found that residents who have not had any social contact with open gay or lesbian individuals have more-negative stereotypes about them (Duyan and Duyan 2005; Sakalh 2003). For Turks who do not know any LGBTQ individuals, information presented about them in the media could provide an opportunity to virtually meet them and possibly empathize with the challenges they face. However, government censorship may limit more-positive and less stereotypical or sensational stories about them.

Despite the government's actions to limit access to information and discussions about homosexuality, there have been some exceptions. The private media gives some attention to gay and lesbian characters and individuals. Indeed, my research team and I found that 23% of the newspaper articles from the *Turkish Daily News* that mentioned homosexuality also included discussions about LGBTQ characters (i.e., Harvey Milk) and artists, including the Turkish-born director Ferzan Özpetek, whose films have included gay themes. Conversely, portrayals in the local media (i.e., local television and newspapers) do not seem as positive or inclusive. As political scientists Arat and Nuñez (2014) explain, "While the private media may employ gay entertainers, show films and programs that include gay characters, or report incidents of violence that involve LGBTQ people, they also often ridicule and make fun of them or present them as threats to society" (26). As a result of these portrayals, ordinary Turks may be less likely to connect with LGBTQ individuals and thereby empathize with the challenges they face.

RELIGION AND ATTITUDES ABOUT
HOMOSEXUALITY IN TURKEY

Along with a limited public press and strong government disapproval, religion also seems to have a role, albeit a complicated one, in shaping Turks' attitudes. In Turkey 98% of the population adheres to Islam. This is a higher proportion than in either Indonesia (i.e., 79%) or Malaysia (i.e., 57%). Despite the high percentage, Turkey is one of a handful of Islamic nations that have long been secular. In 2008 Turkey's government regulation of religion rating was 5.1, where higher numbers indicate more regulation. Relative to Malaysia, which has a score of 7.8, and Indonesia, which has a score of 6.5, Turkey has less government regulation of religion, as well as less government favoritism. Indeed, of all the Muslim countries, Turkey has some of the least religious regulation.

Compared with the Malaysian and Indonesian papers, my research team and I found that the *Turkish Daily News* had a much higher proportion of articles that mentioned homosexuality and discussed religion (see figure 20). The high percentage is similar to that found in the Ugandan papers. However, in contrast to the Ugandan papers, in the *Turkish Daily News* there were few articles that used religion to condemn homosexuality. When negativity was expressed it was often in the context of summarizing the statements or actions of people in other countries, such as Iranian President Mahmoud Ahmadinejad's 2007 speech at Columbia University where he was reported as saying, "There are no gays in Iran" (Cooper 2007).

Because it is geographically close to other, less tolerant Muslim-majority nations and is partially located in Europe and aspires to join the EU, Turkey has to balance both European ideals that support homosexual rights and conservative Islamic views that condemn them. Many of the articles about homosexuality that my research team and I analyzed from the *Turkish Daily News* highlight the tension between conservative Muslim values and pressure from other European countries and the EU. Ozan Gezmiş, an activist, explained in one of the articles we analyzed, "Turkey should vote for human rights on this [gay rights] issue, if it regards itself as a European country. But, we all know this is Turkey's contradiction, where it tries to be European while on the other hand, acting parallel to Islam countries" (Turkish Daily News 2008).

Like Malaysia and Indonesia, a high proportion of Turks disapprove not only of homosexuality but, as shown in figure 22, also of premarital and extramarital sex. Of the six countries presented, Turkey is the only one for which a higher proportion of residents find premarital (i.e., 91%) and extramarital sex (i.e., 94%) more problematic than homosexuality (i.e., 78%). One possible reason why homosexuality has not received the same level of disapproval as these other behaviors may be Turkey's much more liberal European neighbors, who either through direct pressure or unintentional cultural, social, and political influence may very slowly be changing public opinion about homosexuality in this sexually conservative nation. Indeed, measures taken from the WVS suggest that there may be some slight increase in acceptance. In 1990 84% of residents reported that homosexuality is never justified, but in 2011 79% of Turks felt this way. Likewise, WVS data show that in 1990 92% of Turks reported that they did not want a homosexual neighbor, but the figure appears to be declining and was down to 85% in 2011.[5] Of course, during this same period things like education, economic development, and urbanization were also increasing, and I am unable to sort out the causal process and the most important factors.

MUSLIM-MAJORITY NATIONS

As I noted in the introduction to this chapter, all of the countries where homosexuality is punished with death have Muslim-majority populations. Additionally, as I show in table 3, these nations tend to have highly disapproving views. While some of these countries appear to have become somewhat more supportive over time, residents of some societies, like Albania and Malaysia, seem to have developed more-disapproving attitudes. There are some concerns about the survey data used to assess attitudes over time. WVS surveyors did not collect data on any Muslim countries during the first wave of the WVS, and only a handful of countries have more than two time points for comparison. The lack of measures makes it more difficult to have confidence that the data are providing a valid assessment of changes over time. Surveys conducted in non-Muslim nations also suffer from some of the same data concerns. Even with these challenges, a combination of survey data, legislation, and an analysis of the media seems to make clear that residents from Muslim-majority nations on average have highly disapproving views, though there appear to be some modest changes within some of these countries.

TABLE 3   PERCENTAGE OF RESIDENTS IN MUSLIM-MAJORITY NATIONS WHO
REPORT THAT HOMOSEXUALITY IS NEVER JUSTIFIED, OVER TIME

	W2	W3	W4	W5	W6	Change: Less (−) vs. more (+) disapproving
	1990–1994	1995–1998	1999–2004	2005–2009	2010–2014	
Albania		68	81			+13
Algeria			93		63	−30
Azerbaijan		89			93	+4
Bangladesh			99			
Bosnia			72			
Burkina Faso				79		
Egypt			100			
Indonesia			95	89		−6
Iran			94	82		−12
Iraq					73	
Jordan			98	100	87	−11
Kazakhstan					67	
Kyrgyzstan			81		69	−12
Lebanon					48	
Libya					79	
Malaysia				43	60	+17
Mali				63		
Morocco					90	
Nigeria	72	79	78		64	−8
Pakistan			96		73	−23
Palestine					81	
Saudi Arabia			85			
Tunisia					97	
Turkey	84			73	79	−5
Uzbekistan					77	
Yemen					88	
Overall change for nations with at least two time points						−7

SOURCE: Weighted estimates from the WVS.

NOTE: Change in attitudes is indicated for the two waves that are furthest apart. During W1 no data were collected on Muslim-majority countries.

At the end of the previous chapter I showed how differences in attitudes among nations dominated by Protestantism largely disappear when economic development, democracy, and religious salience are considered. Can differences between Muslim-majority countries and others be explained by these same factors? In appendix B, table 8, model 5, I show that even after these other characteristics are considered, residents of Muslim nations remain significantly more likely than those of Catholic-majority countries to disapprove of homosexuality. In a separate analysis I also found that after controlling for these other factions, they are more likely than people living in nations dominated by mainline Protestant, Catholic, and Hindu faiths to find homosexuality problematic. Hence, attitudinal distinctions between residents of Muslim-majority nations and these other countries do not appear to be the result of differences in democracy, economic development, or religious salience.

Why are residents from Muslim-majority nations more disapproving than people living in Catholic, Hindu, and mainline Protestant countries? Part of the reason is that high proportions of residents from Muslim-majority countries, as well as their governments, feel strongly about religious proscriptions that find not only homosexuality, but a wide-range of sex-related behaviors, problematic. Additionally, Islam seems to generate high levels of religious belief and engagement in some of the same ways that strict or conservative Protestant groups do. As a result, many adherents take their religion quite seriously, which, as noted in the second chapter, also has implications for the views of other residents. Finally, even in nations like Turkey and Indonesia, which are classified as democracies, the governments tend to have a closer relationship with religion than can be found in many other countries. This close relationship is going to lead to religious sentiment infusing government decisions and discussions about homosexuality, limiting alternative perspectives, and encouraging religion-inspired views that find homosexuality problematic.

CHAPTER 5

The Relatively Liberal Views of People from Catholic-Majority Countries

An Examination of Spain, Italy, and Brazil

Homosexuals have gifts and qualities to offer to the Christian community. Are we capable of providing for these people . . .? Without denying the moral problems associated with homosexual unions, there are instances where mutual assistance to the point of sacrifice is a valuable support in the life of these persons.

—Cardinal Péter Erdő, archbishop of Esztergom-Budapest

In 2014 Roman Catholic bishops released a draft document calling for the church to welcome gays, unmarried couples, and people who have divorced (Povoledo and Goodstein 2014). Although several public-opinion polls have found that many Catholics around the world are ready to accept these changes, the text was seen as highly controversial among conservative Catholics, and as a result revisions were quickly implemented (Bialik 2014). In the second chapter I showed that on average the Catholics of the world tend to have views more liberal than those of adherents of many of the other major religions, though there is a lot of variation.

Taking a comparative case-study approach and drawing on the theoretical processes discussed at the beginning of this book, in this chapter I look at the factors that have shaped public opinion about homosexuality in Spain, Italy, and Brazil. These nations were chosen because they were included in recent waves of the WVS, and they have high proportions of Catholics. They also differ in their views of homosexuality, as well as in their level of economic development and strength of democracy, offering

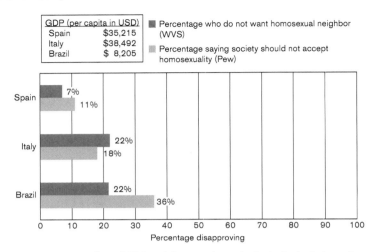

FIGURE 23. Snapshot of GDP and disapproving attitudes in Spain, Italy, and Brazil.

SOURCES: Spring Pew Global Attitudes Survey (Pew Research Center 2013); WVS, wave 5; ARDA's Cross-National Socio-Economic and Religion Data, 2011.

some key points of comparison. Of the three, Spain is the most liberal and has been declared the friendliest place in the world (or at least one of them) for LGBTQ individuals (Tallantyre 2014). Figure 23 shows that only about 11% of Spaniards feel that society should not accept homosexuality. The other two nations are a bit more conservative, with a little over 20% of Brazilians and Italians feeling this way. All three nations are relatively large and stable, with strong research infrastructures, especially Spain and Italy[1]—making the study of attitudes about homosexuality feasible.

This chapter begins with an assessment of Spain and then moves on to an examination of Italy before discussing Brazil. I begin each section with a brief overview of the recent historical and social context of attitudes about homosexuality-related issues and then discuss the roles of democracy, religion, and economic development in shaping public opinion. As each new nation is introduced, additional comparisons are made with the Catholic countries already discussed.

PUBLIC OPINION IN SPAIN

Spaniards have some of the most liberal views about homosexuality in the world. Their attitudes have mostly stabilized, and there is not much more room on the WVS justification measure for them to exhibit even more tolerant views. In table 4, I use data from the WVS to show that in the early 1990s 38% of residents felt that homosexuality was never justified. In the 2000s the percentage dropped to about 10% when same-sex marriage also became legal. Today, less than 10% of Spaniards feel that homosexuality is never justified. In the fifth wave of the WVS, which is the last one to include all three nations, about 32% of Brazilians felt this way and 51% of Italians reported feeling that homosexuality is never justified. In July 2005 Spain became the third country in the world to legalize same-sex marriage (McLean 2005). As of 2016, neither Italy nor Brazil had legalized it. While other nations, like Norway, France, and Germany, have opened the way to same-sex unions by allowing for registered cohabiting partnerships, Spain (along with the Netherlands, Belgium, and Canada) was among the first to provide a direct equivalence to heterosexual marriage.

The legalization of same-sex marriage was the result of a long history of reforms and changes in attitudes. From 1936 until 1975 Spain was ruled by a dictator, Francisco Franco. He supported a vision of Spanish nationalism that tried to promote traditions like bullfighting and flamenco dancing (Brandes 2009; M.H. Hayes 2009). Under his rule all cultural activities were subject to censorship, Spanish became the official language, and the official use of other languages was forbidden (Beer and Jacob 1985). Catholicism became the state religion, with religious norms being officially enforced. During this period homosexuality was criminalized, and as Valiente (2002) points out, many of the guilty (mostly men) were sent to special prisons called "galleries of deviants." Shortly after the end of Franco's reign in 1979 same-sex sexual activity became legal, with the same age of consent for heterosexual and homosexual sex behaviors. As I discuss below, rather than having its origins in a movement that encouraged Spanish gay and lesbian individuals to come out, acceptance of homosexuality seems to have grown out of the post–Franco dictatorship release from suppressive norms, a decline in the church's influence, and the resulting embrace of liberal values.

CHANGING ATTITUDES THROUGH DEMOCRACY AND POLITICS

In the second chapter I explained that democracy can shape views about homosexuality by increasing awareness and knowledge of behaviors and ideas that may be considered new or different, by encouraging

TABLE 4 PERCENTAGE OF RESIDENTS IN CATHOLIC-MAJORITY NATIONS WHO REPORT THAT HOMOSEXUALITY IS NEVER JUSTIFIED, OVER TIME

	W1	W2	W3	W4	W5	W6	Change: Less (−) vs. more (+) disapproving
	1981–1984	1990–1994	1995–1998	1999–2004	2005–2009	2010–2014	
Andorra					8		
Argentina	68	60	32	40	33	19	−49
Australia	41		31		23	13	−27
Brazil		70			32	36	−33
Canada				27	21		−6
Chile		77	44	37	28	14	−63
Colombia			61		46	45	0
Ecuador						49	
France					15		
Germany			21		10	18	−2
Guatemala					46		
Hungary	87		46		33		−54
Italy					51		
Mexico	72	55	52	53	34	40	−33
Netherlands					16	13	−4
Peru			44	57		32	−12
Philippines			29	29		31	+3
Poland		79	60		53	47	−31
Puerto Rico			60	51			−9
Rwanda					76	63	−13
Slovenia			50		26	34	−16
Spain		38	24	12	10	8	−30
Switzerland		40	17		11		−29
Uruguay			46		18	19	−27
Venezuela			71	62			−9
Overall change for nations with at least two time points							−22

SOURCE: Weighted estimates from the WVS.
NOTE: Change in attitudes is indicated for the two waves that are furthest apart.

exposure to and active participation in democratic processes, and by witnessing the government upholding individuals' rights and liberties. In Spain democracy seems to have had a role in increasing tolerance of homosexuality. Franco's regime ended in 1975, at the same time as his death, and the nation transitioned (relatively peacefully) into democracy. Although things began to soften toward the end, throughout much of his thirty-seven-year rule Spaniards were subject to a wide range of behavioral constraints related to sex, marriage, and procreation. In part because of the close relationship between the state and the Catholic Church, abortion, homosexuality, and the selling of birth-control aids were illegal, and divorce was not allowed (Herzog 2011). When the dictatorship ended a lot changed.

By the mid-1970s in other parts of the world such as the United States and Great Britain, residents had experienced an exciting period of sexual liberation, as well as an increase in protest and social-movement activity. Spain, too, had some of this, which occurred as Franco's regime was beginning to thaw. With Franco's death, Spaniards began espousing more-liberal views, which seemed to have implications for how some residents viewed same-sex behaviors. As the Spanish researcher Alberto Mira (2000) explains, "Homosexuality was just one more taboo that had to be broken, so for a while it was fashionable to include references to homosexuality in popular and high culture. This often had very little to do with gay politics and was hardly more than a response to long years of sexual repression" (345).

As ideas began to change and residents became more tolerant, Spain's LGBTQ-movement organizations, which were granted much more freedom under democracy, increased their activities (Guasch 2011). In the mid-1980s a political opportunity arose for the movement to align with the nation's major leftist Communist party, Partido Comunista de España (PCE). The PCE was facing electoral challenges (Linz and Montero 1999). In 1986 the party saw a chance to revive itself by joining a group of smaller leftist and civil organizations and creating a political party with new ideas and leaders, called Izquierda Unida (IU) (Calvo 2007; Platero 2007). Consistent with its leftist political orientation, the IU supported many LGBTQ-related issues, and in 1986 the party's manifesto for the general election included a section devoted to the LGBTQ community's legal and social challenges.

Even with its merger the IU still lacked electoral success (Calvo 2007). During the late 1980s and early 1990s the Partido Socialista Obrero Española (PSOE) was Spain's ruling party and initially did not have much connection with LGBTQ organization leaders. But, as Calvo (2007) explains, when the PSOE started to lose support in the mid-1990s, it decided to develop a stronger relationship with the movement. When it came back into power in 2000, it supported Spain's national same-sex marriage bill, which passed in 2005. A number of scholars have argued that as LGBTQ individuals and organizations were advocating for legislation, they did not draw on identity politics (Calvo 2005, 2007; de Fluviá 1978). Rather, they linked the movement with sexual liberation and Marxist politics, presenting themselves as another actor in solidarity with the working class against the bourgeoisie.

While political opportunity was certainly important for securing same-sex marriage in Spain, I show in table 4 that residents' attitudes had already become a lot more tolerant by the time same-sex marriage was passed in 2005. One mechanism through which democracy can have an influence is through freedom of the press, which increases residents' exposure to a wider range of views and over time can increase tolerance. In the late 1990s, when partnership laws were being discussed at the regional level, major Spanish newspapers printed editorials encouraging support (El Mundo 1996; Tejeda 1998). Today, Spain's freedom-of-the-press score is very good, and Freedom House classifies the press as free (Freedom House 2015). Conversely, Brazil and Italy are categorized as having only partial freedom of the press.

A final political factor that seems to have contributed to more-liberal views and related legislation was the European Union (EU). Some scholars have suggested that the opportunity for Spain to portray itself as very tolerant to the EU may have pushed the country to legalize same-sex marriage (Platero 2007). In this way Spain is somewhat similar to other nations like Turkey in responding to outside pressure and opportunities to present itself as tolerant on issues related to equality, citizenship, and the inclusion of sexual minorities.

CHANGES IN RELIGION AND ATTITUDES ABOUT HOMOSEXUALITY IN SPAIN

Along with democracy, the declining influence of religion seems to have had a role in shaping attitudes about homosexuality and related legislation in Spain. When Franco came to power he implemented a form of Catholic nationalism based on the idea that Catholicism was the historical crux of Spaniards' national identity (Box 2010). With Catholicism becoming the official state religion, the church was sometimes used to justify Franco's power, legitimize Catholic-inspired policies, and enforce religious norms. Particularly important was a Catholic-inspired view of the family where women were primarily seen as caretakers. To work, for example, women often needed the permission of their husbands, and married women were strongly discouraged from working (Skupas 2007). Additionally, from a Catholic perspective the primary reason for sexual intercourse is procreation. Under Franco's rule abortion and homosexuality were illegal and birth control not allowed, though many women were still able to obtain contraception (Ortiz-Gómez and Ignaciuk 2010).

By the early 1970s the state no longer had the same close relationship that it once had with the church (Perez-Agote 2010). Nevertheless, after the dictatorship ended in the mid-1970s, the Catholic Church experienced a sharp decline in adherents' religious engagement (Perez-Agote 2010; Requena 2005; Requena and Stanek 2014). There is evidence that the decrease was related to the implementation of democracy and religious freedom. Requena and Stanek (2014) note that the sharpest drop in the proportion of practicing Catholics (going from 58% to 48%) occurred between 1975 and 1980, when democracy was first implemented and religious freedom granted. During the 1980s the decrease began to slow, with 42% of Spaniards actively engaging the Catholic faith. Some of the people who stopped attending appear to have left religion completely. Between 1975 and 1995 the proportion of atheists, agnostics, and people indifferent to religion increased from 2% to 14%. The decrease in religious engagement happened around the same time that many Spaniards were developing more-liberal views. Today, many Spaniards still consider themselves Catholic (Association of Religious Data Archives, n.d.).[2] However, the level of religious engagement is quite low, and academics typically classify Spain as a secular nation (Perez-Agote 2010; Requena 2005; Requena and Stanek 2014).

In the 1960s Rome enacted Vatican II, which revised many Catholic rituals and softened restrictions to encourage a more individualized and less institutionalized view of the faith (Vatican II—Voice of the Church, n.d.). Vatican II was partially prompted by the church's desire to be more modern (McCarthy 2012; Lakeland 2006). However, by demanding less the Catholic Church may have undermined itself. A number of studies have found that after Vatican II the church's influence declined and people were less religiously engaged, with some scholars attributing the decrease to the church's changes (Ignazi and Wellhofer 2013; Stark and Finke 2000; Stark and Iannaccone 1996).

With fewer people adhering to the Catholic faith and the church losing its privileged position with the state, fewer Spaniards had a religious basis on which to object to homosexuality. Indeed, in the decades after Franco's rule Spaniards' tolerance for a range of sexual behaviors that the Catholic church condemns increased (Solsten and Meditz 1990). In chapter 4, I showed that compared with Muslim countries, Protestant nations in general have more-tolerant views about the moral acceptability of extramarital affairs and premarital sex, as well as homosexuality.

But Catholic nations are even more liberal (see note for figure 22), and among them Spain has some of the most accepting views.[3] Like attitudes, laws regarding a range of sexual-morality issues have also changed. Hence, in addition to the legalization of same-sex marriage, prostitution is legal in Spain, and the nation has very liberal abortion legislation (Associated Press 2010; Fotheringham 2011; Kassam 2014).

ECONOMIC DEVELOPMENT AND PUBLIC OPINION ABOUT HOMOSEXUALITY IN SPAIN

In previous chapters I explained the important role that economic development and many of the factors included with it—like residential mobility, consumer consumption (i.e., televisions and the Internet), and lower birthrates—can have in shaping attitudes about homosexuality. In Spain economic development may have had some role in changing attitudes, but other factors may have also been more important. Spain has had a fairly high level of economic development for some time. Because Franco was stanchly opposed to Communism, many Western nations were willing to trade with Spain (Schmitz 1999), and the country was not isolated in the same way that Catholic countries that were part of the Communist bloc (e.g., Poland) were. That said, beginning in the mid-1980s Spain's economy began to expand rapidly (Solsten and Meditz 1988). A high proportion of residents moved from rural to urban areas (World Bank 2013b). There has been a proliferation of media that includes television shows with LGBTQ characters and information on Spain's well-attended gay pride parades (Guasch, n.d.).

These changes would have contributed to some normalization of same-sex behaviors and relationships. Once Franco's repressive gender-related policies were lifted, the society also became much more egalitarian (Solsten and Meditz 1988). Related to increases in education and women's workforce participation, the traditional family size has shrunk, fertility rates have declined, and more residents are cohabiting (Davia and Legazpe 2014; Dominguez-Folgueras and Castro-Martin 2013; Lesthaeghe 2010; Requena and Salazar 2014). As a result, Spaniards have increasingly gotten exposure to alternative family forms and new perspectives on the meaning of love, commitment, and the family.

All of these changes could have contributed to a more accepting environment. But, given the timing of changes in laws and attitudes, religious secularization and the transition to democracy are likely to have been even more important in increasing residents' tolerance for homosexuality. The next section focuses on Italy, which is the Catholic Church's religious home. Like Spain and many other European nations, Italy's level of religious attendance is lower than in other parts of the world. That said, the Catholic Church seems to have brought a level of religious infusion into public institutions and discussions about morality that today is minimal in Spain.

ATTITUDES ABOUT HOMOSEXUALITY IN ITALY: A LESS TOLERANT EUROPEAN COUNTRY

Compared with the Spanish, Italians are more conservative in their views about homosexuality, but relative to residents in many other nations they are still quite liberal. Same-sex behaviors have been legal since 1890, when Italian unification consolidated the peninsula's different states. In conformity with an EU directive, in 2003 Italy made discrimination on the basis of sexual orientation illegal. However, there are no other areas (e.g., housing, schooling) that offer protection against discrimination. Italy does not allow same-sex couples to adopt, nor does it recognize any form of same-sex union (Moscati 2010). That said, some Italian municipalities have allowed same-sex couples to register their unions, but these are not legally binding (Lavers 2015). While it is more conservative in offering rights to same-sex couples than several other EU countries, including Spain, in 1982 Italy became only the third nation in the world that allowed transgender individuals to legally change their gender and official name. Spain now offers this option without requiring applicants to undergo sex-reassignment surgery.

Relative to both Spain and Brazil, public opinion about homosexuality in Italy is more conservative. Using data from Pew Global Attitudes Survey, figure 23 shows that in 2013 18% of Italians felt that society should not accept homosexuality, but only 11% of Spaniards shared these feelings. Conversely, 36% of Brazilians felt this way. The proportion of Brazilians who said that they did not want a homosexual neighbor was the same as for the Italians. Having relatively liberal views about homosexuality, especially compared with nations outside of Europe, Italy has, as its next big issues regarding homosexuality, extending antidiscrimination laws and enacting same-sex-union legislation (Holzhacker 2012).

There have been a lot of discussions about same-sex unions in Italy's public press. In 2015, when Ireland, also an EU Catholic-majority country, became the first nation in the world to legalize same-sex marriage through popular vote, several Italian politicians, including lieutenants for the prime minister, proclaimed that their nation would be next to enact a civil-partnership law (Vogt 2015). Even before Ireland's vote, political discussions about same-sex unions in Italy were becoming increasingly common in newspapers, in academic circles, and on television talk shows (Moscati 2010). Compared with Spain, religion has been given more reverence in Italy, which seems related at least in part to the Catholic Church being located next to Rome. As I explain below, the church often comments on moral issues like homosexuality, and compared with the Spanish, the Italians and their political leaders seem to give it greater heed.

THE CATHOLIC CHURCH'S IMPORTANT ROLE IN ITALY

The headquarters of the Roman Catholic Church are located at the Vatican, which is across the river from the nation's political capital in Rome. Prior to World War II the Catholic Church at times had a lot of power over politics, but following the war Italy became democratic. As Schmitt, Euchner, and Preidel (2013) explain, one way the church has maintained its relevance and position is by establishing authority over ethical and moral issues. The church is highly opposed to homosexuality and unsupportive of even same-sex unions.

There may be some direct influence of the church's views on residents' attitudes about homosexuality, especially since religious engagement in Italy seems to have increased in recent years. Compared with many other parts of the world, most European nations, especially those located in the western part, have relatively low levels of religious belief and engagement. Hence, for all the countries included in the last three waves of the WVS, 72% of survey respondents say that religion is rather or very important. But in Europe the level is one of the lowest in the world at 56%. Compared with the rest of Europe, Italy has a much higher proportion of people (i.e., 74%) who report that religion is rather or very important. Additionally, over the last four decades Italians appear to have become somewhat more religious. While the percentage of Italians in 1981 who meditated or prayed was 73%, by 2005 it had incrementally increased to 78% (Association of Religious Data Archives, n.d.). A similar change can be found for other religion measures, including the percent believing in God, which went from 89% in 1981 to 94% in 1999.[4] Likewise, the proportion believing in life after death went from 59% in 1981 to 73% in 1999, and the percent feeling that God is *not* important decreased from 9% in 1981 to just 2% in 2005 (Association of Religious Data Archives, n.d.). Even more important for understanding attitudes about homosexuality, the percentage of residents who believe that churches give answers to moral problems went from 51% in 1981 to 64% in 2005.

Why have there been recent increases in support for religion in Italy?[5] The previous discussion of religion in Spain noted that with Vatican II the church eased some restrictions to make the Catholic faith more accessible. Some social scientists have argued that when religions make such changes they may inadvertently lead some respondents to feel that less is expected of them (Iannaccone 1994). As a result, some adherents may feel less assurance of otherworldly rewards, which can weaken belief (Stark and Finke 2000). Following Vatican II this may have happened in Italy. While religious belief has increased some, overall levels are still lower than they were in the late 1950s, when Vatican II was enacted (Vezzoni and Biolcati-Rinaldi 2015).

Introvigne and Stark (2005) attribute more-recent upturns to an increase in religious competition within Italy, where non-Catholic faiths have increased and the state has revised some policies, like paying for the salaries of Catholic parish priests. Religious leaders may be responding to increases in religious competition and the loss of some guaranteed state support by working harder to capture the public's attention, which could increase religious engagement. Also, new religious groups (i.e., Pentecostals) seem to be offering religious alternatives that some residents are finding more appealing, strengthening religious belief (Introvigne and Stark 2005).

Since the Catholic Church is clear in its condemnation of homosexuality, Italians who take their faith very seriously are going to be less approving of homosexuality. Indeed, research done in Italy shows that more-religious individuals are less supportive (Baiocco et al. 2014; Lingiardi, Falanga, and D'Augelli 2005). Additionally, Italy provides the physical home for the Catholic Church, and its historical presence has resulted in substantial religious topography, art, and festivals. Because of the church's physical presence and history in the country, many Italians are likely to feel a strong cultural connection to the Catholic Church. Indeed, research shows that even if Italians are not regularly attending Mass, many see themselves as culturally Catholic (Garelli 2012).

The church has also been vocal in its views about moral issues, and popes like John Paul II have been particularly charismatic and communicative, increasing media visibility (Marzano 2013). Unlike in Spain, the Catholic Church in Italy has a greater role in political decisions and discussions. Researchers have noted that Italian politicians, especially those who are right-wing and conservative, tend to seriously consider the church's position on relevant issues like homosexuality (Moscati 2010). Social-movement leaders. too. seem to have been careful to strategize with the church in mind. Hence, in his research on Arcigay, which is the largest Italian LGBTQ group, Holzhacker (2012) explains that at the end of the 2000s the organization strategically chose to focus on same-sex-union legislation rather than marriage to appease Catholic adherents and "diminish debates about the word 'marriage' with the Vatican and the Catholic Church hierarchy" (30).

How might the recent uptick in religious engagement shape public opinion and related legislation in Italy? Italy has a well-developed economy and a fairly strong democracy, and has also experienced some pressure from the EU. Not surprisingly, compared with many countries in the rest of the world, public opinion in Italy is quite liberal, and some increase in religious engagement is not likely to seriously affect the nation's upward trajectory of acceptance. However, compared with marriage, same-sex unions are likely to be a lot more palatable to the church and the general public. Additionally, unlike in Spain, there is a higher percentage of Italians who take their religion very seriously, including religious proscriptions regarding homosexuality. As a result, the media and government are likely to be more careful about how homosexuality is framed in public discussions.

DEMOCRACY AND POLITICS FOR SHAPING ATTITUDES IN ITALY

In 1946 Italy transitioned to a democracy with a constitutional republic and a multiparty system. Italy has a slightly stronger democracy score (7.98) than Brazil (7.38) and a slightly weaker one than Spain (8.45) (Economist 2008). Freedom of speech is protected, but the media and political leaders in Italy have closely collaborated, leading to concerns about political intrusions into the media (Ciaglia 2013). As a result of this and some other issues (i.e., no national freedom-of-information law), in 2014 Italy's media was categorized as only partially free, though its democracy is classified as free (Freedom House, n.d., "Italy: Freedom of the Press, 2014").

Democracy should increase awareness and knowledge of behaviors and ideas that are new or different, make clear that the government is upholding individuals' rights and liberties, and encourage residents to engage in the political process and support other people's rights. This mostly seems to be happening in Italy. The issues related to democracy that arose in the scholarly research I did for this chapter tended to focus on the depiction of LGBTQ individuals. Some scholars (i.e., Moscati 2010) have argued that the portrayal of these people is not as positive as it could be, and compared with Italy's LGBTQ press, the nation's mainstream daily newspapers have been slower to offer more-complex discussions about the challenges (e.g., becoming parents) that these individuals encounter. That said, in 2013 the government announced guidelines for the media in how to discuss LGBTQ individuals and related issues and avoid stereotypes and particularly negative portrayals (Dipartimento per le Pari Opportunità 2013).

As I was writing this book, surveys were showing that the majority of Italians approved of same-sex unions (Hooper 2014; Hudson 2015). Some prominent politicians, including the nation's prime minister, Matteo Renzi, have also been supportive. Leaving aside microstates like Monaco, in 2015 Italy was the only Western European nation that did have some sort of nationally recognized same-sex-union legislation. Hence, there is some outside pressure from other European nations to provide same-sex-union legislation (see BBC News 2015). Homosexuality-related legislation can follow public opinion (i.e., United States), or it may first be enacted and then contribute to changes in the public's view (i.e., South Africa). Given Italians' relatively high level of acceptability but the lack of more-basic legal protections (i.e., housing discrimination), homosexuality-related laws and policies seem to be following residents' increasingly liberal views.

Though it certainly has a strong presence, the Catholic Church in Italy has been more careful about engaging in politics than it did in Spain during Franco's regime, and its actions seem to have had implications for homosexuality-related legislation. Beginning in the early 1940s and lasting for about fifty years, the Christian Democrat Party played a dominant role in Italy's multiparty system. Rather than attaching itself to only conservative or liberal Catholics, the Christian Democrat Party aligned itself with Catholics in general, becoming a party that was inclusive of all adherents.

In the early 1990s the Christian Democrat Party dissolved, in part, because of high levels of corruption (C. M. Warner 2013). In Spain, Franco's government had aligned itself with the Catholic Church, and when the regime ended, Spaniards seemed to lose some confidence in the church. Because the Vatican largely let the Christian Democratic Party function without direct intervention (Warner 2013), when the party disintegrated, Italians in general did not seem to lose a lot of confidence in the church.

In the early 1990s the Catholic Church abandoned "its policy of relative non-involvement in Italian and Roman political issues" (Mudu 2002), which may have had implications for homosexuality-related legislation. As Schmitt, Euchner, and Preidel (2013) point out, in 1992 the Vatican published an appeal to the electorate to not vote for political leaders that supported same-sex unions, in 2003 it directly urged Catholic politicians not to be supportive, and in 2007 the Italian Episcopal Conference rejected the recognition of any sort of same-sex relationship that differed from the traditional concept of family. A number of scholars have noted that Italian politicians have been more inclined to listen to the church and to seriously consider its perspective in proposing and voting on homosexuality-related legislation (Moscati 2010; Scappucci 2001). Researchers have found that when there are objections to same-sex unions in Italy, the discourse tends to focus on concerns about children and the family and how same-sex parents may inadvertently cause harm (Anaya 2014; Bernini 2010). Conversely, in Spain when same-sex marriage legislation was being proposed, the discourse focused on equality and the right of all Spanish children to grow up in a family with married parents, regardless of the parents' gender (Moscati 2010; Villagrasa Alcaide 2005).

ECONOMIC DEVELOPMENT IN ITALY: THE ENVIRONMENT HAS ALREADY CHANGED

As discussed previously, nations with higher levels of economic development are more likely to cultivate a culture that values self-expression and individual uniqueness over and above group solidarity and loyalty (Inglehart and Baker 2000; Schwartz 2014). Like many western European nations, Italy has a relatively high level of economic development, especially in relation to other countries across the world. Industrialization in Italy began in the mid-1890s (Cohen 1967), and today about 74% of Italy's economy lies in the service sector, which is a similar percentage to that found in other European nations (e.g.., Germany, France, and Spain) (Central Intelligence Agency, n.d., "GDP"). Educational attainment has continued to advance, with 19% of young people completing university in 2000 and approximately 32% finishing in

2010 (OECD 2012). Italian women have increasingly entered the work-force, which along with other changes (e.g., higher levels of education and a greater interest in personal achievement) has resulted in a higher percentage of females choosing to remain childless (Tanturri and Men-carini 2008). All of these factors should contribute to a more liberal and accepting environment, changing views of the family and relationships.

With Italy's relatively high level of economic development, residents' views about homosexuality are relatively liberal. That said, since the 1980s the nation has encountered a lot of economic challenges, and there remain large economic differences between the nation's northern and southern regions. Additionally, since the 1990s labor costs in Italy have risen more than in other European nations, there have been large budget deficits, and consumption and investment have fallen (De Cecco 2007).

If we take a regional perspective that focuses only on Europe, or western Europe, Italy may seem to be losing some of its standing. How-ever, a more macro perspective that considers nations across the world suggests that Italy is doing quite well. The nation has a high base level of economic development and all of the factors (i.e., a stable political system, relatively high levels of education, lower fertility rates) that tend to accompany it. As a result, economic vibrations are not going to pro-foundly change the more tolerant trajectory of residents' attitudes, espe-cially with EU pressure to support same-sex unions, democracy remain-ing strong, and religious importance increasing some but still being far lower than that found in many Muslim and non-European Protestant countries. Below I discuss Brazil, which has a much lower level of eco-nomic development, though like those of its European counterparts, its attitudes about homosexuality are still quite liberal.

BRAZIL AND MOSTLY SUPPORTIVE ATTITUDES

Brazil is South America's largest nation, and with over two hundred million people it is the world's fifth-most-populous country. Like many Catholic societies, its residents have relatively liberal views about homo-sexuality. In the past twenty years, attitudes regarding homosexuality in Brazil have grown even more liberal, with 70% reporting in the early 1990s that it is never justified and then dropping to about 30% twenty years later.[6] As I show in table 4, a similar decrease can be found in many South American nations.

Consistent with these accepting attitudes, in 2013 Brazil became the eleventh nation in the world (following Denmark and just before France) to allow same-sex marriage. Other South American (and Catholic) nations have also embraced liberal homosexuality-related legislation, with Ecuador, Uruguay, and Argentina legally recognizing some form of same-sex civil union (Freedom to Marry 2015). Brazil has long had fairly liberal policies regarding same-sex relations. In 1830, when its imperial penal code was signed, all references to sodomy were removed, essentially making homosexuality legal. Since 2004 Brazil has been recognizing same-sex unions, and before marriage became legal across the nation some judges were converting civil unions into full marriages (see Polaski 2012). While the country as a whole does not have a separate antidiscrimination law that applies to LGBTQ individuals, some cities do.

Some researchers have argued that because same-sex relations have long been legal, Brazil's LGBTQ population has not been segregated from mainstream society in the same way that it has been in other countries (de Albuquerque Júnior, Ceballos, and Hallewell 2002). As a result, the LGBTQ community has had a particularly visible and vibrant presence (La Pastina 2002). Indeed, Brazil's LGBTQ organizations have garnered international recognition, and the community is known across the globe for hosting the world's largest pride parade (Outtraveler Editors 2013).

While many Brazilians seem supportive, there is still resistance. In a nation where same-sex relations have been allowed for 150 years, same-sex unions have been legal since the mid-2000s, and marriage is now possible, we might expect an even higher proportion of residents to express support. Research conducted in Rio de Janeiro in the mid-2000s found that 60% of LGBTQ respondents had been victims of some form of discrimination or violence (referenced in Vianna and Carrara 2007). Likewise, Brazil has one of the highest LGBTQ murder rates in the world (Rodgers 2013), though its homicide rate in general is very high (Bevins 2015; Marszal and Alexander 2015). Police officers appear responsible for at least some of the homosexuality-related hate crimes that at times are directed at transgender individuals, especially poor trans women of color (Lavers 2013). Below I explain how democracy, religion, and economic development have contributed to high levels of acceptance in this relatively new democracy where the Catholic Church has a strong presence and the country has undergone a roller coaster of economic changes.

RECENT DEMOCRACY AND CHANGING ATTITUDES

Like Spain and Italy, Brazil was dominated by a dictatorship, which began in 1964 and lasted for twenty-one years. Under the military dictatorship a restrictive constitution was implemented, and freedom of speech was severely curtailed. In the late 1970s Brazil started the process of redemocratization (Bandeira 2006). In 1988 a new constitution was adopted. Marsiaj (2006) and Vianna and Carrara (2007) point out that at the time, LGBTQ organizations lobbied to have their rights and liberties included in the constitution but they were unsuccessful. WVS data for Brazil goes back only to the early 1990s, which is a few years after the constitution was adopted. At that point 70% of Brazilians felt that homosexuality was never justified (see table 4) and 30% said they did not want a homosexual neighbor. About twenty years later, when the nation was making same-sex marriage legal, only about 11% of Brazilians felt that homosexuality was never justified.

Although Brazil has hit some bumps (e.g., government corruption) along the way, scholars generally see the country's transition to democracy as successful (French and Fortes 2012; Rubin 2010). Today it has a democracy score of 7.38, which is only slightly less than that of Spain (8.45) and Italy (7.98). By increasing exposure to and awareness of seemingly new or nontraditional behaviors and demonstrating that the government upholds rights and liberties, democracy can foster more-tolerant views (Guérin, Petry, and Crête 2004; Peffley and Rohrschneider 2003). To some extent this seems to have happened in Brazil. Since the end of the military dictatorship, Brazil's television and newspaper outlets have given a lot of visibility to homosexuality-related events, including the very large annual gay pride parade and the International Lesbian and Gay Association meetings (i.e., 1995 and 2010). The government has also had a more direct role in combating homophobia. For example, in the mid-2000s the Citizen Rights Regional Attorney in São Paulo successful brought a civil suit against a TV network (Omega Ltda.) that had a show (*Hot Afternoons*) that contained offensive jokes related to people's sexual orientation (Vianna and Carrara 2007). There have also been several initiatives led by public institutions and nongovernmental organization to developed projects to help combat and prevent homophobia (e.g., the Permanent Mission of Brazil to the United Nations Office in Geneva 2015).

THE ROLE OF THE CATHOLIC CHURCH IN BRAZIL

As in Italy, religion is important to the majority of Brazilians. The nation has the largest Catholic population in the world, though the proportion has been shifting and not everyone is actively engaged. In 2010 about

65% of Brazilians identified as Catholic, 22% affiliated with a Protestant faith, and many of the remaining belonged to Afro-Brazilian and spiritualist faiths (Ogland and Verona 2014).[7] Over time the proportion of people who consider themselves non-Catholic has increased, so that in 1950 only about 3% self-affiliated with a Protestant faith, but by 2010 the figure was 22%, with the majority being Pentecostal and Evangelical. There has also been a small increase in the proportion of Brazilians claiming no religious affiliation, going from almost nothing in 1950 to about 8% in 2010 (Association of Religious Data Archives, n.d.).

In contrast to Spain and Italy, Brazilian Catholicism is much more heterogeneous, including, for example, Catholic Charismatic Renewal and Christian Base Community (Pierucci and Prandi 2000). These other variants of Catholicism may include charismatic practices (i.e., singing in tongues), emphasize a personal relationship with God, and encourage religious reorientation—features that also tend to be found in many charismatic (and conservative) Protestant faiths.

Compared with Spaniards and Italians, a higher proportion of Brazilians are actively engaged in their faith. While 22.5% of Spaniards reported attending church at least once a month in 2005 and 54% of Italians said they did, 65% of Brazilians did (Association of Religious Data Archives 2013). Additionally, somewhat similarly to Italy, religious engagement and devotion (i.e., attending religious services once a month or more) in Brazil has remained above 50% since 1990, when the WVS begin collecting data in both countries. All three nations experienced a dictatorship. But unlike Spain, where the Catholic Church (at least initially) supported authoritarian rule, in both Brazil and Italy the church maintained a high level of autonomy (Philpott 2004). In Brazil there was also popular support for liberation theology, a doctrine of social justice for the poor that inspired many Latin Americans to mobilize against the existing authoritarian regimes (Smith 1991). Scholars have argued that when the transition to democracy happened in the 1980s, many Brazilians saw the Catholic Church as clearly separate from the military dictatorship and did not become disenchanted (Philpott 2004; Serbin 1999).

Today, researchers tend to see the major opposition to more-liberal views and related legislation as coming from religious individuals and organizations, which often support conservative political lobbies (Marsiaj 2006; Vianna and Carrara 2007). Catholic and Protestant Brazilians have at times made their religion-inspired objections to homosexuality clear. For example, in 2015 religious organizations mobilized to boycott both a well-known perfumery that featured same-sex couples in its Valentine's Day advertisements and a prime-time telenovela that broadcast an episode with an elderly lesbian couple kissing (Stycer 2015). The church's continued relevance offers some insight into why Brazilians are less supportive of homosexuality than Spaniards, even though Brazil has also legalized same-sex marriage and has long had a vibrant LGBTQ subculture and heavy media presence.

ECONOMIC DEVELOPMENT AND ATTITUDES IN BRAZIL

Although Brazil, with a GDP of about eight thousand dollars per capita, has only about a quarter of the GDP of Italy and Spain, Brazilians' attitudes are quite liberal. Approximately 34% of Brazilians reported in 2008 that homosexuality is never justified. With this GDP, the regression line (see figures 7 and 8) shows that closer to 65% of residents should report that it is never justified. Based on GDP alone, Brazil seems like an anomaly in expressing more-liberal views. However, it shares a lot of similarities with other Latin American nations (Uruguay, Chile, Argentina, Mexico, Peru, and Guatemala), which are also Catholic and have been ruled by a dictatorship but also have views more liberal than their GDPs alone would suggest (see table 4). As I argue below, the economic development that Brazil has experienced could have contributed to friendlier attitudes by breeding a culture that is more supportive of individualism and self-expression. However, over the last twenty years democracy and the relatively liberal Catholic faith seem to have been more important for driving changes in attitudes.

Since the dictatorship ended in the 1980s Brazil has experienced a roller coaster of economic changes. Between 1980 and 1994 the nation had ambitions to reduce large differentials in standards of living by implementing many government-supported programs. To pay for them the government printed more money, which resulted in so much hyperinflation that goods that cost a certain amount one day would be much more expensive the next. This created obvious problems for the government's and residents' ability to plan for the future and save money. By the mid-1990s inflation was under control, and from 2000 to 2012 Brazil experienced an annual GDP growth rate of 3.8% (World Bank Development Indicators 2014), making it the sixth-largest economy in the world (Inman 2012). However, in whiplash-like fashion, in 2013 growth began to decelerate, in 2014 there was almost no liquid growth, and by 2015 the nation's economy was contracting (Leahy 2015).

Even as the nation has endured an economic roller coaster and income inequality remains very high, Brazilians' standard of living has increased, women have made important strides, and the institutions of family and marriage have undergone major changes. Whereas in 1980 the average Brazilian had 2.6 years of schooling, by 2013 it was 7.2 (United Nations Development Programme 2014). In 1980 30% of Brazilians lived in rural areas, but by 2014 it was just 15%, as residents continued to switch from agriculture and manufacturing to service-sector jobs (World Bank, n.d.). Women have increased their labor-force participation, which went from 45% in 1990 to 59% in 2013 (World Bank, n.d.). Consistent with these other developments, fertility rates have dropped and there has been an increase in the number of cohabiting couples (Esteve, Lesthaeghe, and López-Gay 2012; Forero 2012). Today many Brazilians can travel and have access to television, movies, and the Internet—all of which increase the possibility of exposure to gay and lesbian individuals.

As discussed in previous chapters, all of the economic-related changes that Brazil has experienced since the ending of the military dictatorship (i.e., a decline in fertility rates, higher education, women's advancement, etc.) could contribute to a self-expressive culture where individual uniqueness and individualism are encouraged. However, Brazil has long had a moderate level of economic development, which has provided a baseline level of security. Rather than economics being the major driver of change, the transition to democracy, which made LGBTQ-related organizing activities possible, seems to have contributed to more-liberal views. Additionally, the dominance of the relatively liberal Catholic faith, which has not been as successful at proscribing sex-related behaviors as other religions (i.e., conservative Protestantism and Islam), seems to have contributed to the more limited influence of religious beliefs on Brazilians' attitudes about homosexuality.

CONCLUDING THOUGHTS AND OTHER CATHOLIC NATIONS

This chapter has examined how religion, economic development, and democracy have shaped attitudes within Spain, Italy, and Brazil. Although the majority of residents in these countries identify as Catholic, the importance they give to their religion tends to be lower than that found in Muslim and many (non-European) Protestant nations. The lower levels of religious engagement can also provide insight into why these residents are more supportive. For all three nations, changes brought about with Vatican II may have inadvertently contributed to some religious decline, especially in Spain. The type of relationship that the Catholic Church had with the previous dictatorship provides additional insight into why Spaniards are less religious and even more supportive of homosexuality than Italians and Brazilians. Finally, for many Latin American nations like Brazil, the greater varieties of Catholicism and emphasis on liberation theology may have at times diverted the church's and adherents' attention away from sexual-morality issues like homosexuality.

While the Catholic nations discussed in this chapter are relatively liberal, they are not that different from the many other Catholic-majority countries across the world. Over the last twenty years several of these countries have developed more-supportive attitudes about homosexuality. In table 4, I presented information on changes in attitudes about homosexuality for the twenty-five Catholic-majority countries that are included in the WVS. Several of these nations have survey data for multiple years. For countries that were surveyed at least twice, all but one show an increase in support for homosexuality, with many of them, including Chile, Hungary, Argentina, and Brazil, having had a substantial increase in support of at least 30%. The Philippines is the only Catholic country that does not appear to have increased support. However, attitudes in the Philippines are quite liberal. In the mid-1990s only 29% of people disapproved, and during the last wave of data collection in the early 2010s 33% disapproved—which is a very small increase and may be related to fluctuations in the data.

While residents of almost all Catholic nations for which data are available appear to have developed more-liberal views, the Catholic Church is opposed to same-sex relationships, which is unlikely to change anytime soon. In some countries the church has been very vocal in its condemnation of homosexuality, making the lives of many people who engage in same-sex sexual behaviors quite difficult even as many residents have become increasingly liberal (O'Dwyer and Schwartz 2010). Likewise, in some nations the public discourse regarding homosexuality draws heavily on conservative Catholic frames and claimsmakers (Tereškinas 2002).

Finally, for the latter part of the twentieth century Spain and Italy have maintained a high level of economic development, and Brazil's economy is doing much better than many countries in Africa and Asia (World Bank 2013a). Differences in the level of economic development could, in part, explain why these three countries are more tolerant than their counterparts in other parts of the world. However, because these nations have continued to have relatively high levels of economic development, within-country economic changes do not seem to be substantially shaping within-country increases in support for homosexuality. Conversely, for all three nations the transition to democracy increased LGBTQ organizing opportunities and contributed to a more open media, likely adding to an increase in the public's exposure to gay and lesbian individuals and the challenges they encounter.

Christianity, which includes Protestant and Catholic faiths, is the largest religion in the world, and it is followed by Islam. Both Christianity and Islam are monotheistic faiths that have a single, demanding God. The next section takes a closer look at nations with Confucian cultures, many of which are dominated by Buddhism—which, unlike Islam and Christianity, is a polytheistic faith that has a strong presence in East Asia.

PART THREE

Views on Homosexuality in East Asia

CHAPTER 6

Investigating Public Opinion in Confucian Nations

Buddhism and the Importance of Family Ties in East Asia

The previous three chapters focused on the factors that shape attitudes about homosexuality within nations with substantial proportions of Protestant, Muslim, and Catholic adherents. The vast majority of social science research that has been done on public opinion about same-sex behaviors has focused on nations located in North America, Europe, and Australia, and on differences between nations with monotheistic religious traditions (i.e., Christianity and Islam). See van den Akker, van der Ploeg, and Scheepers 2013; Scheepers, Te Grotenhuis, and Van Der Slik 2002; and Stulhofer and Rimac 2009. Very little research attention has been given to the factors that shape tolerance for homosexuality in Confucian countries[1] (i.e., societies that are influenced by Chinese Confucian culture and history), which constitute nearly a fifth of the global population. These societies are China, Taiwan, Hong Kong, North and South Korea, Japan, Singapore, and Vietnam. Figure 24 shows that the Confucian countries for which there is available data (i.e., Japan, South Korea, China, Taiwan, and Vietnam) are more tolerant of homosexuality than India and some Middle Eastern nations. But they are less tolerant than their neighbors in Europe, Australia, and the Americas, and the proportion of Confucian residents who say homosexuality is never justified (63%) is very similar to that found in African countries (64%).

As shown in the second chapter, economic development is an important predictor of cross-national variation in attitudes about homosexuality. However, many societies with a Confucian heritage, such as Taiwan,

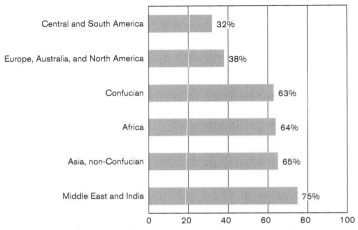

FIGURE 24. Percentage disapproving of homosexuality in Confucian and non-Confucian nations. (Society N = 47)

SOURCE: WVS, wave 5.

NOTE: The societies included in the category for the Middle East and India are India, Turkey, Iran, Jordan. The African societies are South Africa, Ghana, Burkina Faso, Ethiopia, Mali, Rwanda, and Zambia. The Asian non-Confucian societies are Thailand and Indonesia. The Confucian societies are Japan, South Korea, China, Taiwan, and Vietnam. The Central and South American societies are Mexico, Argentina, Brazil, Chile, Uruguay, and Trinidad and Tobago. The European, Australian, and North American societies are France, Great Britain, Netherlands, Spain, the United States, Canada, Australia, Norway, Sweden, Finland, Poland, Switzerland, Slovenia, Bulgaria, Romania, Ukraine, Russia, Moldova, Georgia, Serbia, Cyprus, Andorra, and Germany.

Hong Kong, South Korea, Japan, and Singapore, have well-developed economies. In 2013, for example, Singapore had a higher per capital GDP ($55,128) than the United States ($53,042), and Taiwan, Hong Kong, South Korea, and Japan all have per capita GDPs above $25,000 (World Bank 2013a). The remaining Confucian countries (China and Vietnam) are far from the poorest in the world.[2] Some Confucian nations have only recently held democratic elections, and countries like China are known to have much less transparent and democratic governments. However, some Confucian societies like Taiwan have a higher democracy score (7.82) than some South American nations like Venezuela (5.34), Guatemala (6.07), and Peru (0.61), even though residents from the latter countries express more-liberal views about homosexuality (Economist 2008).

Finally, none of the Confucian countries have conservative Protestantism or Islam as a dominant religion—both of which, as shown in the first chapter, express some of the most disapproving views. The Confucian nations tend to be dominated by Buddhism or systems of ancestral beliefs, all of which include multiple deities. These faiths often generate lower levels of religious belief and devotion (Stark and Finke 2000). Indeed, among the Confucian societies presented in figure 24, only 7% of residents report that religion is very important. These countries are followed by Europe, Australia, and North America (27%), South America (39%), India and the Middle East (69%), Africa (77%), and the other non-Confucian Asian nations (77%), including Indonesia (WVS, Wave 5).

Hence, although they have relatively high levels of economic development and low levels of religious importance, these countries lag behind others in Europe and the Americas in regard to their residents' support of homosexuality. Likewise, several of these societies have been slow to change laws and policies regarding homosexuality-related rights. As of 2015, Singapore still had a colonial-era law that criminalizes sexual acts between men. Although the law has never been enforced, in 2007 the nation's parliament voted to uphold it after two gay men challenged its constitutionality (Economist 2013). Similarly, up until 2001 China still considered homosexuality a mental illness (Wu 2003), and as of 2016 none of the Confucian societies had laws that recognized same-sex unions.

The cross-national quantitative analysis presented in the first two chapters included several Confucian nations. The findings on the influence of economic development and democracy have relevance for understanding attitudes in Confucian societies. For example, amongst the Confucian countries, Vietnam and China have the lowest levels of economic development and also the highest percentage of residents disapproving. Likewise, Japan is considered to have the strongest democracy among these nations, and it has a higher democracy score than the United States (Economist 2008). It also has more-supportive residents. (See figures 17 and 26.) The low levels of religious belief and lack of a monotheistic religious tradition provide less insight into why these nations tend to have lower levels of support for homosexuality. As I explain below, there is reason to think that these nations' Confucian culture may be able to provide additional insight into how people from Confucian nations view homosexuality.

One reason offered for differences in attitudes between Confucian residents and those in other nations are Confucian values, which emphasize hierarchical authority, a strong community orientation, and family and filial piety (K. Cheng 1944; Tu 1988). There is a rich history of work that has tried to separate the values seen as prevalent in many Confucian and Asian societies from those found elsewhere (Hofstede and Bond 1988; Hofstede and McCrae 2004; Monkhouse, Barnes, and Pham 2013). Likewise, there have been some challenges to the idea that there is a unique set of "Asian" or "Confucian" values that set these nations apart from others (Dalton and Ong 2005; S. Y. Kim 2010).

This chapter examines whether there is a unique cultural influence that could be described as Confucian and shapes residents' attitudes about homosexuality. After presenting the quantitative findings, the next chapter uses interviews with several key informants living in Taiwan to better understand the survey results as well as explore additional issues that the public-opinion data could not address. This type of mixed-methods design is referred to as *explanatory sequential* (Creswell et al. 2003) and is especially useful when the quantitative findings would benefit from further explanation and understanding.

CONFUCIAN VALUES

Based on the influence of Confucius, the impression has arisen that countries with Chinese heritage and history have cultural values that are distinctly different from those found in other nations (M. Hill 2000; Zakaria and Yew 1994). The general argument is that Confucian societies are more likely to accept hierarchical authority, be paternalistic, place a heavy emphasis on family, and have a stronger community orientation—all of which increase order and consensus. Conversely, Western nations are seen as rights-based and individualistic. There are some important implications to the idea that there is a unique Confucian culture (Dalton and Ong 2005). For example, the former Singaporean prime minister Lee Kuan Yew suggested that a Confucian cultural tradition could justify nondemocratic governments in East Asia (Zakaria and Yew 1994). Former Korean president Kim Dae Jung (1994) critically responded to these comments, arguing that "Asia should lose no time in firmly establishing democracy and strengthening human rights. The biggest obstacle is not its cultural heritage but the resistance of authoritarian rules and their apologists" (194). A number of academics have also focused on differences between residents of Confucian and non-Confucian societies to better understand variations in economic development, values, and organizational style (Hyun 2001; Y.-M. Kim 1997; Robertson and Hoffman 2000). Despite research on differences in other areas, social scientists who study homosexuality have given minimal attention to dissimilarities between Confucian and non-Confucian cultures.

While there is almost no research investigating differences in attitudes about same-sex relations in Confucian and non-Confucian nations, there is some work that has examined the factors that shape sex-related attitudes and behaviors, including the acceptability of premarital sex, within Confucian societies (Feng et al. 2012; Gao et al. 2012; Monkhouse, Barnes, and Pham 2013). Some of these studies have found a relationship between values that may be described as "Confucian" and disapproval of behaviors like homosexuality and premarital sex (Feng et al. 2012; Gao et al. 2012). For example, Gao et al. (2012) found that respondents with more-traditional perspectives were less likely to engage in sexual activity. Likewise, Feng et al. (2012) found that young people living in Shanghai, Hanoi, and Taipei who had more-traditional views of the family, gender roles, and premarital sex were less likely to find homosexuality acceptable. In their conclusion the authors attribute their findings to Confucian values: "Confucian tenets characterize an individual's way of viewing the world—including homosexuality. Family values, gender role values, and premarital sexual attitudes are elements of traditional Confucian values. . . . Individuals who hold more traditional Confucian values would be likely to have a more negative perception of homosexuality because they see homosexuality as threatening the traditional values they hold dear" (S59).

While some research has attributed residents' sex-related attitudes and behaviors to Confucian values, this work typically does not make any comparisons with non-Confucian samples. For example, Feng et al. (2012) focus on differences *within* Confucian countries. However, some of the values (e.g., traditional gender roles) that they argue are shaping attitudes may also be found in other nations and may not be the result of a unique Confucian cultural influence. A comparison with non-Confucian societies is necessary to determine which cultural values found in Confucian nations are indeed unique and may be shaping differences in public opinion about homosexuality.

MICRO VERSUS MACRO CONFUCIAN INFLUENCES IN SHAPING ATTITUDES

To assess whether there is anything unique about the culture found in Confucian nations, a distinction needs to be made between individual differences and influences emanating from the larger society. As established in the first chapter, a distinction can be made between an individual or micro influence in shaping attitudes and a contextual effect emerging from the larger culture. Individuals may, for example, have religious beliefs that proscribe homosexuality, and through their personal involvement with a religious institution and other religious adherents, their beliefs may come to shape their views about homosexuality. Similarly, some people may place a heavy emphasis on hierarchy, authority, respect for parents, and the importance of keeping the family intact. These are personal values that can shape the extent to which people, regardless of where they live, disapprove of same-sex behaviors.

When a high proportion of people share the same values and regularly interact, their combined energy may produce an influence that Durkheim referred to as "sui generis," meaning a force that exists over and above people's personal values and beliefs (Durkheim 1912, 1951). This macro influence may be understood as the force of culture. Even if some residents do not hold the same values as other people in society, the larger culture may still shape their attitudes and behaviors (Adamczyk and Hayes 2012; Finke and Adamczyk 2008). Empirically, researchers can assess the existence of a cultural influence by examining whether cultural values and beliefs shape individuals' attitudes about homosexuality over and above the influence of their personal values (e.g., importance of hierarchy and respect for family) and beliefs (Adamczyk and Pitt 2009). In the first chapter I explained that a high proportion of residents who feel that religion is important can contribute to a religious culture that influences all residents' attitudes regarding same-sex behaviors. Similarly, a Confucian culture may also exist that shapes individuals' attitudes, even after accounting for personal values like obedience and respect for authority.

How is a Confucian cultural influence assessed? The first step is to look at whether nations that have a Confucian heritage or history of Chinese occupation express cooler feelings toward homosexuality than people living in other parts of the word, after accounting for key country-level characteristics like economic development, which might otherwise shape differences. As shown in figure 24, residents from Confucian nations appear less tolerant of homosexuality than people living in Europe, Australia, and the Americas. This distinction remains, even after accounting for economic development and a host of micro factors such as religious importance, age, gender, and level of education. (See table 5, model 2.)

The nations that would be considered Confucian are located in southern and eastern parts of Asia. Aside from these Confucian societies, there

TABLE 5   HLM ANALYSIS OF INDIVIDUAL- AND SOCIETAL-LEVEL FACTORS FOR EXPLAINING INDIVIDUALS' DISAPPROVAL OF HOMOSEXUALITY (WVS, FIFTH WAVE) *(Society N = 47; Individual N = 66,096[a])*

	Model 1	Model 2	Model 3	Model 4	Model 5[b]
Intercept	7.59 ***	7.54 ***	7.54 ***	7.52 ***	7.53 ***
Individual-level variables[c]					
Individual values:					
Main goal is to make parents proud	0.08 ***	0.08 ***	0.08 ***	0.08 ***	0.08 ***
Obedience mentioned as a good quality	0.23 ***	0.23 ***	0.23 ***	0.23 ***	0.23 ***
Important to behave properly	0.05 ***	0.05 ***	0.05 ***	0.05 ***	0.05 ***
Prostitution not justified	0.51 ***	0.51 ***	0.51 ***	0.51 ***	0.51 ***
Divorce not justified	0.20 ***	0.20 ***	0.20 ***	0.20 ***	0.20 ***
Traditional gender-role values	0.07 ***	0.07 ***	0.07 ***	0.07 ***	0.07 ***
Religious importance	0.08 **	0.08 **	0.08 **	0.08 **	0.08 **
Protestant (reference: Muslim)	-0.14	-0.13	-0.13	-0.13	-0.12
Catholic	-0.30 **	-0.30 **	-0.30 **	-0.30 **	-0.29 **
Orthodox	-0.16	-0.16	-0.16	-0.16	-0.14
Buddhist	-0.18	-0.19	-0.19	-0.18	-0.17
Other religion	-0.02	-0.02	-0.02	-0.02	-0.01
No religion	-0.42 ***	-0.42 ***	-0.42 ***	-0.42 ***	-0.41 ***
Society-level variables					
Confucian society		0.43 *		0.65 ***	0.43 *
GDP		-0.04 ***	-0.04 ***	-0.04 ***	-0.03 ***
Asian society			0.28		
Proportion Buddhist				-0.01 ***	-0.01 ***

(continued)

TABLE 5   *(continued)*

	Model 1	Model 2	Model 3	Model 4	Model 5[b]
Society mean:[d]					
Obedience as a good quality					NS
Important to behave properly					NS
Traditional gender-role values					NS
Prostitution not justified[e]					NS
Important to make parents proud					NS
Divorce not justified[f]					0.31 ***
Individual variance component (σ^2)	3.93 ***	3.93 ***	3.93 ***	3.93 ***	3.93 ***
Society intercept variance component (τ_{00})	1.19 ***	0.34 ***	0.35 ***	0.33 ***	0.21 ***

[a]Multiple imputation techniques were used to replace missing values. The results presented here are very similar to results produced using list-wise deletion.

[b]This model explains 95% of the variation that is occurring between societies and 63% of the total variation (i.e., individual and society) in attitudes about homosexuality. The largest standardized societal-level variable is GDP.

[c]The following individual-level variables are also included in all models: age, gender, financial satisfaction, highest educational level obtained, and marital status.

[d]To preserve degrees of freedom and to see whether there was an independent influence of any of the societal mean variables, each one was entered by itself with only the Confucian variable, proportion of Buddhist residents, and GDP. I also looked at whether the questions about values could be combined. The Cronbach's alpha was not large enough to suggest that these variables contribute to some underlying construct.

[e]In an initial analysis prostitution was significant, but it was no longer significant when included with the societal mean for divorce not being justified. Since attitudes about prostitution were initially significant in a separate analysis, I also included a variable measuring prostitution laws that was taken from www.ProCon.org. However, the correlation (i.e., 0.34, p < .01) between prostitution laws and attitudes about prostitution is relatively low. Prostitution laws did not have any effect on attitudes about homosexuality.

[f]Since the society measures of prostitution and divorce were the only two that were significant when entered alone, I also tried combining the two measures since they could both be viewed as assessing a dimension of sexual morality. The combined variable was significant when entered along with GDP, Confucian country, and proportion of Buddhist residents. However, when this variable was added, the Confucian society variable remained significant, and the inclusion of this variable explained less of the country-level variance than when the single divorce attitudinal variable was included (i.e., 29% vs. 36%). While attitudes about divorce and prostitution explain a lot of the same variation in attitudes about homosexuality, divorce attitudes appear to have a unique influence on feelings about homosexuality. In a separate HLM analysis I assessed the macro influence of the proportion of divorced and married, and the divorced-to-married ratio, using information about the marital status of the respondents in the sample. None of these variables were significant.

are many other Asian countries in this region (e.g., Malaysia, Indonesia, the Philippines, and Thailand) that would not be considered Confucian because they do not have a strong Chinese history or culture. Some of these countries have very different religious, political, and historical backgrounds. For example, Indonesia has the largest Muslim population in the world. Conversely, in the Philippines the majority of residents are Catholic, and English is one of the official languages. Because they are located within the same geographical area of the world, these countries are sometimes grouped together, and writers sometimes refer to the "Asian" culture that these societies or residents from this region of the globe share (see D. K. Chung 1992; B. S. K. Kim, Atkinson, and Yang 1999).

Could the Confucian cultural influence that seems related to cooler feelings about homosexuality really be the result of a larger Asian influence that is shaping the attitudes of people living in this region of the world? If so, then the more similarly disapproving views regarding homosexuality among residents in these nations would not be indicative of a Confucian culture. Rather, there may be something unique to Asia in general. When the Confucian variable is replaced with an indicator for Southeast Asian nations, which includes the five Confucian countries for which there are data (i.e., Japan, South Korea, China, Taiwan, and Vietnam) as well as Thailand and Indonesia, there is no significant effect of simply living in an Asian country. Likewise, as shown in figure 24 above, the Confucian nations appear more tolerant than some of these other Asian nations. Hence, there is a unique influence of living in a country with a Chinese history, even after accounting for factors like economic development.

Finally, Buddhism is prevalent in East and Southeast Asia. In Vietnam, for example, 49% of the population would be classified as Buddhist, 26% in Taiwan, 25% in South Korea, and 15% in China and Hong Kong (Association of Religious Data Archives, n.d.). For nations where less than 50% of people are Buddhist, the remaining residents tend to be Chinese universalists, agnostics, or atheists, or follow indigenous and ancestral beliefs. South Korea is an exception whereby a substantial proportion (i.e., 33%) of this East Asian nation affiliates as Christian (Association of Religious Data Archives, n.d.). Buddhism can be seen as supporting both more-conservative views about homosexuality and more-liberal and flexible interpretations (Bao 2012; Cabezón 1993). In the first chapter I showed that Buddhists tend to fall in the middle of the world's religions in the extent to which their adherents view homosexuality as problematic. Likewise, the first chapter showed that residents living in nations that would be classified as Buddhist do not differ from people living in countries dominated by Hindus, mixed Protestant faiths, Muslims, or the Eastern Orthodox faith in the extent to which they view homosexuality as acceptable. However, people living in nations with a substantial proportion of Buddhists[3] tend to have more-conservative views than residents living in countries where Catholicism and mainline Protestantism are the major faiths. Conversely, they tend to have more liberal attitudes than those of residents from Muslim-majority societies.

Since Buddhists and residents of Buddhist-dominated nations tend to fall in the middle of other major religions in terms of their views about homosexuality, it is unlikely that Buddhism could explain why Confucian nations tend to be less tolerant. When the proportion of Buddhist residents is included in the same analysis that assesses differences between Confucian and non-Confucian nations, countries with and without Chinese histories continue to differ from each other in the extent to which homosexuality is seen as problematic. (See table 5, model 4.) The proportion of Buddhist residents within a nation accounts for a tiny amount of the variation (about 1%[4]) in attitudes about homosexuality across the world. More important, the effect of living in a Confucian nation on attitudes actually becomes stronger, suggesting that the proportion of Buddhist residents may be slightly suppressing the otherwise negative influence that living in a Confucian nation has. If there is a Confucian effect that cannot be reduced to the influence of Buddhism or of living in an East Asian society, what specific Confucian values may be shaping public opinion about homosexuality? In the next section I begin to unravel the values that may be understood as "Confucian" in order to assess which ones are most likely responsible for the cooler attitudes Confucian residents seem to exhibit.

CONFUCIAN CULTURAL INFLUENCES AND ATTITUDES ABOUT HOMOSEXUALITY

Unlike religious affiliations such as Islam and Christianity, people who support Confucian values would not necessarily identify as "Confucian." Rather, Confucianism can be viewed as a set of interconnected values and morals about how to interact and behave. People who abide by and support Confucian values may also claim a religious identity. When discussing Confucian values, researchers and writers often explain how the traits they are defining fit within a larger Confucian value system. For example, Tong (1994) describes Confucian values as entailing "a sense of community and nationhood, a disciplined and hardworking people, strong moral values, and family ties" (417). Shin and Dalton (2006) identify concern for collective well-being and respect of hierarchy as important features of a Confucian value system.

The fifth wave of the WVS, which was collected between 2005 and 2007 and covers forty-seven nations,[5] including five Confucian societies (i.e., Japan, South Korea, China, Taiwan, and Vietnam), asked residents the extent to which they think homosexuality is ever justified. These data also include several survey questions that could be described as assessing different dimensions of Confucianism and can be used to create a set of "Confucian" values.[6] These are obedience and the importance of behaving properly, traditional gender roles, sexual morality, and family connectedness (i.e., making parents proud and keeping family intact). These data make it possible to assess whether Confucian countries have a unique system of values and beliefs that may increase the likelihood that residents find same-sex behaviors problematic. As discussed below, there is reason to think that many values that could be described as "Confucian" would be associated with disapproving views about homosexuality for people across the globe.

Obedience and Respect for Authority

Confucianism emphasizes interdependence between individuals and others, and as a result, the success of an individual can be seen as depending on the harmony and strength of the group (Bond 1991; Hsu 1981). Because of these values, residents of Confucian societies may be seen as having stronger obedience and conforming orientations. As I discussed in the first chapter, researchers (Altemeyer 1998; Haddock and Zanna 1998) have found that people who value obedience and convention may have a stronger attachment to the status quo. As a result, they may be opposed to activities that are new or different from what they already know, including behaviors that may be seen as challenging establishments like the traditional family (Haddock and Zanna 1998). They may also be more likely to react punitively toward people whose behavior is unconventional (Abrams and Della Fave 1976). Indeed, researchers have found that individuals with stronger obedience and conforming orientations are more likely to display prejudicial attitudes related to homosexuality (Detenber et al. 2013; K. Kelley et al.

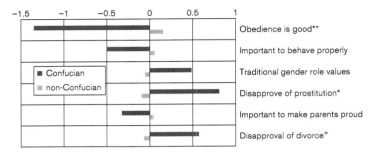

FIGURE 25. Amount of difference between Confucian and non-Confucian nations in standardized values. (Society N = 47)

+ = p < .10; * p <. 05; ** p <.01

SOURCE: WVS, wave 5.

NOTE: Numbers less than zero indicate that the nations are lower than the others on the measure, and numbers above zero indicate that the nations are higher. Zero is the mean value for the full sample. Significant differences between Confucian and non-Confucian countries on each measure are indicated.

1997; Vicario, Liddle, and Luzzo 2005; Whitley and Lee 2000), as well as other types of prejudice (e.g., race, ethnicity) (Billig and Cramer 1990). These ideas suggest that residents of Confucian societies may be more likely to disapprove of homosexuality because the larger culture is particularly likely to value conformity and obedience.

The fifth wave of the WVS includes a question that asks respondents whether obedience is a quality that children should be encouraged to learn. Likewise, the survey asks people to indicate the extent to which the following description of a person is very much like them: "It is important to this person to always behave properly; to avoid doing anything people would say is wrong." Figure 25 presents the standardized measures of these two questions for Confucian and non-Confucian nations. The sample mean for the forty-seven countries in this analysis is zero, so values above zero indicate greater support and those below it indicate less support. Figure 25 shows that on average the five Confucian societies are a lot less likely than other countries in the sample to report that obedience is a good quality for children to have. This difference is highly significant. A separate analysis reveals that among residents of Confucian societies, the Japanese are the least likely to report that obedience is a good quality for children, and Vietnam is the most approving. Nevertheless, the mean measure of obedience for all Confucian nations is below the sample mean, indicating that on average they are less likely to say that obedience is a good quality for children.

For assessing differences in the importance of behaving properly, the Confucian nations have a score that is again below the sample mean. However, the difference is not statistically significant, meaning that people in Confucian countries are not any more or less likely than people living in other parts of the world to value "behaving properly." A separate analysis shows that among the Confucian countries, the Japanese again appear particularly unlikely to report that it is important to behave properly. On every remaining measure for the Confucian countries the Japanese express some of the most progressive and nontraditional views. Japan also has the highest level of economic development among the Confucian societies and has a strong and stable democracy. These factors may, in part, be driving these liberal leanings.

Table 5 shows whether there is a significant cultural influence of behaving properly or valuing obedience in Confucian nations that could explain why these residents tend to have cooler attitudes. Regardless of where they live and after accounting for a host of other characteristics (e.g., gender, age), people who place greater value on behaving properly or valuing obedience are less likely to approve of homosexuality. These findings are consistent with previous work finding a similar relationship between these personal characteristics and feelings about homosexuality (Haddock and Zanna 1998). However, in model 5 of table 5, I show that there is no cultural effect of a nation's residents placing greater importance on obedience and behaving properly that results in cooler attitudes about homosexuality.

Some writers and politicians, including former Singaporean prime minister Lee Kuan Yew, have argued that Confucian and non-Confucian residents differ in the extent to which they are oriented toward the larger group and are willing to behave properly and follow the existing order (Hofstede and Bond 1988; Zakaria and Yew 1994). As shown in figure 25, even when very simple comparisons are made using the WVS, differences in obedience and the importance of behaving properly are not found. Indeed, people in Confucian nations are actually less likely to value obedience. Similarly, some social science research has not found clear differences between residents of Asian and non-Asian (or Western) societies in their likelihood of valuing convention and obedience (Dalton and Ong 2005; S. Y. Kim 2010).

Traditional Gender Roles

Some researchers have argued that Confucian societies tend to empha-size distinct gender roles for men and women (Feng et al. 2012; W.S. Yang and Yen 2011). As a result, even if women participate in the labor force, they are still seen as responsible for the majority of the housework and child care, and men are viewed as leaders and most likely to be the primary breadwinner (Raymo and Ono 2007; Xu and Lai 2004). People who heavily value traditional gender roles may find homosexuality problematic because it does not allow for clearly delineated responsibili-ties for men and women. Research in both Asian and non-Asian societies has found that individuals who value a clear gender division are more likely to disapprove of homosexuality (Feng et al. 2012; Herek 1991; Kerns and Fine 1994; Whitley 2001). Are Confucian societies more likely than others to have a culture that values traditional gender roles, which could explain why their residents tend to have cooler attitudes?

The WVS includes four questions that can be used to assess the extent to which people value traditional gender roles. The first one asks whether respondents agree with the statement "When jobs are scarce, men should have more right to a job than women." The remaining questions ask the extent to which respondents agree with the following statements: (1) "On the whole, men make better political leaders than women do;" (2) "A university education is more important for a boy than for a girl;" (3) "On the whole, men make better business execu-tives than women do." These four questions can be combined into a single measure of traditional gender role values.[7]

I show in Figure 25 that, as a whole, the Confucian nations have a score above zero, indicating more-conservative gender-role attitudes, but this score is not statistically higher than the sample mean. Table 5 looks at whether the fact that a culture values traditional gender roles can explain why residents from Confucian nations have cooler atti-tudes. Consistent with previous research, table 5 shows that, regardless of where in the world they live, people who value conservative gender roles are less supportive of same-sex behaviors. But there is no cultural effect and certainly not one that could explain differences in public opinion between residents of Confucian and non-Confucian nations. Turkey, Malaysia, and Indonesia could all be described as having patri-archal cultures where women's roles may be seen as less valuable than those of men. Many nations may support traditional gender roles; this is not necessarily indicative of a unique cultural influence.

Keeping the Family Together and Respecting Parents

Within the Confucian context, some writers (Zakaria and Yew 1994) have argued that the family is given particular importance. It may be seen as laying the basis for people's expectations for their roles in public life, giving rise to a community of trust modeled on the family (Tu 1988). Over the past few decades, crude divorce rates in many Confucian societies have grown (United Nations Population Division 2009). However, compared with many Western countries, the proportion of divorced people in East Asia is especially low. In the current study, Confucian countries have a lower proportion of divorced people than nations in Europe, Australia, North America, Central and South America, and Africa.[8] In the United States, for example, the number of divorces per one thousand people in 2011 was 2.8 and in Australia it was 2.2 (World Divorce Statistics, n.d.). Conversely, in Japan it was 1.8 and in China it was 1.6.

People who put a heavy emphasis on keeping the family together and on family lineage may be less accepting of same-sex relationships because they may be viewed as a challenging the traditional family structure, since same-sex couples cannot on their own create a child. Indeed, in many Western countries a threat to the family has been one of the key rationales used to justify why same-sex couples should not be granted the legal right to marry or adopt children (Pullella 2012; Sprig, n.d.). Research conducted in Europe shows that one of the best predictors of whether a nation recognizes same-sex marriage is the importance of marriage as an institution, as indicated by a change in marriage rates (Festy 2007). Despite the rising prevalence of divorce in East Asia, keeping the family intact, even when it is very difficult, may be prioritized. Additionally, for many people living in Confucian nations, divorce may be stigmatizing for parents and children.

I show in Figure 25 that Confucian residents are more likely to disapprove of divorce than other people in the sample, and this difference is marginally significant ($p < .10$). A separate analysis shows that while the Japanese are more approving of divorce than respondents in the larger sample, Vietnam and China, which also have much lower GDPs than Japan, are a lot more likely to disapprove. Does this difference in attitudes about divorce remain even after accounting for GDP, which previous research (Trent and South 1989) has shown can affect the likelihood of divorce?

In model 5 of table 5, I show that there is a significant cultural effect of attitudes about divorce. In nations where people are more likely to disapprove of divorce, all residents, regardless of personal views about divorce and marital status, are less likely to support homosexuality. Moreover, societal attitudes about divorce partially explain why nations with Confucian cultures are less tolerant of same-sex behaviors.[9] In a separate analysis I looked at whether the proportion of divorced or married people, or the divorce-to-marriage ratio, was statistically significant for explaining attitudes. None of these other measures had a macro effect. Hence, regardless of one's marital status or how one personally feels about the acceptability of divorce, living in a society where a high proportion of people disapprove of divorce has a macro cultural influence on attitudes about homosexuality, and it can partially explain differences in public opinion between residents of Confucian and non-Confucian countries.

Figure 25 shows that there are not any statistically significant differences in the extent to which residents of Confucian and other countries feel that it is important to make parents proud. Table 5 shows that people who report that a major goal is making their parents proud are more likely to disapprove of homosexuality. However, across nations a culture that supports the importance of making parents proud does not appear to exist, and does not shape differences in attitudes between residents of Confucian and non-Confucian countries.

Conservative Sex-Related Attitudes

Finally, societies can vary substantially in the extent to which they disapprove of various sex-related behaviors. For example, in chapter 4, I showed that Muslim nations in general tend to consistently disapprove of a range of sex-related issues. Some scholars have also argued that people who have been influenced by Asian cultures and subcultures tend to be more conservative in their attitudes regarding a range of sex-related behaviors (Kennedy and Gorzalka 2002; Okazaki 2002), including prostitution (Anderson and Gil 1994). There seems to be some consistency between laws and attitudes regarding prostitution in Confucian countries. Once Mao came to power in 1949 prostitution was eliminated in China, and it is currently illegal (Gronewold 1982). Likewise, prostitution is illegal in all of the Confucian societies, except for Japan, where it has restricted legality, and Singapore, where it is legal.[10] Attitudinal research done in China suggests that residents are very disapproving of prostitution, viewing it as possibly destabilizing the family (Cao and Stack 2010). Likewise, research on other sexual-morality issues, like premarital sex, in Confucian countries has found that the vast majority of young people have fairly conservative views (Y. Cheng et al. 2012) and tend to have first sex later in adulthood or after marriage (Gao et al. 2012). Are residents of Confucian nations less approving of homosexuality because in general they have more-conservative views about sex-related issues like prostitution?

The WVS includes a question about approval of prostitution, which can be used to assess attitudes about this particular issue, as well as sexual morality more generally.[11] It asks the extent to which prostitution is ever justified. On average residents from Confucian nations tend to be more disapproving than others in the sample, and this difference is statistically significant. While the Taiwanese express the most-liberal views, the Chinese have the most-conservative ones. As shown in figure 25, residents of Confucian nations have more conservative views than those of people living in other countries.

Table 5 presents the multivariate analysis. In an initial analysis, the societal measure of prostitution was significant. However, when societal attitudes about divorce were included, attitudes about prostitution no longer had a statistically significant effect. These two variables explain some of the same variation, and both can be seen as related to the family. Prostitution can be a potentially destabilizing force within families (Cao and Stack 2010), and divorce dissolves the marital union. Yet, for understanding why residents from Confucian nations are more likely to disapprove of homosexuality, feelings about divorce appear more important. Moreover, as I discussed above, societal attitudes that disapprove of divorce, rather than divorce rates, are the key factor for explaining why Confucian residents are less tolerant than other people in the sample.

DISCUSSION AND CONCLUSION

Very little research has examined the factors that shape public opinion about homosexuality in Confucian and non-Confucian nations. Individuals living in Confucian countries have attitudes about same-sex behaviors that are less tolerant than those of residents in other nations. "Asian" values are sometimes described as being different from those found in other countries (D. K. Chung 1992; B. S. Kim, Atkinson, and Yang 1999). However, the findings here show that Asian residents in general do not have distinctly different attitudes. At least in regard to homosexuality, the cultural distinction seems to be between Confucian and non-Confucian societies.

To understand better why Confucian nations are different, I examined several Confucian-inspired values, including obedience and behaving properly, making parents proud, and conservative views about gender roles and prostitution. None of these resulted in a societal-level cultural influence on public opinion about homosexuality. In separate analyses, I also considered several other measures (e.g., importance of the family, independence, and respect for authority) from the WVS,[12] as well as macro variables such as those from Hofstede and his colleagues' research on cultural differences[13] (Hofstede and McCrae 2004); legal measures such as prostitution laws; and behavioral indicators like divorce rates. These analyses helped eliminate several alternative explanations for why Confucian residents appear less tolerant. Confucian residents do not differ significantly from people in other countries in their views about obedience, behaving properly, gender role values, or making their parents proud. Moreover, these views do not shape their level of support for same-sex behaviors.

This is not the first study to show that some values that may be described as "Confucian" are not necessarily more prevalent in those societies. Other research has also found that so-called Confucian values can also be found in many non-Confucian countries (Dalton and Ong 2005; Kim 2010). However, because many well-known politicians and writers, and even some social scientists, have maintained that such differences exist (i.e., Hofstede and Bond 1988; Kim 1994; Zakaria and Yew 1994), stereotypes about residents from Confucian societies have been difficult to shake. Strong interest in drawing a distinction between Confucian and non-Confucian cultures may have obscured many of the similarities among residents across the globe.

Among all of the different values examined, culture-wide disapproval of divorce appears to be the one that has an influence on public opinion about homosexuality, even after accounting for marital status and personal feelings about divorce. When enough people in a nation endorse the importance of keeping the family intact, residents may be inclined to follow the sentiments of the larger group, regardless of their personal feelings. Durkheim (1912, 1951) referred to this force as "sui generis," an influence that exists over and above personal feelings and characteristics. The findings presented here show evidence of a sui generis influence of feelings about divorce. Moreover, it is societal disapproval of divorce, rather than the proportion or ratio of divorces within the country, that shapes views about same-sex behaviors.

Societal views about divorce can account for some of the difference between people living in Confucian and non-Confucian societies in their level of disapproval of same-sex behaviors. One of the limitations of survey research is that it often does not provide much in-depth information about why a given factor (e.g., divorce attitudes) has an influence. Previous work (Tu 1988) has indicated that residents of Confucian societies are particularly concerned about keeping the family together, putting forth a positive and united impression of the family, and maintaining the family lineage. Along with the finding about divorce, these ideas suggest that people living in Confucian societies may view homosexuality as deviating from the Confucian family norm, undermining family lineage and the traditional family structure.

As with any research using secondary survey data, analyses are limited to the questions that administrators decide to include in the survey. Many of the WVS questions are not ideal for carefully capturing Confucian values, but in a multination study, these data are some of the best available. The multivariate analysis presented here shows that all of the individual values (e.g., obedience, traditional gender role values) are significantly related to attitudes about homosexuality. Hence, even though some measures are less than ideal, at the individual level they have the theoretically expected effect.[14] While attitudes about divorce explain a portion of the difference in views about homosexuality for people in Confucian and non-Confucian societies, other societal factors that could not be accounted for using questions from the WVS may also have an influence.

Having ruled out several other processes and establishing that views about keeping the family intact and avoiding divorce are related to public opinion about homosexuality, in the next chapter I take Taiwan, which is one of the Confucian countries included in this analysis, as a case study. The quantitative analysis in this chapter has helped to narrow down one of the factors that can, in part, explain why Confucian residents have a cooler feeling toward homosexuality. Through interviews with twenty-six key informants, in the next chapter I further explore the survey findings, focusing on how the Taiwanese's view of marriage, divorce, and the importance of maintaining the family structure are related to disapproval of homosexuality. I also use the qualitative data to assess whether there are key concepts or ideas that were not captured in the WVS analysis that are important for understanding public opinion about homosexuality in Taiwan, which may also have relevance for understanding public opinion in other Confucian societies.

CHAPTER 7

Shaping Attitudes in Taiwan

A Case Study (OK, but Not in My Family)

While across the globe economic development, democracy, and religion are major forces shaping public opinion, the Confucian nations offer some challenges because, among other things, they have relatively low levels of religious belief and Buddhism tends to have an important presence. Compared with adherents of some other religions (e.g., Islam), Buddhists tend to have more-tolerant views. (See figure 3.) In the previous chapter I showed that feelings about keeping the family intact—specifically, disapproval of divorce—partly explain why Confucian residents are not as tolerant as might otherwise be expected. In this chapter I draw on interviews with key informants, as well as public-opinion data and existing research, to provide additional insight into the factors most likely shaping attitudes and the processes through which they have an effect in Taiwan, which also offers some insight into the factors working in other Confucian countries.

Of the available Confucian nations, I selected Taiwan for a case study, in part, because it has a strong research infrastructure that is open to international scholars, and there is some acceptance of homosexuality, which makes asking about the public's attitudes much easier. Among Confucian societies for which data are available, Taiwan is second only to Japan in residents' level of tolerance for homosexuality. As I show in figure 26, in the sixth wave of the World Values Survey only one-quarter of Taiwanese respondents reported that homosexuality was never justified. Conversely, 61% of respondents from mainland China felt this way. Taiwan has never had a Western-style sodomy law,

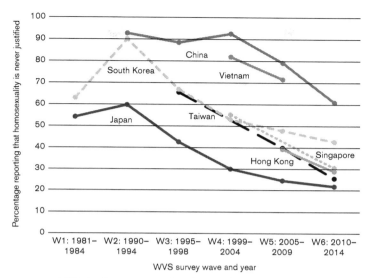

FIGURE 26. Weighted percentages of residents within Confucian societies who report that homosexuality is never justified, over time.

and unlike mainline China and Hong Kong, it has never systematically prosecuted homosexual individuals (Haggerty 2000). As of 2016, none of the Confucian nations allowed for same-sex marriage. However, Taiwan's legislature has been discussing the issue, prompting speculation that it may become the first Asian nation to legalize same-sex marriage (Y.-T. Lin 2013; Wiseman 2004).

In this chapter I use semistructured interviews to further explore underlying processes discovered in the previous chapter's analysis, as well as to identify other key influences that seem to be shaping views. In August and December 2013 and January 2014, I conducted twenty-six systematizing expert interviews[1] (Bogner, Littig, and Menz 2009). To contextualize the interviewees' responses, the next section provides a brief history of homosexuality-related issues in Taiwan. I then provide more information on how the interviewees were selected and move into a discussion of the interview findings.

HISTORY AND CONTEXT

In less than twenty years, attitudes about homosexuality have become dramatically more accepting in Taiwan. Figure 26 shows that the percentage of Taiwanese reporting that homosexuality is never justified fell by over half, from 65% in 1995–98 to 25% in 2010–14. Until 1987 Taiwan was under martial law, which, among other things, meant that residents could not freely assemble, petition, criticize the government, or form new political parties, and newspapers were heavily regulated (Gluck 2007). Perhaps not surprisingly, once martial law was lifted, there was an increase in civic engagement (Chuang 2013).

Following the transition to democracy, the 1990s saw the emergence of several LGBTQ organizations (Damm 2005; E. Lin 1998). At this time the AIDS crisis was also beginning to gain global attention. In the mid-1990s LGBTQ individuals and supporters had their first demonstration against the defamation of gay and lesbian individuals (Damm 2011). As in many other nations, there was also a substantial increase in the number of websites devoted to homosexuality-related issues, as well as novels, magazines, and newspaper columns that addressed relevant issues (S. H. Lim 2008; C.-C. Yang 2000).

Along with other activities, the 2000s brought with it the highly publicized death of an adolescent boy, Yong-Chi Yie, which may have influenced how many Taiwanese see homosexuality. On April 20, 2000, Yong-Chi Yie, who was described as having effeminate gestures, left his classroom to use the bathroom and shortly thereafter was found dead in a pool of his own blood. There were reports that he had been heavily bullied for his looks and mannerisms (Wen-ting 2002), and the media often used the English term *sissy boy* to reference him. Around the same time as his death, legislators were drafting a bill that required the teaching of gender equality within schools (Hsieh 2012). The highly publicized death seemed to prompt Taiwanese officials to include sexual orientation in the bill, ultimately changing its title from "Gender Equality" to "Gender Equity" (Hsieh 2012). Because of this legislation, from the mid-2000s onward all Taiwanese youth should have gotten some classroom exposure to gender-related matters, which could include homosexuality-related issues. As noted below, in their understanding of the factors that shape attitudes, several interviewees mentioned his death and changes to the gender-education bill.

After the millennium the Taiwanese legal movement for gay rights really began to gain momentum. In 2006 the first same-sex marriage bill was proposed (Sheng-en 2013), but with little discussion legislators of the Kuomintang (KMT, also known as the Chinese Nationalist Party), quickly rejected it (Kao 2014). Shortly thereafter, the Employment Service Act, which prohibited discrimination on the basis of a variety of characteristics, including race and religion, was altered to include sexual orientation (Huang 2007).

More recently, in 2013, as I was about to conduct several interviews, the Diverse Family Formation bills were proposed. The bills had three parts: (1) legalizing same-sex marriages; (2) implementing a civil solidarity pact; and (3) legalizing family relationships between individuals without biological or marital ties (Taiwan Alliance to Promote Civil Partnership Rights 2014). The bills were novel in proposing legal protections for people in "non-traditional families." However, a few of my interviewees suggested that some Taiwanese may have been confused by them because the bills also proposed broadening the category of marriage-like relationships to include any group living together and not just same-sex couples. As of 2016, the part that focused on same-sex marriage, which had the greatest chance of support, had not been approved.

Until the 2000s, there did not seem to be much public or vocal resistance to Taiwan's LGBTQ movement. However, in 2009 Christian groups in Taipei organized an anti- homosexuality protest, occurring about a week before that year's gay pride parade. As hundreds marched, they sang Christian hymns and spoke of biblically inspired proscriptions regarding homosexuality (Loa 2009). Only about 5–7% of Taiwanese are Christian (Association of Religious Data Archives, n.d.). However, as I explain in more detail below, Christianity appears to have had a powerful role in shaping the countermovement in Taiwan. While there had been some protests against homosexuality before that, the 2009 event was one of the first to really capture the media's attention.

Consistent with the theoretical framework put forth in the second chapter, the Taiwanese have developed more-liberal views at the same time that their nation's economy has grown and democracy has strengthened.[2] Over the span of four decades, Taiwan's GDP per capita has increased twenty times (DGBAS 2014). In 2011 the nation's GDP per capita was $38,200, ranking it twenty-ninth worldwide and positioning it between Belgium ($38,200) and Denmark ($37,600) (Index Mundi, n.d.). Economic changes have been simultaneously accompanied by increases in education. Whereas in 1975 only 12% of Taiwanese had a secondary education, by 2012 31% had graduated from high school, and there have been substantial increases in the percentage graduating from college (Department of Household Registration 2013). Finally, today Taiwan is seen as having transitioned relatively successfully from authoritarian rule to democracy (Cao, Huang, and Sun 2015).

While residents in many Confucian nations, including Taiwan, have developed more-supportive views about same-sex behaviors, there is still resistance to acceptance. In the next section I draw on the expert interviews to explain how Taiwan's Confucian culture—which, like that in many other Confucian nations, places heavy importance on keeping the family intact—may be related to views about homosexuality. The interviews are also able to provide insight into other important factors shaping public opinion in Taiwan and the processes through which they have an effect.

The twenty-six interviewees included people whose jobs or activities brought them insight into how the Taiwanese public views homosexuality. These would be considered "expert interviews," where the respondent is treated "as a guide who possesses certain valid pieces of knowledge and information" and can enlighten the researcher on "objective" matters (Bogner and Menz 2009, 46). Using a theoretical sampling approach (Coyne 1997), I drew the first set of respondents from a list of potential experts and organizations from the Taipei area.[3] After I completed five initial interviews, I started to focus my recruitment efforts on groups (i.e., religious officials) and views (i.e., unsupportive) that at least initially were not well represented.[4] The interviews lasted between one and three hours, were conducted with most Taipei-based organizations and officials who would have had a stake in the public's views, and represented an array of people from a wide range of backgrounds: academics (N = 7), religious officials and leaders (N = 5), reporters (N = 4), politicians (N = 2), and representatives of NGOs (N = 8). All of the respondents were guaranteed confidentially, which is the typical ethics-related protocol offered by researchers from American universities.

I asked all participants a core set of open interview questions and followed up with questions related to the respondents' specific areas of expertise (e.g., politics, Buddhism, conservative Christianity). The vast majority of interviewees spoke English, but when a translator was requested,[5] one whose native language is Mandarin was made available.[6] After the interviews were transcribed,[7] I coded for major and minor themes and ones that reappeared within the same interview and across a variety of them. I also looked for concepts (e.g., bestiality, incest) that did not receive much attention, and for ideas that I presented (e.g., biology versus socialization) and thought might be important but were mostly dismissed by interviewees. Below I discuss the results of the interviews, beginning first with the theme of reproduction and bloodlines and then moving on to the challenge of homosexuality for children, coming out, and generational differences. The chapter ends with an examination of religion, especially the important role of Christianity in Taiwan for shaping public discourse about homosexuality, as well as concerns about China in shaping views.

REPRODUCTION AND BLOODLINES

My quantitative findings from the previous chapter suggested that keeping the family intact is important for shaping differences in attitudes about homosexuality in Confucian and non-Confucian nations. Not surprisingly, I found that this was a key theme in all of my interviews. In discussing why homosexuality might be a problem,[8] the overwhelming majority of interviewees told me that it was a challenge for the Confucian family. Indeed, there was not a single interview in which family and children were not specifically discussed in the context of why the public might find same-sex behaviors and relationships problematic. As one representative of an NGO explained, "It's deeply rooted in the Chinese culture that everyone is tied closely to each other in one's family. So it's hard for you to just be yourself."

Several interviewees told me that a key reason why homosexuality was viewed as a challenge for the family was that gay and lesbian individuals were seen as unlikely to get married to someone of the opposite sex and carry on the bloodline. As one NGO representative explained, "There's an old traditional theme about 'you having to perpetuate the family, you have to have kids.' . . . You get grandkids for the parents. So the recognition that they are not gonna get grandkids would be upsetting for a lot of parents. . . . I think that's one of the main aspects actually." Several other respondents stated that homosexuality in general is not a big issue for the average Taiwanese, "but it's another thing if my kids are gay."

From a demographic perspective, there are some good reasons why the possibility of not having kids would be such a big concern for potential grandparents and Taiwanese society more generally. Over the last two decades, Taiwan's fertility rate has dropped substantially, going from 1.78 in 1995 to 1.12 in 2005 (G. W. Jones 2007) and then mostly stabilizing (Central Intelligence Agency, n.d., "Country Comparison"). In 2011 it was the lowest in the world, and there has been a lot of media commentary about it being too low (Branigan 2012; Jennings 2011). A reporter I interviewed elaborated on the role of Taiwan's low fertility rates for understanding public opinion, explaining,

Taiwan currently has the lowest birth rate of the world. And their population is aging rapidly. And they basically are not making babies. So you want to come out and support same-sex marriage? One can easily make the case that if we do not have traditional families, where there is a husband and wife, and biologically this is the only unit that can actually produce the offspring; if we allow the same-sex units, those people won't be making babies. That unfortunately runs into problems because the homosexuals that exist today, whether they can legally get married or not, they are still not making babies.

There are several other nations in the region that have very low fertility rates (e.g., Japan, South Korean, Hong Kong, and Singapore).[9] Some research has suggested that the reason their rates are so low is that a smaller proportion of people are getting married or people are delaying marriage until a later age (Jones, Straughan, and Chan 2008). Many Western nations have experienced a similar decrease in the marriage rate. But many residents living in Europe and the Americas have exchanged marriage for living together, and a substantial number have children while cohabiting (Bumpass, Sweet, and Cherlin 1991; G. W. Jones and Ramdas 2004). Although cohabitation is increasing some in Pacific Asian nations like Taiwan (Lesthaeghe 2010), it still has not gained general acceptance (G. W. Jones 2007). As a result, many residents in the region are unlikely to get married, cohabit, or have children (G. W. Jones 2007).

The pressure to get married and have a least one child seemed to highlight current concerns about childbearing, as well as the importance placed on the traditional family, which same-sex relationships may be seen as threatening. As one respondent told me, "The Asian Chinese thinks family is the most important unit in the society: 'You have to build a good family, so we will have a good society, and we will have a good country.' . . . So the society is concerned about gays or lesbians, not because gays or lesbians will harm the society, but because they will harm the family."

Divorce rates have also been increasing in Taiwan (Y. A. Cheng 2015) and other Confucian nations (Dommaraju and Jones 2011). Indeed, current divorce rates are higher in Taiwan (i.e., 2.5 crude divorce rate) than they are in the United Kingdom, Sweden, France, or Germany (Sustainable Demographic Dividend 2011). As shown in the previous chapter, actual divorce rates in Confucian nations do not have a statistically significant effect on attitudes. Rather, people's views about the acceptability of divorce (i.e., what people think people ought to do rather than what is happening) are important for shaping support for homosexuality. Even though fertility rates are low and divorce rates are high, the general public seems to be holding on to a traditional view of the family.

Of course, many same-sex couples can have children through other means, like adoption. So, why is there such concern about having biological children? Part of the problem is that domestic adoption between people who are unrelated by blood is not particularly common in Taiwan (Ju 2012; Yan-chih 2005). As a religious official told me, "People don't tend to want to include another person who's not [biological] family."

For many Taiwanese, adoption may not garner a lot of interest because the culture places heavy importance on bloodlines and ancestor worship. As one interviewee explained, "In Chinese culture you have to have the blood of this family, otherwise you cannot worship, you cannot descend the blood of the family." Before China became Communist, almost every home had an altar where offerings were regularly made to ancestors (Tang 1995). The practice has continued in Taiwan, where the majority of residents engage in an amalgam of beliefs that mix Buddhism, Confucianism, animism, and ancestor worship (Lee and Sun 1995). The standard thinking seems to be that ancestors need descendants to worship them so that they do not have to wander the world as ghosts, with their existence being threatened. Descendants worship them, in part, because ancestors may use their supernatural powers to help. Ancestor worship and Confucianism have played a role in shaping fertility patterns in Asia, with some researchers crediting them with China's high population growth in the twenty-first century (Tang 1995). Several interviewees confirmed that having biological children to pass on the family name and worship ancestors has remained important. As one openly gay middle-age male running for political office explained to me, "I have a duty, I have to marry, I have to have my son, so my son will carry the family name. . . . . It is very important to make sure that there is someone who can carry the family name, especially for males in our society. I have a very important role, to make sure every generation has someone who carries the family name, because we have to worship our ancestors."

Despite the pressure, many Taiwanese are not getting married, and many married couples are having only one child. Additionally, with sex-selective abortions prohibited and renewed government directives against gender screenings of fetuses, many couples may not know the sex of their child before birth. Hence, they cannot be sure that they will have a son to carry on the family name, worship ancestors, and inherit property (Chan 2013). One female reporter challenged some ideas about the importance of bloodlines, explaining to me that "the concept of carrying on the family line is not so important in Taiwan, because in Taiwan now many people don't get married, I mean even though they are heterosexual. They don't get married, and they don't have children." Nevertheless, throughout the majority of interviews most people told me that the concept of bloodlines—making sure that there would be someone to worship ancestors and inherit property, having a traditional family structure and keeping it fully intact—was seen as a challenge to acceptance of same-sex behaviors and relationships.

SOCIALIZATION AND MAKING LIFE DIFFICULT FOR CHILDREN

In addition to providing insight into how concerns about the family in Taiwan may shape views, the interviews were also able to provide insight into other factors shaping attitudes. In the United States and in many other countries there has been a big debate about whether homosexuality is the result of biological forces or socialization (G.B. Lewis 2009). The biological argument posits that same-sex desire is innate and either immutable or not easily changed, and therefore LGBTQ individuals should not be stigmatized for their sexual orientation. The alternative perspective is that same-sex desire is learned in some way, and can be unlearned. Empirical work on these differences has found that people who feel that sexual orientation is innate tend to be more accepting of homosexuality (Herek and Capitanio 1995; Lewis 2009; Schmalz 1993).

Since this has been an important aspect of public discussions about homosexuality in other parts of the world, I asked subjects how they thought the public viewed the origins of sexual orientation. Very few interviewees seemed to think that these distinctions were prevalent in the Taiwanese view of homosexuality. That said, one view that emerged repeatedly and was related to the socialization perspective was that LGBT parents might harm their children. This concern was framed in several different ways. With a moderate degree of frequency this fear centered on gay and lesbian parents somehow making their children gay. This issue tended to emerge in discussions about adoption by same-sex parents, which the same-sex marriage bill mentioned above would also make possible (Engbarth 2013). As one researcher whom I interviewed told me, "They [i.e., Taiwanese] would think [their] kids might be influenced to be gay or lesbian in the future, if they [were] adopted by gay parents."

Interviewees also mentioned the danger of confusing children by having two parents of the same sex, especially in relation to teaching them about appropriate gender roles. As one reporter I interviewed told me, "They have essential imaginations for men and women, like a man has to be like this, and a woman has to be like that. So if a child has both a father and a mother, then he knows from his young age that 'oh a man is like this, and a woman is like this.'" Across all of the interviews, only one respondent suggested that same-sex parents might physically harm their children. In this case, an older male religious official told me that "gay parents sexually abuse their children; the rate is higher than heterosexual families."

While some interviewees noted that same-sex parents might confuse their children or turn them gay, many felt that the major issue with gay and lesbian individuals is that they or their children would have a difficult life. As one researcher interviewee explained, "It's also likely for kids with gay parents to be bullied at school, in the campus. People would say, 'Your parents are gay, lesbian,' something like that, because most people don't really accept LGBT in the society." A young male religious official added that "being gay is a very big disadvantage in society, just by who you are. Imagine that you got beat up all the time at school and being yelled at. So nobody wants that for their kid, right?" In many of these conversations the "sissy boy" incident was mentioned, but interviewees tended to clarify that "it's really an accident. And we are really not so violent." That said, several interviewees told me that the boy had been heavily harassed and bullied, which they seemed to think was a key concern for children who might be different in the same ways he was.

Several of my interviews suggested that people's concerns about gay or lesbian children having a difficult life extended to adults. Some of the interviewees who openly identified as gay or lesbian spoke about spending years trying to convince their parents that they had a good life, were doing fine, and in some cases had found someone they loved. For understanding the public's views, if people think that children who have same-sex parents or exhibit seemingly "gay" characteristics are going to have a very difficult life, they may feel that it is better for LGBTQ individuals to act in more normative (i.e., heterosexual) ways, even if this causes them internal distress.

Concerns about lesbian and gay individuals, especially children, having a difficult time are likely to be found in most other societies, even in places that allow for same-sex marriage and have very high levels of acceptance (Euronews 2013; Takács 2006). Hence this worry is not unique to Taiwan. In fact, there was some irony to the high level of Taiwanese concern about gay and lesbian individuals being teased and harassed when they are in fact not encountering serious threats to their physical safety, especially when compared with the treatment of their counterparts in many other countries (Wiseman 2004). When asked how LGBTQ individuals are treated, all of the respondents, even those who thought the Taiwanese were not supportive of homosexuality, said that harassment almost never included physical threats. As a young male religious leader explained to me, "I have never heard of people going around looking for gay people to beat them up, whereas in the States you have that. Even in Europe you have that." A middle-age white reporter added, "Views in general on homosexuality are—it's quite tolerant. . . . I've not heard stories of people being spat upon, beaten, and insults shouted."

Even though LGBTQ individuals in Taiwan are unlikely to endure physical harm, and they have legal protection against employment discrimination, more-minor forms of harassment, like name-calling and dirty looks, can have a major impact on individuals' well-being (Huebner, Rebchook, and Kegeles 2004; Kuang and Nojima 2005). This seemed to be an important concern in Taiwan, especially given the Taiwanese emphasis on kindness. Throughout the interviews, respondents spoke about the importance of being nice and accepted, and the problem of hurt feelings. Several interviewees also thought that being openly opposed to homosexuality could be viewed as "not being nice." As one female reporter told me, "Taiwanese will be easily moved, and it's about the feelings. If they say it's not good [i.e., homosexuality], they will be criticized, like, 'You are not open-minded, you are not so cool, you need to be nice to these persons, because they are very poor.'"

COMING OUT?

I noted in the first chapter that knowing someone who is gay or lesbian can foster more-supportive attitudes. Not surprisingly, research done in Taiwan and other Confucian nations has also found that contact with openly gay or lesbian individuals can increase tolerance of homosexuality. For example, in a study of nurses in southern Taiwan, Yen et al. (2007) found that those who had friends or relatives with a same-sex orientation were more likely to have positive attitudes toward homosexuality. Similarly, Kan et al. (2009), in their research done in neighboring Hong Kong, found that medical students who had a homosexual friend or coworker were more likely to exhibit supportive views.

Through my interviews I was able to investigate the role that contact with LGBTQ individuals might have in shaping attitudes.

Across the world there is a lot of variation in the extent to which LGBTQ individuals disclose their identity. In societies where homosexuality is illegal, publicly revealing one's identity or same-sex orientation can put one's life in danger. In other nations the idea of coming out has become increasingly popular and is seen as having a number of benefits. Research has suggested that individuals who come out tend to experience less isolation and depression, and greater self-esteem (Bohan 1996; Juster et al. 2013). Additionally, as more LGBTQ individuals come out, the number of people who know, connect with, and empathize with them tends to increase, thereby building momentum for the movement (Bohan 1996; Signorile 2003). However, some scholars and social-movement leaders have not encouraged coming out to the same extent as in many Western nations (Wang, Bih, and Brennan 2009).

What role does coming out have in shaping overall attitudes about homosexuality in Taiwan? Because of the worry it may bring parents, and because of strong traditional-family norms, many LGBTQ individuals in Taiwan and other Chinese cultures may be especially likely to struggle with coming out to their relatives. As one male politician explained, "I think more and more people in Taiwan have a friend who is gay or lesbian, but because the family is still a big problem, he may come out to his friend, not his family. So maybe people have a gay friend, but they don't have a gay cousin. Maybe his cousin is gay, he doesn't know. But he has a gay friend."

As mentioned above, when I was conducting many of the interviews, the same-sex marriage bill had successfully gotten a first reading in parliament. Respondents who were supportive of homosexuality tended to back the bill. At the same time, a number of supportive interviewees noted that even if the bill was successful, most same-sex couples were not going to get married, and hence the bill would not have much effect on LGBTQ marriage rates. As one representative from a LGBTQ-friendly NGO told me, "In Taiwan the main battle of the gay movement might be our own family. If your parents don't really accept you, you don't have a good relationship with your family, you can't even think about getting married, because your parents wouldn't support that." Another NGO representative explained, "More women groups support the bills rather than homosexual NGOs. Because for homosexual people, they have to consider, 'Am I going to reveal my identity to my family?' They might be worried." Unlike in some Western nations, many LGBTQ Taiwanese did not seem to be embracing the idea of "coming out," which, as discussed in the first chapter, can bring about more-positive attitudes in some nations. As I explain below, a lack of interaction with openly gay and lesbian individuals may be an important factor in explaining why there have been fewer attitudinal changes for older Taiwanese than for younger ones.

GENERATIONAL DIFFERENCES

Overall, support for homosexuality in Taiwan has changed rapidly and is clearly moving in a friendlier direction, yet generational differences remain. As discussed in the first chapter, younger people tend to have more-liberal views. This trend can also be found in Taiwan. Data from the sixth wave of the WVS reveal that only 10% of residents thirty-five and under feel that homosexuality is never justified. This number increases to 28% for people thirty-six to fifty-five and goes up to 47% for people older than fifty-five. While these numbers provide insight into the generational divide, most Taiwanese, even older people, could have developed more-supportive views over time. When attitudes change through cohort succession, older cohorts turn over and are replaced by younger ones. Alternatively, with intracohort change both older and younger people may develop more-liberal attitudes during a similar time period. As I explained in the third chapter, in the United States a lot of change in attitudes appears to be the result of all cohorts becoming more liberal. What process is responsible for attitude change in Taiwan?

In Taiwan, cohort succession seems to have had a greater role than intracohort change. Examining changes in attitudes between 1995 and 2012, Y. A. Cheng, Wu, and Adamczyk (2016) used a decomposition analysis to show that while some (i.e., 34%) of the change in the attitudes of the Taiwanese over the last twenty years occurred across cohorts, the majority of the change (i.e., 66%) is the result of younger cohorts replacing older ones. A number of interviewees mentioned this deep generational divide. As one academic interviewee noted, "For the younger generations, it's much easier for them to accept. . . . For the elder people, their traditional values are so deeply rooted in their minds, so maybe we'll just wait for the time, for the generation rotation."

Why hasn't the whole nation been susceptible to more-supportive views? One reason that emerged from the interviews was that there were so few people coming out in earlier years that it would have been difficult for interpersonal contact to have had much of an effect on the older generation's attitudes. One representative of an NGO that provides counseling to LGBTQ individuals told me, "For the people we have been working with, they are about fifty or sixty years old. Most of them have been married and entered heterosexual marriages in their generations. So they didn't really come out in their daily life. Or they don't even have the concept of coming out."

Additionally, as I noted above, all Taiwanese who attended school beginning in the mid-2000s would have had some school-based exposure to gender-related topics, which could have introduced younger people to homosexuality-related issues. While it's not clear how much of an impact that would have had, some interviewees mentioned it as a source of change, with one conservative religious official explaining, "Younger people are basically open to the homosexuals because of the education." Finally, LGBTQ characters and individuals do not appear to have penetrated Taiwan's broadcast media in the same way that they have in other countries, like the United States.[10] However, the Internet offers a wealth of knowledge to people who actively look for information on homosexuality, though older generations may be less inclined to seek it out (Pew Research Center 2009).

RELIGION AND ORGANIZED RESISTANCE

One area of discussion that came up repeatedly in the interviews and was somewhat surprising was the role of Christianity. In previous chapters I have shown that religion can play a powerful role in shaping attitudes about homosexuality. The majority of Taiwanese would be classified as Buddhist (Association of Religious Data Archives, n.d.), and, as mentioned above, many residents mix Buddhism with other systems of belief, including Taoism and ancestor worship. Across the world Buddhists are more accepting of homosexuality than Protestants and Muslims but do not significantly differ from Catholics, Hindus, or Eastern Orthodox Christians (see figure 3). Additionally, people who find their religion very important are more likely to disapprove. In the last three waves of the WVS, respondents were asked about the importance of religion. Approximately 14% of Taiwanese reported that religion is very important, which is quite low. Among the major religions, Buddhists have the smallest percentage (33%) of adherents reporting that religion is very important. In contrast, 48% of Catholics, 60% of Protestants, and 78% of Muslims report that religion is very important.

Consistent with the low levels of religious belief for Buddhists, interviewees rarely mentioned Buddhism as an important factor shaping attitudes about homosexuality. One reporter explained, "Except for some Christians, not all of them in Taiwan, most people's attitude toward homosexuality, I think it's not shaped by religion." That said, Christianity emerged in discussions about individuals and organizations who were opposing homosexuality-friendly policies. One of the biggest rallies against homosexuality occurred in Taipei on November 30, 2013, shortly before I conducted several interviews. This event included tens of thousands of people protesting against the same-sex marriage bill (Loa 2013). The emergence of such a large gathering of people was a surprise for many interviewees, except, of course, for those who helped organize the event, some of whom I interviewed. As one white male representative of a human rights NGO explained about the rally, "Yeah, the pushback is interesting, because until a couple of months ago, most of us are not really thinking about the pushback too much, we knew they were there, but we thought they were insignificant."

Initially, information about the group that helped organize the rally was difficult to obtain. Newspapers reported that a group calling itself "Happiness for Our Next Generation" was a key sponsor (Bohon 2013; Loa 2013). But this group did not have a website, which is odd given that Taiwan has very high Internet usage.[11] When I asked about this, one politician I interviewed explained that they regularly change their name: "They have several names, they always have a new name—'Protect Family Union,' or another union called 'Protect Our Next Generation Union.' And they will have a new name, I think." Initially, there were also some challenges finding people who were a part of the opposition who were willing to be interviewed, and some of the reporters I interviewed mentioned having a similar problem.

As I completed my first set of interviews, a key question emerged: Why would the organizers and larger opposition want to keep their identity hidden? Almost all of the interviewees noted that the organizers were a coalition of religious groups consisting mostly of Christians. Two interviewees from Christian organizations also confirmed their involvement, with one explaining, "[They were] mostly Christian. So, the church they like from all over Taiwan, took buses, and they just came out." Another religious leader added, "This countermovement is basically mobilized by the church. Because they have foreign countries' experiences, they know this is a serious problem." As noted above, Christians are a minority group in Taiwan (Association of Religious Data Archives, n.d.). Several interviewees suggested that if they want to persuade the larger population that homosexuality is problematic, they will have to draw on justifications other than Christianity. As one reporter told me, "Although everybody knows that they are from the church, they just want to pretend that it's not just Christians who stand up against homosexuality but also other people, including the non-Christian people."

If they want to use something other than a biblical framework to protest homosexuality, what ideas should they use? Several interviews explained that, given the importance of family and children in Taiwan, they are linking their agenda to concerns about the family. As one politician explained, "The church emphasizes the family value, and the family value is very important for the traditional society." An NGO representative referred to the "cleverness" of these Christian groups in using a family-values discourse.

> *Interviewee:* In Taiwan we don't have so many Christians. I think it's only five percent; however, I think they are clever. They tried to mix the family values with the religious values together to talk to the public.
>
> *Me:* To persuade the public.
>
> *Interviewee:* Yes. It's not about the God, because in Taiwan we don't talk about God—I mean Christian God—so much. But when you talk about family values, then people will be involved. People will be convinced.

Additionally, because the organizers were concerned that the rally and their larger message might be perceived as mostly Christian, they also included other religious groups—most notably Buddhists, whose involvement was also confirmed by one of their representatives. An NGO interviewee explained to me the different religious groups' commonality: "Basically they support the same goal, and that's the family value. So they unite together very fast. And they don't have to spend too much time on it."

CHRISTIANITY'S POSITION IN TAIWAN

Like gay and lesbian individuals, Christians are also a minority in Taiwan. Hence, it is somewhat ironic that Christians are helping lead the countermovement. Additionally, they are a proselytizing faith, meaning that unlike some religions (e.g., Judaism), they are actively recruiting people to join their religion. There were mixed views on whether focusing on homosexuality was a challenge for them because they are also trying to recruit people to their religion. As one Christian representative explained to me, "Some Christians would say there would be conflicts between the two, so we shouldn't oppose homosexuality. Some fear that we are not able to spread the words of God. . . . [But] just because of a small group of people [who] dislike this, we should not ignore the whole social problem. Because it's getting more and more serious." One Christian pastor noted that by linking it to the family, they could really engage homosexuality as an issue in Taiwan. But other issues, like abortion, which the larger church and many Christians strongly oppose, have not gotten the same level of attention. Not only is abortion legal in Taiwan, but there are reports that the nation has a particularly high rate (Asia Sentinel 2011; Westley 1995). Several people I interviewed suggested that Christian leaders are acutely aware of their minority status within Taiwan and the issues with which they can and cannot make inroads. As a result, they have given less attention to issues like abortion, where views may be more established and difficult to change.

Although Christians are a small minority in Taiwan, residents seem to have a lot of respect for them. Indeed, few respondents said anything disparaging about Christians. However, there was a lot of criticism of LGBTQ individuals, with the harshest comments coming from Christian representatives. One reason why Christians seem to have a good reputation in the country may be related to their history in Taiwan of helping people (Rubinstein 1990). As one NGO representative explained, "Taiwanese people basically accept and respect Christians, no matter [whether] Catholics or Protestants, because the missionaries came here and did many service projects." A reporter added that the Taiwanese "don't view them [i.e., Christians] as really bizarre. They have positive views about Christians." One correlate of these relatively tolerant views is the high level of religious freedom in Taiwan. Since the removal of martial law in the 1980s, Taiwan has increasingly given religions freedom to minority faiths (Hu and Leamaster 2013). For at least the last fifteen years Taiwan has had one of the highest religious-freedom scores in the world (Association of Religious Data Archives, n.d.). As one very tolerant Buddhist representative explained to me, "Some countries have conflicts about their religions. They [i.e., religions] actually share the same ideas—for example, they have similar morality, and they all teach people to be nice and kind to others . . . So in Taiwan, if you are religious, . . . we carry the same missions. We need to protect the security of society, we need to protect the social order, and also we want everyone to have a peaceful mind—um, peaceful spirit."

Finally, many Taiwanese may also have a relatively positive view of Christianity because they may not fully realize the importance that Christians place on monotheism.[12] The religions and practices in which the majority of Taiwanese participate (e.g., Buddhism, ancestor worship, Taoism) allow for worship of more than one deity (i.e., polytheism), which some may see as including the Christian God. Conversely, Christianity allows for only one god (i.e., monotheism), which can create some challenges. As one Christian pastor told me, "We have people whose parents come to church really mad because their kid became Christian. They will yell at us that 'when I die there's nobody to venerate me.' So, we have that happen a few times."

In contrast to Christianity, there was minimal mention of Buddhism or Buddhist leaders. As one reporter explained, "If one day they were to come out, and a large number would say, 'You know what, we are a predominantly Buddhist society. And as religious leaders, we support same-sex marriage,' the impact would be humongous. Because then political leaders could not afford to ignore them." That said, my interviews did not present a clear consensus on the Buddhist view of homosexuality. Some respondents felt that Buddhism sanctions homosexuality, and supported such statements by explaining that they knew of Buddhist masters who had given their blessing at same-sex marriage ceremonies. Conversely, when I asked one Buddhist representative how his religion viewed homosexuality, he explained, "We don't consider homosexual people perverse; it would be more like their values are so chaotic, they don't know what they want; they are unclear about themselves. They just want to enjoy the freedom of sex." He further explained that as they get older, they would realize that sex is not so important and focus on spirituality.

A number of interviewees told me that many Taiwanese have not thought that much about homosexuality. As a representative of an LGBTQ-friendly church explained, "The traditional society does not have [an] opinion about this. So, we just don't have opinion." As a result, the views of many Taiwanese may still be in the process of formation, which opens them up to a lot of influences. While Buddhism in Taiwan has not been vocal about homosexuality, some Christian groups have been, giving them more power to shape the discourse, especially since many Taiwanese seem to have a relatively positive view of Christians.

As illustrated by the November 30, 2013, protest, the Christian organizations that are opposing same-sex marriage seem particularly well organized. As one reporter told me, "They have a lot of resources. For example, they bought the front page that is on the nation's four major newspapers. They organized rallies. They have people hand out flyers." Conversely, some representatives from LGBTQ NGOs felt that amid the pushback they were struggling to gain support. The final section of this chapter discusses how these organizations have tried to draw on a human rights discourse, in part, to distinguish themselves from mainland China, with the hope that this will help garner support for the LGBTQ movement.

HUMAN RIGHTS, CHINA, AND THE POSITION OF THE TAIWANESE IN THE WORLD

Taiwan is a densely populated sovereign state that is located on an island near China. It has a complicated relationship with mainland China, which has the second-largest land mass in the world. When the Communist Party took full control of the mainland in 1949, the ousted leadership fled to Taiwan. Until 1971 Taiwan represented China in the United Nations. But at that point the government of mainland China (i.e., PRC) took the seat. Although Taiwan no longer does this, for many years one of the country's political goals was to retake China. Conversely, the much larger PRC views Taiwan as its twenty-third province and has tried to assert itself as the sole legal representative of China. International recognition of Taiwan has increasingly eroded, in part, because with over a billion people China is so much larger and economically and politically more powerful. Today, only twenty-one members of the United Nations and the Holy See maintain diplomatic relations with Taiwan (Tiezzi 2013). One interviewee described Taiwan as an "international orphan." The issue of China seemed to loom large in the minds of many Taiwanese, and compared with homosexuality, concerns about national identity seemed a lot more important. One reporter told me, "I think these are the issues [i.e., China, identity] that are far more troubling to ordinary Taiwanese than the issues of one's sexuality, or chastity or stuff like that. . . . They are already overwhelmed by questions about who they are. They simply do not have time or energy to fight all these other issues as well."

Taiwan has tried to differentiate itself from China and has been able to do this with its fast-growing economy, high levels of education, democratic government, and, perhaps most important for understanding the public's view of homosexuality, human rights. China's human rights record is dismal (Cook 2013; Human Rights Watch, n.d.). Conversely, Taiwan has a very good human-rights record (U.S. Department of State 2014), which is a source of pride. In recent years the international community has increasingly given attention to the importance of providing protection to LGBTQ individuals (Howard 2014). Some of the interviewees told me that a human rights discourse was useful for framing homosexuality-related issues in Taiwan. As one researcher explained, "We have quite isolated diplomacy in the international community. So we try to emphasize the protection of human rights. And I think the protection of sexual minorities is a very good cause." Other interviewees noted that while they think this frame is important, they do not feel that the public truly understands what human rights mean. As one NGO representative explained, "When most people think of rights, they think, 'As long as it doesn't violate my own rights.' But they won't think further for other people—that if you want to protect your own rights, you have to get involved in the social movement, you have to fight for it."

Some of my interviewees suggested that the human rights frame may have been inspired by Western nations. In some countries, like Uganda, public discussions have included the idea that homosexuality is something that came from Western nations. This topic rarely emerged in my interviews. In only two did anyone offer support for the idea that same-sex behaviors are a Western phenomenon brought by foreigners, or something some Taiwanese acquired while abroad. Conversely, a number of respondents mentioned that movement strategies were taken from other nations. Indeed, some of the NGO representatives were explicit in explaining to me that when they were developing the ideas that became the foundation for the Diverse Family Formation bills, they looked at what other (mostly Western) countries had done. Finally, some interviewees suggested that if homosexuality were not so significant in the Global North, Taiwan would not find it so important. Said one interviewee, "I think today if gay marriage is not accepted in most European countries, like most western European countries, or North European countries and America, it would probably not be debated in Taiwan. Taiwan wouldn't be the first nation to do that. But then in Taiwan right now a lot of people are proposing that 'let's be the first nation in Asia to beat the rest of them,' . . . because Taiwan always takes pride in being the most democratic society, among the Chinese society." While same-sex behaviors have largely not been framed as coming from other countries, there were suggestions that political and social changes in Western nations may be inspiring Taiwan to consider extending rights and liberties to LGBTQ individuals. These ideas are consistent with the research finding that nations that have had problems gaining international recognition tend to be more likely than others to adopt international norms, in part, to improve their global reputations (Ayoub 2015; Towns 2012).

CONCLUSIONS

The previous chapter established that concern about divorce is an important factor in shaping differences in attitudes about homosexuality in Confucian and non-Confucian countries. Using a sequential explanatory research design (Creswell 2004; Creswell et al. 2003), the current chapter drew on twenty-six open-ended interviews to better understand the way that views about the family—as well as other influences, like religion—are shaping public opinion in Taiwan. With Taiwan having relatively low levels of religious belief, we might expect the Taiwanese to express more-supportive views. A strong desire for a traditional family structure, concern about low fertility rates, the fact that few people have come out, and a heavy emphasis on bloodlines and the importance of worshiping ancestors all offer some challenges. Additionally, more recently there has been a nascent, but seemingly strong, countermovement against more-supportive views, which is largely being driven by Christian groups and the Unitarian Church.

In the previous chapter I looked at how the Confucian context may differentially shape attitudes, providing comparative information. This chapter focused only on Taiwan, though some of the findings are likely relevant for understanding attitudes in other Confucian nations. For example, the emphasis on family ties and a traditional family structure is likely to be relevant in other Confucian societies. Indeed, like Taiwan, other Confucian countries such as South Korea and Japan are also experiencing very low rates of fertility and marriage. Conversely, some factors are likely to be different. For example, Taiwan is focused on human rights in a way that China is not, and China loomed large in some discussions about homosexuality. Because of their different histories, China is likely to be less of a concern for Confucian countries like Japan and South Korea.

Conclusion

Other Religions, Outliers, and the Future

Using a wealth of data, the research presented in this book has isolated the key factors shaping cross-national public opinion about homosexuality and has shown how these forces play out within specific sets of countries. The aim has been to provide an understanding of why nations across the world differ so substantially in how they view homosexuality. This is a large undertaking, and it is not possible to consider all nations in a single volume. However, I have tried to cover the most impactful and parsimonious characteristics underlying variation in cross-national public opinion about homosexuality. In this concluding chapter, I highlight the major contributions and discuss religions that have not yet gotten much attention and nations that do not appear to fit the patterns previously outlined. I also consider how homosexuality-related cross-national legislation has proceeded in the past and may develop in the future.

THE POWER OF RELIGIOUS CONTEXTS

Throughout this book I have argued that a society's religious context can have a powerful influence on attitudes about homosexuality, resulting in some nations being stanchly opposed and others offering a much more sympathetic view. Countries with a substantial proportion of Muslims or a mixture of different Protestant groups are less likely to support homosexuality, as are Eastern Orthodox nations. But even more important than the dominant religion is the proportion of residents who feel that their faith is a very important aspect of their lives. The interesting thing about these country-level influences is that they affect the attitudes of all residents within the nation. Hence, even for individuals who are not very religious or fail to adhere to the dominant faith, the national religious context is likely to shape how they view homosexuality. This is powerful.

How do national-level religious forces shape individuals' attitudes? The religious context can work through both the surrounding culture and dominant institutions. For example, on Sunday mornings in various parts of the United States, many people are likely to wake up relatively early, get dressed up, and attend religious services with family, friends, and local community members. On their way to church, some will drive past religious billboards proclaiming "The Coming of the Lord," and they may listen to religious programming. After church there might be a small-group Bible study, Sunday school for children, and a potluck where people will gather with fellow congregants to discuss the week's activities. Alcohol, which some conservative Protestants view as inconsistent with religious precepts (see Barrick 2007), may not be served at these events, and in many areas of the nation alcohol is not sold on Sundays.

In the first chapter I explained that many conservative or strict Protestant faiths have been particularly successful at getting their followers to abide by religious proscriptions. It may seem that strict faiths that make a lot of demands (e.g., no alcohol) of their adherents would ultimately discourage religious belief, weakening support for religious proscriptions. However, the opposite may occur, resulting in the strengthening of religious belief and commitment (Iannaccone 1994; Stark 1996; Stark and Finke 2000). When people feel that they are giving a lot to their faith, they become more invested and develop a stronger connection with their religion, increasing their expectations that they will receive otherworldly rewards (Iannaccone 1994). Additionally, religious organizations tend to offset the church's demands and social restrictions (e.g., alcohol use, interactions with nonreligious people) with their own fun and fulfilling activities (Stark and Finke 2000).

Many of those living in Muslim nations experience a life similarly imbued with religious imagery, ritual, and social activities. Instead of the Sunday ritual, many residents living in Muslim-majority countries will stop what they are doing five times a day to pray with their fellow Muslims (Pew Research Center 2012d). Many women will happily cover their hair, wearing a hijab to show their devotion to Islam (see

Haddad 2007; Hessini 1994). During Ramadan the vast majority of residents may fast during the daylight hours, stopping to eat only after sundown and often with fellow Muslims who have also been fasting all day (Pew Research Center 2012d). Like some conservative Protestants living in America, many Muslims do not drink alcohol, wait to have first sex until marriage, and are regularly involved with religious activities and other adherents.

The religious climate is going to affect feelings about homosexuality by reminding people of religion-inspired proscriptions. In some countries there are going to be legal restrictions against homosexuality, and when religious leaders, politicians, and media elites publicly discuss these issues, religious justifications may enter into the discourse, reinforcing dominant views. Relatedly, even if homosexuality is not being explicitly discussed, people may be regularly reminded through the culture (e.g., women wearing the hijab, religious billboards) and structure (e.g., limits on alcohol sales, religious police) in which they are embedded that they live in a society that values religion and generally tries to abide by religious proscriptions. Secular people living in religious nations may support long-standing religious proscriptions because they are familiar to them and hence seem "natural" and moral. There is also likely to be a lot of social pressure to support religious proscriptions, since most people are either religious or at the very least nominally support religion-inspired norms, values, and beliefs.

OTHER MAJOR RELIGIONS

In the case-study chapters, I have given particular attention to Protestantism, Islam, and Catholicism. The analysis of Confucian nations touched on Buddhism. Less attention has been given to three other major religions: the Eastern Orthodox faith, Hinduism, and Judaism. With about fourteen million adherents across the world, Judaism is the smallest major religion (Pew Research Center 2012b). Although it is a dominant religion of only one country, Israel, Jewish adherents are scattered throughout many nations across the globe. Figure 3 from the first chapter presents the predicted values for all Jews in the mixed modeling analysis. Among the categories presented, including people with no religion, Jews express the most supportive attitudes. However, the figure includes only Jews living outside of Israel, because the survey of that country did not include a measure for religious importance, which was needed for inclusion in this analysis. (See appendix B, table 8, model 1.)

Although the WVS did not ask about religious importance, Israel participated in its fourth wave, which took place in the early 2000s. In a separate analysis I found that the percentage of Israelis who said homosexuality is never acceptable is 38%, which is much lower than it is for the overall fourth-wave sample (i.e., 69%). Similar to figure 3, my analysis of Jews (the majority residing in Israel) during the fourth wave shows that they express views that are more supportive than those of adherents of any of the other major religions. Some of Israel's homosexuality-related policies seem to reflect these liberal leanings. As of 2016, Israel was the only nation on the Asian continent to recognize same-sex marriages performed in other countries, there are protections against employment discrimination, and same-sex couples can adopt children together. That said, LGBTQ individuals do not necessarily have an easy time in Israel, especially in interactions with traditional communities (Puar 2007). There has also been a lot of resistance to more-liberal legislation, and as of 2016 same-sex couples still could not get married in Israel (Hoare 2013).

Within the Jewish community there has long been an emphasis on civil liberties and rights, in part, because Judaism has almost always been the minority faith in countries where adherents reside, and there is a long history of followers being prosecuted (Svonkin 1997). Many adherents also put a heavy emphasis on the religion's cultural elements. A 2016 survey of Israelis found that the share of Jews who say being Jewish is very important to them is 54%, compared with 30% who say religion is very important in their lives (Pew Research Center 2016). Similarly, in the United States, which has almost as many Jews as Israel, 62% say that being Jewish is a matter of ancestry and culture, while just 15% report that it is mainly a matter of religion (Pew Research Center 2013). The continuing significance of a Jewish identity, even if one is not regularly practicing, and the importance of civil liberties, along with adherents often residing in relatively rich and democratic nations (i.e., Israel and the United States), can provide some insight into why many Israelis and Jews more generally tend to express liberal views.

Like Judaism, Hinduism is the dominant religion in just a few nations—India, Nepal, and Mauritius (Pew Research Center 2012b). However, because India is home to such a large population, Hinduism is the third-largest religion in the world,[1] following Christianity and Islam. Homosexuality is criminalized in India, and sodomy can be punished with life imprisonment, though this is rare (George 2014; Qureshi 2014). Figure 3 shows that Hindus have views that are more conservative than those of Jews and do not significantly differ from the other religious groups.

Residents of India, which is the only Hindu country in the WVS, initially appear to have attitudes that are less supportive than those of people living in mainline Protestant and Catholic countries. (See figure 5.) However, these differences disappear after other macro characteristics are considered. Once country religious importance is included, attitudinal differences between Hindus and Catholics decrease substantially. (See appendix B, table 8, model 3.) Once GDP is included there are no longer any significant differences between people living in Hindu and Catholic nations. (See appendix B, table 8, model 4.) Hence, a lot of the differences between residents from India and those from other, seemingly more liberal nations appear related to economic development and overall religious importance rather than the nation's Hindu religious culture.

ORTHODOX CHRISTIANITY

Unlike Judaism and Hinduism, the Eastern Orthodox faith is prominent in a number of different nations. Many of the countries where this faith dominates have Communist histories. Recently, Russia, which houses a substantial number of the worlds' Eastern Orthodox population (Pew-Templeton Global Religious Futures Project 2011), has received a lot of media attention for enacting stricter homosexuality-related policies. Below I provide some additional information on how this faith is likely to influence attitudes and on the factors most likely shaping public opinion about homosexuality in Russia.

About 12% of the world's Christian population is Eastern Orthodox (Pew-Templeton Global Religious Futures Project 2011). The nations with the largest proportion of residents adhering to this religion are Armenia, Greece, Moldova, and Romania. For about one thousand years after Jesus's death, Catholicism and the Eastern Orthodox Church were part of the same religious branch. In 1054 the "Great Schism" occurred, whereby people who identified with the Western church gradually began to adopt the label "Catholic," and those from the Eastern church began referring to themselves as "Orthodox" (Dennis 1990). One reason for the schism relates to disagreements about who had jurisdiction over various geographical regions. Today, there are a number of doctrinal differences between the two branches of Christianity. Perhaps the most well-known is that Roman Catholics give special status to the pope, who is viewed as the interpreter of the Catholic tradition. Within the Orthodox Church there are different ranks, but relative to the Catholic hierarchy there tends to be more equality (R. Allen 2016).

In terms of attitudes about homosexuality, there are some key similarities between Catholicism and the Eastern Orthodox faith. As shown in the first chapter, Eastern Orthodox adherents' level of disapproval is very similar to that of Catholics, with both groups being statistically less likely than Protestants, Muslims, and Hindus to disapprove of homosexuality. (See figure 3.) Like Catholics, Eastern Orthodox adherents also have relatively low levels of religious importance. Across the last three waves of the WVS only 43% of Eastern Orthodox Christians and 48% of Catholics reported that religion is very important. Conversely, 78% of Muslims and 60% of Protestants said that it is very important.

An important distinction between Catholic-majority nations and those where the Eastern Orthodox faith dominates is that many more of the latter are societies that were either a part of or aligned with the Soviet Union. Russia, Romania, Serbia, Ukraine, and Bulgaria all have substantial proportions of Eastern Orthodox adherents (Pew-Templeton Global Religious Futures Project 2011). Under Communist rule, religious organizations and believers were somewhat tolerated, but religious leaders were not permitted to comment publicly on social or political issues, and at times government officials would confiscate religious property and harass believers (Szostkiewicz 1999). The Soviet Union sought to eliminate religion altogether (Froese 2004b). Not surprisingly, religious belief declined substantially under Communism. As the Soviet Union was dissolving in 1990, 34% of Russians reported that they belonged to a religious denomination (Association of Religious Data Archives, n.d.). Today, the governments in many formerly Communist nations support religious freedom. The percentage of Russians who affiliate with a religion has increased so drastically that by 2011, 73% adhered to one.

While many people from former Soviet-bloc nations affiliate with the Eastern Orthodox faith, as noted above, religious belief is not nearly as important for them as it is for Muslims and Protestants. That said, in the first chapter I pointed out that while Eastern Orthodox adherents are not as disapproving as Protestants and Muslims, residents from nations with a high proportion of Eastern Orthodox adherents tend to have particularly unsupportive views. Indeed, people from these countries have attitudes that are as unsupportive as those of people from Muslim and mixed Protestant-majority countries. The similarity in attitudes remains robust even after accounting for overall levels of religious salience, economic development, and democracy.

Because of the discrepancy in the level of disapproval among Eastern Orthodox adherents in general and people living in Eastern Orthodox nations, it seems that country-level factors other than Eastern Orthodox beliefs may be responsible for the more-conservative views of residents from Eastern Orthodox countries. There has, for example, been a movement in some Eastern Orthodox nations to embrace "traditional values," which are being promoted as a key part of national identity (Stan and Turcescu 2000). Likewise, some of these countries seem to have concerns about Western imperialism, especially given their history with western Europe and the United States (Wilkinson 2014) and the fact that western Europe has been leading the global fight for homosexuality-related rights (Kollman 2013). Finally, since the ending of Communism, the Eastern Orthodox Church in nations like Romania has been working to shape attitudes and lifestyles (Turcescu and Stan 2005), even though religious engagement is not particularly high. It seems that for at least some of these countries political struggles, nationalistic concerns, and a respected church may be more important than strong personal Eastern Orthodox religious beliefs for explaining attitudes.

SPOTLIGHT ON RUSSIA

In the mid-2010s Russia was receiving a lot of attention for its views and policies on homosexuality-related issues. Under Communist rule, homosexuality was punishable with prison and hard labor, but in 1993 the nation's anti-homosexual law was repealed. Today, same-sex relations in Russia are legal; however, in 2013 the government approved a law prohibiting "the promotion of nontraditional sexual relationships." The law was being used to, among other things, limit homosexuality-related organizing activities and associated media attention (Keating 2014). In 2014 the nation also began banning adoptions of Russian-born children to foreign same-sex couples and single people from nations that allow same-sex marriage, presumably because these potential parents might be gay (Black and Eshchenko 2014). A number of government officials have made negative comments about homosexuality. For example, in a 2014 televised interview President Vladimir Putin said that Russia needs to "cleanse" itself of homosexuality if it wants to increase its birth rate (Berry 2014). Likewise, the Saint Petersburg lawmaker behind the law prohibiting "the promotion of nontraditional sexual relationships" was quoted as saying that any Russians who want a same-sex marriage should move to the West "where they belong" (Chance 2014).

Recent legislation and negative comments by public officials have put a spotlight on the nation, prompting questions about why Russia and its leaders appear so homophobic (Chance 2014; Khazan 2013; Pappas 2014). Is there anything particularly unique about what is happening in Russia that would suggest that economic development, democracy, and the nation's religious context cannot help explain residents' attitudes? Given the long-lasting effects of Communism and the nation's moderate GDP, Russians' attitudes are about where we would expect them to be. In figure 7 from the second chapter I show the proportion of Russians who disapprove relative to their nation's GDP. With Russia having a 2008 per capita GDP of $11,832, 63% of Russians report that homosexuality is never justified. Based on the regression line, a country with this GDP should have a slightly smaller percentage (i.e., about 59%) of residents disapproving. So Russians are just a little less tolerant of homosexuality than we would expect purely on the basis of economic development. Likewise, table 6 shows that that since the early 1990s Russians have actually become more tolerant. While in the early 1990s 88% reported that homosexuality is never justified, about fifteen years later only 60% felt this way. Though comments about homosexuality may be couched in discourse related to the Eastern Orthodox faith (Pappas 2014), Eastern Orthodox affiliation may not have a major effect on attitudes, in part, because many Russians are only nominally engaged with their religion.

In contrast to the influence of Eastern Orthodox religious beliefs, Russia's Communist past and relatively new democratic status are likely important in shaping contemporary views about homosexuality. During Communism homosexuality was sometimes erroneously conflated with pedophilia and rape, and to some extent the association has remained in the public discourse (Berry 2014; Pappas 2014). If Russia didn't now limit homosexuality-related movement activities and the extent to which the media can discuss related issues, tolerance might be more moderate. There are also some factors that are unique to Russia and its position in the world that may be affecting attitudes and the surrounding discourse. These include ongoing rivalries with the United States and several European nations, as well as unwanted international pressure as homosexuality-related rights enter the global stage (Wilkinson 2014). There is also some research suggesting that beginning in the

TABLE 6   PERCENTAGE OF RESIDENTS IN EASTERN ORTHODOX–MAJORITY
NATIONS WHO REPORT THAT HOMOSEXUALITY IS NEVER JUSTIFIED, OVER TIME

	W2	W3	W4	W5	W6	Change: Less (−) vs. more (+) disapproving
	1990–1994	1995–1998	1999–2004	2005–2009	2010–2014	
Armenia		71			96	+25
Belarus	80	68			58	−23
Bulgaria		51		33		−17
Cyprus				37	38	0
Estonia		66			46	−19
Ethiopia				76		
Georgia		82		91	87	+5
Macedonia		81	76			−5
Moldova		74	65	62		−12
Montenegro		68	86			+18
Romania		67		73	71	+4
Russia	88	80		66	60	−28
Serbia		65	75			+10
Ukraine		71		57	53	−19
Overall change for nations with at least two time points						−5

SOURCE: Weighted estimates from the WVS.

NOTE: Change in attitudes is indicated for the two waves that are furthest apart. During W1 no data were collected on Eastern Orthodox–majority countries.

mid-2000s Russian officials began promoting "traditional values" as part of a national identity (Erofeeva 2013; Wilkinson 2014). That said, given the country's level of economic development, strength of democracy, dominant religion, and overall level of religious belief, Russians' attitudes do not seem radically different from what we would expect.

DEMOCRACY AND ECONOMIC DEVELOPMENT

My primary thesis is that tolerance for homosexuality tends to be reduced by overall levels of religious importance, affected by the dominant religion, and boosted by economic development and democracy. How do economic development and democracy shape residents' attitudes? In the second chapter I drew on the work of several cultural social scientists (Hofstede 2001; Inglehart and Baker 2000; Schwartz 2006) to explain that as economic development increases, a nation's cultural values shift in predictable ways. In less economically developed countries cultural orientations are more likely to focus on survival, group membership, and solidarity. In nations with particularly low levels of economic development and a lot of political instability, much of the population is likely to be oriented towards survival-related concerns. By working with people they trust and pooling their resources, to the best of their abilities residents can try to increase feelings of security and protection. In environments where basic survival and safety are precarious, residents tend to be less concerned about civil rights or self-actualization (Inglehart and Baker 2000).

A number of theorists have argued that as nations become more economically developed, cultural orientations begin to shift and people become more secure, increasingly functioning on their own and away from the watchful eye of the larger group (Hofstede and McCrae 2004; Inglehart and Oyserman 2004; Schwartz 2006). As resources become available to improve the lives of everyone, some residents will advocate for laws that require all residents to partake of collective goods, like universal health care. This interest in improving the lives of all people seems to apply not only to physical and educational needs, but also to providing other residents with civil liberties and rights (Inglehart and Oyserman 2004; Welzel, Inglehart, and Kligemann 2003).

Many of the case-study nations fit the hypothesized trends related to attitudes about homosexuality, level of economic development, democracy, and the nation's religious context. For example, Uganda, which only recently instituted major democratic reforms, has particularly unfriendly views of homosexuality, a low level of economic development, and a high proportion of residents who take their religion very seriously. While many societies follow the trend, there are outliers. Several of the Persian Gulf nations have high GDPs. Qatar, for example, has one of the highest levels of economic development in the world.[2] However, like many of its Arab neighbors, Qatar has made homosexuality illegal, and regional government officials have been vocal about their disapproval. For example, in 2015 Kuwait's director of health, Yousouf Mindkar, was quoted as saying that health centers in Gulf Cooperation Council (GCC) countries, which include Qatar as well as Saudi Arabia, Kuwait, Bahrain, Oman, and the United Arab Emirates, will be taking "stricter measures" to help "detect gays who will be then barred from entering Kuwait or any of the GCC member states" (Thornhill 2013; Toumi 2013). There are also reports of people being punished in Qatar and other Gulf nations for same-sex behaviors (Global Gayz 2009; Resource Information Center 2001).

How can this seemingly inconsistent relationship between high levels of economic development and the enforcement of laws criminalizing homosexuality be explained? Several nations located in the Middle East are strongly opposed to homosexuality, in part, because Islam is the dominant religious faith, religious belief is high, and governments are nondemocratic. Sandi Arabia, for example, is the birthplace of Islam and home to the faith's two holiest shrines, in Mecca and Medina. Along with many of its neighbors, it is one of a minority of the world's countries where Sharia has a high degree of influence over the legal system (Sacirbey 2015).[3] In many of the Gulf nations the legal code prohibits a wide range of behaviors, including smoking, drinking, attending discos, and socializing with unrelated people of the opposite sex. Many behaviors that are legal in other parts of the world (e.g., extramarital and premarital sex, alcohol consumption) are illegal here, so homosexuality is not necessarily being singled out for special attention.

As the strict laws suggest, many of these nations are not democracies. Rather, most are monarchies ruled by a king who is often commander in chief of the military. Since 1999, when Freedom House began publishing democracy and freedom-of-the-press scores, several of the Gulf nations (e.g., Oman, Qatar, United Arab Emirates, and Saudi Arabia) have been consistently awarded some of the worst possible scores for freedom, civil liberties, and political rights, positioning them as some of the most undemocratic nations in the world (Freedom House 2015). This being the case, many people living in this region of the globe are unlikely to know much about homosexuality, and there are limits to any visible and active LGBTQ movement activity.[4] Any increase in support for homosexuality that higher levels of economic development might bring is offset by the lack of democracy, restrictions on freedom, and a government-regulated press, as well as by a very close relationship between Islam and the state. For other nations that are outliers in one dimension (e.g., economic development), another factor (e.g., religion or democracy) is likely to help swing them back into place. The combination of these three forces can explain a lot of the differences in cross-national support for homosexuality.

RELIGION AND ECONOMIC DEVELOPMENT

Many European nations have high levels of economic development, stable democracies, and low levels of religious belief.[5] Additionally, several of these societies, especially those located in northern and western Europe, have some of the most liberal homosexuality-related legislation in the world. For example, between 2009 and 2015 all of Europe's Nordic countries (i.e., Sweden, Finland, Norway, Denmark, and Iceland) legalized same-sex marriage (Pew Research Center 2015b). Likewise, they all have 2008 GDPs that were over $55,000 (World Bank, n.d.). According to data from the last three waves of the WVS, the percentage who say religion is very important is low, with 8% in Sweden, 10% in Finland, and 17% in Norway. For this same time period 49% of people across the world report that religion is very important. These differences might suggest that overall levels of religious belief are spuriously related to attitudes, whereby economic development influences both factors. There has been a lot of debate about what characteristics (e.g., economic development, a lack of religious diversity) weaken religious belief.

Secularization theorists have long predicted that as nations become more economically developed, religious belief will decline (Inglehart 1997; Voyé and Dobbelaere 1994; B. Wilson 1968). Part of the reasoning is that economic development and modernity may erode religion's plausibility, intensity, and authority. Likewise, the expanding social and cultural pluralism that emerges in modern societies could introduce people to a greater variety of religions, which undercuts each other's religious authority. The well-known sociologist of religion Peter L. Berger explained that as the number of religious worldviews available increases, the less plausible each will seem and the less likely people will be to adhere to a given faith (Berger 2011). Berger (1997) later changed his position, but the basic idea has remained: as nations become more economically developed, they become more secular.

Beginning in the early 1990s, rational-choice and market-based theories emerged as a direct challenge to the secularization thesis (Finke and Stark 2005; Iannaccone 1991; Iannaccone, Finke, and Stark 1997). These approaches argue that governments differ in the extent to which they regulate religion. Some countries subsidize specific faiths (Messner 2015). In many European nations, for example, the national government helps pay religious leaders' salaries and contributes to the maintenance of church buildings. As a result, some religions and denominations do not have to work as hard as others for survival, which can limit religious innovation and the quest for converts (Stark and Finke 2000). Countries can also make it difficult for new religions (e.g., Latter-Day Saints) or different (and more appealing) versions of existing faiths (e.g., Southern Baptist, nondenominational Protestant) to emerge. Many nations with Communist pasts, for example, have histories of suppressing certain religious groups (Froese 2004a). From a religious-economies perspective, when a nation has a greater number of religions or denominations that are diverse and interesting, more residents are likely to find a faith that matches their religious preferences, bolstering belief (Stark and Finke 2000). Conversely, when religious diversity is limited, people tend to be less interested in religion since they will be less likely to find one that is appealing to them.

If we look only at the relationship between a nation's GDP and mean levels of religious importance, there is a significant and inverse correlation whereby nations with higher levels of economic development tend to have lower overall levels of religious belief. However, there are a number of outliers. While religious belief in Europe is generally low, it is much higher in the United States. Likewise, in many societies outside of Europe and North America, such as Turkey, Malaysia, Mexico, and Venezuela, religious belief has remained relatively high even as these nations have become richer. Studies that focus on religious diversity instead of economic development have also found support for the religious-economies model (Iannaccone 1991; Stark and Finke 2000), though it has also been criticized (Bruce 1993, 1999; Sharot 2002). Given that the governments of several European nations have implemented policies limiting religious diversity, factors other than economic development may be at least partially responsible for lower levels of religious belief in these countries.

For understanding attitudes about homosexuality, the data and analysis presented in appendix B show that the religious context of a nation, economic development, and the political system have independent influences on attitudes. Moreover, these country-level forces have effects even after accounting for residents' personal characteristics, like age, religious importance, and income. When looking across dozens of nations, there should not be any doubt that personal religious beliefs and the religious context of a country (i.e., dominant religion and mean level of religious importance), as well as democracy and economic development, shape how residents in different nations feel about homosexuality.

COMBINING ECONOMIC DEVELOPMENT AND PERSONAL RELIGIOUS BELIEFS

At the end of the second chapter I explained that the effect of personal religious beliefs on attitudes about homosexuality is greater in richer nations than it is in poorer ones. This relationship offers some insight into why highly religious people may disapprove of homosexuality even as many of their fellow residents develop more-accepting views. Research on the anti-ascetic hypothesis argues that religion has its greatest effect on attitudes and behaviors when secular guidelines are unclear (Burkett and White 1974; Hadaway, Elifson, and Petersen 1984; Tittle and Welch 1983). Hence, personal religious beliefs are less likely to influence attitudes and behaviors related to rape and murder. But they tend to have a greater effect on substance use, minor crime, and premarital sex (Adamczyk 2012; Adamczyk and Felson 2006; Adamczyk and Palmer 2008). While most residents in poorer nations may disapprove of homosexuality, personal religious beliefs tend to have less of an influence on the attitudes of more-religious people because religion will be one of many sources of authority (i.e., government, parents, friends, etc.) disapproving of homosexuality.

Because of the security that comes with higher levels of economic development, richer nations have more normative ambiguity about the acceptability of homosexuality. When there is less agreement in the larger culture, personal religious beliefs appear more likely to guide attitudes and behaviors (Adamczyk 2013; Adamczyk and Pitt 2009; Gaskins, Golder, and Siegel 2013). Because public discussions about homosexuality in richer nations tend to incorporate a range of views, religious residents are more likely to turn to religious institutions, religious officials, and trusted religious friends to make judgments about the acceptability of behaviors like homosexuality, as well as other issues like abortion and divorce (Adamczyk 2013). In poorer nations both religious and secular people are more likely to agree that homosexuality is wrong. This rift provides insight into why there remains so much mobilization around homosexuality even in countries where there is very supportive homosexuality-related legislation.

PACE OF CHANGE

Religion, economic development, and democracy are powerful for shaping public opinion. However, within individual countries the process through which they have an effect is by no means simple, and change does not move at a similar pace across nations. I noted in previous chapters that changes in attitudes can occur through cohort succession, where older cohorts turn over and are replaced by younger individuals, or through intracohort change, where both older and younger residents develop more-liberal views.

In the United States many of the recent increases in support for homosexuality have resulted from intracohort changes whereby people of all ages became more supportive of homosexuality over a relatively short time period (Brewer 2003; Loftus 2001; Sherkat et al. 2011; Treas 2002). In this country, economic development brought with it a lot of free time and high incomes that could purchase various forms of media. Additionally, strong democratic institutions provided space for discussions about and interest in LGBTQ individuals. Along with other forces (e.g., active LGBTQ organizations, sympathetic media elites, a movement that promoted "coming out"), democracy and high demand for a wide range of entertainment options resulted in an increase in likable gay and lesbian media characters (e.g., Will from *Will & Grace*). A number of studies have suggested that this programming may have contributed to friendlier attitudes by introducing residents across this large nation to a diverse range of lesbian and gay individuals and subcultures (Garretson 2009; Schiappa, Gregg, and Hewes 2006).

In contrast to the United States, the primary engine of change in Taiwan appears to be cohort succession. Economic development contributed to an increase in the college population and some shifts in cultural values. A number of studies suggest that the strengthening of democracy, changing values, and a more educated populace resulted in younger people becoming more tolerant about a range of issues and increasingly concerned about civil liberties and rights (Wright 1999). Though the attitudes of older generations have adjusted some, there is evidence that changing views about homosexuality in Taiwan are being driven by younger people (Y.A. Cheng, Wu, and Adamczyk 2016). Younger Taiwanese cohorts seem to be gradually replacing older ones, resulting in slowly shifting views.

Across many nations the forces of economic development, democracy, and the religious environment shape attitudes, but the speed of change appears to be influenced by differences in a wide range of other characteristics, like social-movement activity, global status, a culture of "coming out," media influences, and so forth. Unfortunately, quantitative measures for these other forces are not readily available. But even if they can be found or constructed, some of these factors may be important for shaping attitudes only in certain nations, limiting the likelihood that they will appear statistically significant in a large cross-national analysis.

Another challenge with using quantitative data to assess cross-national differences in attitudes about homosexuality is the lack of information about what homosexuality means to survey respondents, how they feel about different LGBTQ individuals, and how intersecting characteristics shape attitudes. Throughout this book these challenges have been there. For example, in South Africa there is a lot of research finding that characteristics like race, gender, and class have a major role in shaping LGBTQ individuals' feelings and treatment by others (Moolman 2013; Smuts 2011; Swarr and Nagar 2004). This work suggests that when considering whether homosexuality is acceptable, the public may draw distinctions based on factors like gender and race. In Turkey some work has found that certain types of behaviors, like being the receiver of oral sex, would not necessarily be categorized as a homosexual act (Oksal 2008; Tapinc 1992). Likewise, many Indonesians may regularly see and interact with *waria,* who in a different country might be described as transgender (Boellstorff 2006; Laurent 2005). However, it's unclear whether Indonesians think of *waria* as "homosexual."

Because all of the available cross-national surveys and many of those conducted within individual countries tend to ask very general questions about homosexuality, it is difficult to know how people differentially see LGBTQ individuals and what they consider homosexual behavior. In cultural studies there is a rich body of work that has examined these differences (El-Tayeb 2011; E.-B. Lim 2013; Reddy 2011). Because survey research has minimally engaged these ideas (Worthen 2013), researchers like me, who want more-detailed cross-national quantitative information on how the public sees homosexuality, do not yet have access to it.

INCREASING SUPPORT FOR HOMOSEXUALITY UNTIL EVERYONE IS TOLERANT? NOT NECESSARILY

Across the world many nations seem to be becoming more democratic and economically developed. Does this mean that all countries will become more supportive of homosexuality, ultimately legalizing same-sex marriage everywhere? Figure 27 provides some insight. Attitudes about homosexuality and laws are moderately correlated, and since it is more difficult to gather data on public opinion than laws, which almost every country in the world has, figure 27 uses same-sex legislation to show how things have changed over the last roughly twenty years.

Between 1996 and 2013 the number of countries with a provision for civil unions or marriage went from 6 to 43, a 617% increase. Over the same period, the number of nations with a tacit ban on homosexuality, where marriage is restricted to heterosexuals but there is no constitutional or legal ban of same-sex marriage, fell from 203 to 150, a 20% drop. These more-liberal changes are consistent with the idea that across the world, nations are becoming more tolerant, in part, because

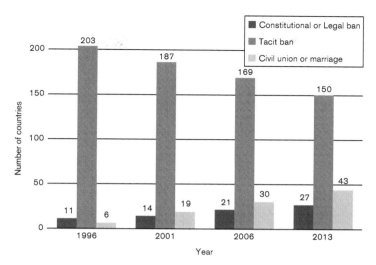

FIGURE 27. Changes in the number of nations (N = 220) with legal or tacit bans on civil unions or marriage between 1996 and 2013.

SOURCE: ILGA 2013 (in Itaborahy and Zhu 2014).

NOTE: "Constitutional or legal ban" means that this applies to same-sex marriage. "Tacit ban" indicates that marriage is restricted to heterosexuals but there is no constitutional or legal ban of same-sex marriage. "Civil union or marriage" indicates legal provision for same-sex marriage or civil unions within part or all of the country.

of advances in democracy and economic development (Asal, Sommer, and Harwood 2013; Hooghe and Meeusen 2013). However, in chapters 3 and 4, I showed that Uganda and Malaysia have not been supportive of more-liberal legislation. The darkest bars in figure 27 capture changes in the number of countries that have implemented a constitutional or legal ban on same-sex relationships. Between 1996 and 2013 the number of nations that have enacted harsher homosexuality-related legislation (e.g., moving from a tacit ban to a constitutional or legal ban) went from 11 to 27, which is a 145% increase. Hence, while there is a trend toward more-liberal legislation, there are a number of countries moving in a more conservative direction.

Between 2006 and 2013 six countries enacted a constitutional or legal ban on same-sex marriage. Four of these nations (i.e., Democratic Republic of the Congo, Kenya, Zambia, and Zimbabwe) are located in Africa. One society is located in Europe (i.e., Montenegro) and another in the Caribbean (i.e., Dominican Republic). During the early part of the twenty-first century some of these countries faced severe hardship.

For example, the Democratic Republic of the Congo and Zimbabwe were both involved in the Second Congo War, which officially ended in July 2003, though hostilities (e.g., the Lord's Resistance Army insurgency) have continued. Additionally, these nations could be categorized as having a lot less political and media power than many European countries like Austria, Ireland, and Switzerland. Between 2006 and 2013 these three European nations enacted friendlier policies, moving from a tacit ban to allowing same-sex marriages or unions.

With the content analysis of newspaper articles presented in chapter 3, I showed that Ugandan government officials, religious leaders, and media elites sometimes framed discussions about homosexuality as something introduced by Western countries. (See figure 14.) At the same time American evangelists like Scott Lively have been accused of galvanizing support for homophobia in Uganda (Kaoma 2009; Oliver 2012). While there may be some legislative backlash that is related to the pressure some countries feel from other, more powerful and richer nations, Grossman (2013) notes that some government officials may also use homosexuality-related issues to distract from more-pressing domestic concerns such as water, health, sanitation, and housing.

Just as some politicians, media, and religious leaders may use homosexuality-related issues to gain attention within their countries, some societies may be inclined to support friendlier policies because they want to gain positive press and affirmation from more-powerful countries and establish themselves as major international players. Focusing on the European Union (EU), Phillip M. Ayoub (2015) found that between 1970 and 2009 the countries that adopted friendlier homosexuality-related legislation most readily were more dependent on international resources. These countries were also more inclined to see policy adoption as a means of improving their reputations and gaining legitimacy (see also Ayoub 2016). While Ayoub's study focused only on the European Union, the findings offer insight into what may be driving countries in other parts of the world to enact more-supportive legislation. Taiwan, for example, is a relatively small nation that China claims as its twenty-third province. Since 1971 Taiwan has gradually been losing support in the United Nations (Tiezzi 2013). Some of the Taiwanese I interviewed explained that becoming the first Asian nation to permit same-sex marriage would be an excellent way to gain more international recognition and distinguish itself from China, which has a much poorer human rights record.

This book has illustrated the powerful roles of religion, economic development, and democracy in shaping cross-national attitudes about homosexuality. However, the march toward greater liberalization is less straightforward than these three factors alone would suggest. Nations are embedded in a global context, and the interrelationship between countries is dynamic (Kollman 2013). As homosexuality-related issues enter the global arena, some nations are pushing other countries to adopt more-liberal legislation, which is creating some backlash. Many nations located in the Global North were among the first to undergo processes of democracy and economic development. Because they were the leaders, they were not subject to the same pressure from more-powerful countries and international organizations that others are currently experiencing. Even as many nations have become more democratic and economically developed, religion continues to be relevant. Responses to international forces, as well as the extent to which religion remains important to many of the world's people, are likely to complicate how attitudes and laws will develop in the future.

Countries Included in the WVS HLM Analysis, by Homosexuality Laws as of 2015 and the Nation's Dominant Religion

TABLE 7 COUNTRIES INCLUDED IN THE WVS HLM ANALYSIS, BY FOUR TYPES OF HOMOSEXUALITY LAWS AS OF 2015 AND THE NATION'S DOMINANT RELIGION *(N = 87)*

Dominant religion and legal status of homosexuality

Catholic countries

Homosexuality legal, but not union

Australia[a]	Philippines
Guatemala	Poland
Italy	Rwanda
Mexico	Venezuela
Peru	

Marriage or marriage-like union allowed

Andorra	Germany[b]
Argentina	Hungary
Brazil	Netherlands[c]
Canada	Puerto Rico
Chile	Slovenia
Colombia	Spain
Ecuador	Switzerland
France	Uruguay

Mixed Protestant/Christian countries

Homosexuality illegal, but not punishable by death

Ghana	Uganda[e]
Tanzania[d]	Zambia
Trinidad and Tobago	Zimbabwe

(continued)

TABLE 7 *(continued)*

Mixed Protestant/Christian countries

Marriage or marriage-like union allowed

South Africa	United States

Mainline Protestant[f] countries

Marriage or marriage-like union allowed

Finland	Norway
Great Britain	Sweden
New Zealand[g]	

Orthodox Christian countries

Homosexuality illegal, but not punishable by death
Ethiopia[h]

Homosexuality legal, but not union

Armenia	Moldova
Belarus	Montenegro
Bulgaria	Romania
Cyprus	Russia
Georgia	Serbia
Macedonia	Ukraine

Marriage or marriage-like union allowed
Estonia

Muslim countries

Death for homosexual acts

Iran	Saudi Arabia
Nigeria[i]	Yemen

Homosexuality illegal, but not punishable by death

Algeria	Malaysia
Bangladesh	Morocco
Egypt	Pakistan
Indonesia	Palestine
Iraq	Tunisia
Lebanon	Uzbekistan
Libya	

Homosexuality legal, but not union

Albania	Kazakhstan
Azerbaijan	Kyrgyzstan
Bosnia	Mali
Burkina Faso	Turkey
Jordan	

Buddhist countries	

Homosexuality illegal, but not punishable by death
Singapore

Homosexuality legal, but not union

China	Taiwan
Hong Kong	Thailand
Japan	Vietnam
South Korea	

Hindu countries	

Homosexuality illegal, but not punishable by death
India

SOURCES: ILGA 2015 (in Carroll and Itaborahy 2015); ARDA's *Cross-National Socio-Economic and Religion Data* (2011); ARDA's national profiles; CIA World Factbook 2013; Pew Research Center 2011.

[a]According to ARDA's national profile for Australia, 72.8% of the population is classified as Christian, with the largest proportion being Catholic. There are also a substantial proportion of other types of Christianity, including Anglicans, which constitute 19% of the population.

[b]According to ARDA's national profile for Germany, 70.1% of the population is classified as Christian, with the largest proportion being Catholic. There is also a substantial proportion of mainline Protestants.

[c]According to ARDA's national profile for the Netherlands, the country has a high proportion of people who do not practice any religion. For those who do practice, the dominant religion is Christianity, with the largest proportion being Catholic, though other Protestant groups, including the Dutch Reformed Church, are well represented.

[d]According to the CIA World Factbook 2013, the majority of residents are Christian (61.4%), though a substantial proportion are also Muslim (35.2%). Zanzibar is almost all Muslim. The Christian population is almost evenly divided between Catholic and Protestant (Pew Research Center 2011). Because there was no clear majority Christian faith and the nation also has a substantial number of Muslims, the country was placed in this category.

[e]According to the CIA World Factbook 2013, Uganda is a majority Christian nation with an almost even divide between Catholics and Protestants, including mainline Protestant groups like Anglicans, as well as conservative Protestants. The Pew Research Center's 2011 report shows that a slightly higher percentage of Ugandans are Protestant rather than Catholic.

[f]These nations tend to be dominated by mainline Protestant denominations, including Anglican and Presbyterian.

[g]The majority religion is Christian, with the largest group being mainline Protestantism, including Anglican, Presbyterian, and Methodist. According to the CIA World Factbook 2013, there is also a substantial number of residents who do not adhere to any religion, as well as a number who adhere to religions and denominations other than mainline Protestantism.

[h]While the religious group with the largest proportion is Orthodox Christianity (43.5%), there are a substantial number of Muslims (33.9%) and Protestants (18.5%) (CIA World Factbook 2013).

[i]According to the CIA World Factbook 2013, about 50% of the population is Muslim and 40% is Christian.

WVS Data and Hierarchical Models

The World Values Survey (WVS) data are used for the hierarchical linear models (HLMs) presented in tables 8 and 9. Using national random and quota sampling, the data were collected through a variety of means, including face-to-face interviews. (For more information on the sampling techniques used in each nation, see the data documentation on the WVS website [http://www.worldvaluessurvey.org /WVSContents.jsp].) The fourth wave of the WVS includes 57,868 respondents clustered within forty societies.[1] The fifth wave of the WVS includes 82,992 respondents clustered within fifty-nine societies, and the sixth wave includes 86,274 respondents clustered within fifty-nine societies.

Several countries where data were collected could not be included in the HLM analysis because they did not have information on the key outcome, independent variables, or controls. Multiple imputation could not be used to replace this missing data for these nations because these techniques are inappropriate when the data are systematically missing (i.e., not asked in the country survey) (Allison 2001). The final analysis included 202,316 individuals from eighty-seven societies, representing over 80% of the world's population. See appendix A for a list of all societies included in the WVS HLM analysis.

TABLE 8 HIERARCHICAL LINEAR MODELS FOR EXAMINING THE INFLUENCE OF INDIVIDUAL CHARACTERISTICS AND RELIGION, GDP, AND DEMOCRACY ON HOMOSEXUALITY *NEVER BEING JUSTIFIED*[a] *(Individual N=202,316; Society N=87)*[b]

	Model 1[c]	Model 2	Model 3	Model 4	Model 5[d]
Constant[e]	115.621***	114.177***	111.386***	114.179***	114.581***
Country-level variables					
Dominant religious faith[f]					
Mixed Protestant/Christian		1.947***	1.227**	1.025**	0.865*[g]
Mainline Protestant		-1.823***	-1.224*	-0.048	-0.074
Orthodox		2.382***	2.295***	1.644***	1.582***
Muslim		2.675***	1.973***	1.530***	1.258***
Buddhist		1.717***	2.125***	1.695***	1.490***
Hindu		1.015**	0.651**	-0.176	-0.139
Mean country religious importance			0.959***	0.353+	0.388*
GDP per capita (in U.S. dollars)				-0.005***	-0.005***
Democracy category					-0.271*
Individual-level variables					
Female	-0.376***	-0.376***	-0.376***	-0.376***	-0.376***
Age	0.016***	0.016***	0.016***	0.016***	0.016***
Education					
Primary or less	0.766***	0.767***	0.766***	0.765***	0.765***
Incomplete secondary school	0.342***	0.342***	0.342***	0.342***	0.342***
Completed secondary school	0.578***	0.578***	0.578***	0.578***	0.578***
Some university	0.259***	0.260***	0.260***	0.259***	0.259***
Religious importance	0.344***	0.344***	0.343***	0.343***	0.343***
Income	-0.102***	-0.102***	-0.102***	-0.102***	-0.102***
Survey year	-0.055***	-0.055***	-0.055***	-0.055***	-0.055***
Marital status[h]					
Living with partner	-0.313***	-0.312***	-0.312***	-0.312***	-0.312***
Divorced/separated	-0.284***	-0.284***	-0.284***	-0.283***	-0.283***

(continued)

TABLE 8 (continued)

	Model 1[c]	Model 2	Model 3	Model 4	Model 5[d]
Constant[e]	115.621***	114.177***	111.386***	114.179***	114.581***
Widowed	0.035	0.035	0.035	0.035	0.035
Single	-0.114**	-0.114**	-0.114**	-0.114**	-0.114**
Religious affiliation[i]					
Protestant	0.417***	0.416***	0.416***	0.416***	0.416***
Orthodox	0.130	0.124	0.123	0.124	0.123
Jewish	-0.496*	-0.499*	-0.499*	-0.499*	-0.499*
Muslim	0.392***	0.384***	0.383***	0.385***	0.384***
Hindu	0.228+	0.224+	0.224+	0.225+	0.225+
Buddhist	0.048	0.044	0.043	0.043	0.043
Other religion	0.495***	0.493***	0.493***	0.493***	0.492***
None	-0.197**	-0.200**	-0.199**	-0.199**	-0.199**
All else	0.030	0.027	0.027	0.027	0.027
Individual-level variance	5.541	5.541	5.541	5.541	5.541
Country-level variance	2.912***	1.079***	0.862***	0.506***	0.483***

+ = p < .05; ** = p < .01; *** = p < .001

[a] The outcome ranges from 0 (= always justified) to 10 (= never justified).

[b] The WVS includes three societies that the United Nations does not recognize as countries. These are Taiwan, Andorra, and Puerto Rico. WVS administrators include these places separately from the larger nations that claim them because they feel that these geographic areas are culturally, politically, or economically distinct in the same way that countries typically are.

[c] The variables included in this model account for 12% of the total variance in attitudes about homosexuality. In an empty model the individual-level variance is 6.00 and the country-level variance is 3.621. Approximately 62% of the variance is occurring at the individual level and 38% is at the country level.

[d] The variables included in this model account for 37% of the overall variance in attitudes, and they explain 87% of the country-level variance.

[e] Variables are not centered.

[f] Catholic is the reference for dominant religious faith.

[g] A separate analysis shows that when mixed Protestant countries are the reference group, there is no significant difference between it and nations that are dominated by mainline Protestantism, Islam, and Buddhism. Catholic- and Hindu-dominated nations appear significantly more liberal, and Eastern Orthodox countries appear more conservative.

[h] Married is the reference of individual marital status.

[i] Catholic is the reference for individual religious affiliation.

TABLE 9 HIERARCHICAL LINEAR MODELS FOR EXAMINING ALTERNATIVE MACRO-LEVEL INFLUENCES AND CROSS-LEVEL INTERACTIONS FOR HOMOSEXUALITY *NEVER BEING JUSTIFIED*[a] (*Individual N = 202,316; Society N = 87*)

	Model 1	Model 2	Model 3	Model 4	Model 5
Constant[b]	115.132***	112.611***	114.522***	112.214***	112.684***
Country-level variables					
Dominant religious faith[c]					
Mixed Protestant/Christian	0.816*	0.959*	0.846*	0.817*	0.817*
Mainline Protestant	-0.132	-1.138*	-0.107	-0.065	-0.065
Orthodox	1.402***	2.227***	1.637***	1.367***	1.367***
Muslim	1.024**	1.563***	1.252***	1.141***	1.141***
Buddhist	1.448***	1.788***	1.498***	1.239***	1.239***
Hindu	-0.324	0.645**	-0.213	-0.307	-0.306
Mean country religious importance	0.470*	0.948***	0.329	-0.501**	-0.362
GDP per capita (U.S. dollars)	-0.005***	-0.005***	-0.005***	-0.008***	-0.008***
Democracy category	-0.277*	-0.410*	-0.280*	-0.222*	-0.221*
Economic inequality (GINI coefficient)[d]	-0.018				
Country mean education		-0.139			
Gender inequality score			0.446		
Cross-level interactions					
Interaction between GDP and individual religious importance				0.001***	0.001***
Interaction between country and individual religious importance					0.039
Individual-level variables					
Female	-0.376***	-0.376***	-0.376***	-0.378***	-0.378***
Age	0.016***	0.016***	0.016***	0.015***	0.015***
Education					
Primary or less	0.765***	0.766***	0.765***	0.762***	0.762***
Incomplete secondary school	0.342***	0.342***	0.342***	0.338***	0.338***
Completed secondary school	0.578***	0.578***	0.578***	0.571***	0.571***
Some university	0.259***	0.260***	0.259***	0.248***	0.248***

(continued)

TABLE 9 (*continued*)

	Model 1	Model 2	Model 3	Model 4	Model 5
Constant[b]	115.132***	112.611***	114.522***	112.214***	112.684***
Religious importance	0.344***	0.343***	0.343***	0.136***	0.005***
Income	-0.102***	-0.102***	-0.102***	-0.100***	-0.100***
Survey year	-0.055***	-0.055***	-0.055***	-0.053***	-0.053***
Marital status[e]					
Living with partner	-0.312***	-0.312***	-0.312***	-0.291***	-0.291***
Divorced/separated	-0.283***	-0.284***	-0.283***	-0.279***	-0.278***
Widowed	0.035	0.035	0.035	0.037	0.037
Single	-0.114**	-0.114**	-0.114**	-0.117**	-0.117**
Religious affiliation[f]					
Protestant	0.416***	0.416***	0.416***	0.429***	0.429***
Orthodox	0.123	0.123	0.123	0.215*	0.215*
Jewish	-0.499*	-0.499*	-0.499*	-0.417*	-0.416*
Muslim	0.384***	0.383***	0.384***	0.467***	0.467***
Hindu	0.225+	0.224+	0.225+	0.291*	0.291*
Buddhist	0.043	0.043	0.043	0.110	0.110
Other religion	0.492***	0.492***	0.492***	0.452***	0.452***
None	-0.199**	-0.200**	-0.199**	-0.108	-0.108
All else	0.027	0.027	0.027	0.051	0.051
Individual-level variance	5.541	5.541	5.541	5.482	5.482
Country-level variance	0.472***	0.802***	0.480***	1.035***	1.028***
Slope				0.045***	0.045***

* = p < .05; ** = p < .01; *** p < .001

[a]The outcome ranges from 0 (= always justified) to 10 (= never justified)

[b]Variables are not centered.

[c]Catholic is the reference for dominant religious faith.

[d]A separate analysis showed that proportion foreigner is also not significant for explaining; individuals' attitudes about homosexuality.

[e]Married is the reference for individual marital status.

[f]Catholic is the reference for individual religious affiliation.

DEPENDENT VARIABLE

The key outcome variable is disapproval of homosexuality, which is measured using a question that asks, "Please tell me for each of the following statements whether you think it can always be justified, never be justified, or something in between: Homosexuality?" Responses could range from 1 (= never justifiable) to 10 (= always justifiable). These responses were reverse-coded so that higher numbers indicate "less justifiable."

INDIVIDUAL-LEVEL RELIGION VARIABLES

The religious-importance variable is created from a question that asks, "For each of the following aspects, indicate how important it is in your life. Would you say it is: Religion?" Responses were reverse-coded so that "1" indicates "not at all important" and "4" indicates "very important."

Religious affiliation is measured with a set of dummy variables: Buddhist, Muslim, Hindu, Jewish, Eastern Orthodox, Protestant, other religion, none, and all else. Catholic is the reference category. Individual country surveys did not consistently include the information needed to make finer-grain religious distinctions such as conservative and mainline Protestant.

ADDITIONAL INDIVIDUAL-LEVEL VARIABLES

The other individual-level variables include gender, age, education, income, and marital status. Gender is assessed with a dichotomous variable where "1" = female and "0" = male. Age is a continuous variable that is measured in number of years. Education is measured with a set of dummy variables; primary school or less, incomplete secondary school, completed secondary school, and some university, where completed university is the reference category. Preliminary analysis revealed that the effect of education on attitudes about homosexuality is not linear. For that reason, a set of dummy variables are included instead of a single education measure.

Income is measured with a question that gave each respondent a card and explained, "On this card is a scale of incomes on which 1 indicates the 'lowest income decile' and 10 the 'highest income decile' in your country. We would like to know in what group your household is. Please, specify the appropriate number, counting all wages, salaries, pensions and other incomes that come in." WVS survey administrators then recoded this question into five categories.

Marital status is measured with a set of dummy variables for living with partner, divorced or separated, widowed, and single, where married is the reference group.

Survey year was also included to account for differences between survey waves. Ideally, multiple waves of data would have been collected for each country, making a cross-sectional longitudinal analysis possible. But very few countries had data for all time periods, and these tended to be the most politically stable and economically developed.

KEY COUNTRY-LEVEL VARIABLES

To create the measure of mean country religious importance, I used individual-level responses to the question about religious importance to create a mean for each country in the survey. Information on the coding of the dominant religious faith and sources used to create it can be found in appendix A.

The measure of 2008 GDP per capita in U.S. dollars (measured in 1,000s) is taken from the Association of Religious Data Archives' "Cross-National Socio-Economic and Religion Data, 2011," which they compiled using data from the United Nations (UN). For societies that did not have an estimate online, open sources were used to create an estimate. GDP is taken from 2008 because this is the same year in which many countries conducted the WVS, and this is year for which the content analysis of newspaper articles was completed.

Democracy was measured with a three categorical variable taken from the Association of Religious Data Archives' "Cross-National Socio-Economic and Religion Data, 2011," which they took from the UN. The measure is coded so that 0 = nondemocratic, 1 = democratic with no alternation, and 2 = democratic.

The score is meant to captures the regime's authority spectrum. The UN initially assigned each society a score on a 21-point scale ranging from -10 (hereditary monarchy) to +10 (consolidated democracy). The UN then converted the scores into three regime categories: "autocracies" (-10 to -6), "anocracies" (-5 to +5), and "democracies" (+6 to +10).

ADDITIONAL COUNTRY-LEVEL VARIABLES

There are three other country-level variables that are considered in the analysis presented in tables 8 and 9. Economic and gender inequality are taken from the Association of Religious Data Archives' "Cross-National Socio-Economic and Religion Data, 2011," which they compiled from the UN. "Country mean education" is the average level of educational attainment based on the individual-level variable described above.

METHODS

The analysis presented in tables 8 and 9 was conducted using generalized mixed models (Breslow and Clayton 1993), which make it possible to discern variance within nations (micro-level effects) from variance between societies (macro-level effects). The multivariate analysis begins by first examining the contribution of individual-level variables for attitudes about homosexuality. To explore the effect of the national context on attitudes, the country-level variables are then included on the intercept. Three additional society-level variables (i.e., economic inequality, country mean education, and gender inequality) are also introduced, with each one being entered into a separate model. The final model examines whether GDP and mean religious importance explain variation in the influence of individual religious importance on disapproval of homosexuality. They are included in the same model to show that the moderating influence of GDP is significant and that the moderating influence of religious importance, which is used to test the moral communities hypothesis, is not significant.

The analysis uses the recommended weights, which account for the unequal probability of selection of persons within nations. To maintain the largest sample size possible, the analysis utilizes multiple imputation techniques, which take full advantage of the available data and avoid some of the bias in standard errors and test statistics that can accompany list-wise deletion (Allison 2001). Missing values are imputed for five datasets. Standard errors from the multiple imputation process are calculated to reflect the uncertainty that is generated through simulated data.

Additional Macro-Level Indicators

TABLE 10 SEVENTY ADDITIONAL INDICATORS CONSIDERED FOR EXPLAINING THE
MEAN PROPORTION OF RESIDENTS WHO REPORT THAT HOMOSEXUALITY IS NEVER
JUSTIFIED

Indicator	Significant relationship between indicator and attitudes	Significant relationship *after* GDP, democracy, and religious context are considered
Religion		
Government regulation of religion index, 2008[a]	Y[b]	N[c]
Government favoritism of religion index, 2008[a]	N	
Modified social regulation of religion index, 2008[a]	Y	N
Democracy	Y	N
Human rights violations score, 2008[d]	Y	N
Percentage of population who voiced their opinion to public officials, 2008[d]	Y	N
Civil war intensity, 2008[d]	Y	N
Press freedom index, 2009[d]	Y	N
Population		
Total population in millions, 2010[d]	N	
Projected percent average annual population growth, 2010–2015[d]	Y	N
Percent population growth rate, 2009–2011[d]	Y	N
Percentage of the total population living in urban areas, 1990[d]	Y	N

Percentage of the total population living in urban areas, 2010[d]	Y	N
Number of births per 1,000 population, 2011[e]	Y	N
Sex ratio at birth (male births per 100 female births), 2010[d]	N	

Fertility

Total fertility rate, 1990–1995[d]	Y	N
Total fertility rate, 2009–2011[e]	Y	N
Projected total fertility rate, 2010–2015[d]	Y	N
Adolescent fertility rate, 1990–2008[d]	Y	N
Contraceptive prevalence rate (percent of married women age 15–49), 1990–2008[d]	Y	N

Age

Median age in years, 2010[d]	Y	N
Percentage of population age 0–14, 2009–2011[e]	Y	N
Percentage of population age 15–64, 2009–2011[e]	Y	N
Percentage of population age 65 and older, 2009–2011[e]	Y	N

Income

Income GINI index, 2000–2010[d]	Y	N
Inequality-adjusted income index, 2010[d]	Y	N
Tax revenue as a percentage of GDP, 2008[d]	N	

Education

Mean educational level[f]	Y	N
Inequality-adjusted education index, 2010[d]	Y	N
Percentage of population with at least one severe deprivation in education, 2000[d]	Y	N

Employment

Ratio of employment to population age 15–64, 1991[d]	N	
Formal employment as a percentage of total employment, 2000–2008[d]	Y	N
Percentage of employed people who live on less than $1.25 a day, 2000–2008[d]	N	
Percentage of children age 5–14 engaged in child labor, 1999–2007[d]	N	

Human development

Human development index value, 2010[d]	Y	N
Inequality-adjusted human development index, 2010[d]	Y	N
Change in human development index rank, 2005–2010[d]	N	N

(continued)

TABLE 10 *(continued)*

Indicator	Significant relationship between indicator and attitudes	Significant relationship *after* GDP, democracy, and religious context are considered
Gender inequality		
Gender inequality index value, 2008[d]	Y	N
Gender inequality index rank, 2008[d]	Y	N
Percentage of seats in parliament held by women, 2008[d]	Y	N
Health		
Percentage of population with at least one severe deprivation in health, 2000–2008[d]	N	
Percent of total population that was undernourished, 2004–2006[d]	Y	N
Percentage of adults age 15–49 with HIV, 2007[d]	N	
HIV/Aids adult prevalence rate as a percentage of the population, 2001–2009[e]	N	
Number of people living with HIV/Aids, 1997–2009[e]	N	
Life expectancy at birth, total population, 2009–2011[e]	Y	N
Life expectancy at birth among males, 2009–2011[e]	Y	N
Life expectancy at birth among females, 2009–2011[e]	Y	N
Inequality-adjusted life expectancy at birth index, 2010[d]	Y	N
Number of calendar days of mandatory paid maternity leave, 2007–2009[d]	N	
Life satisfaction		
Overall life satisfaction, 2006–2009[d]	Y	N
Overall life satisfaction among females, 2006–2009[d]	Y	N
Percentage of employed who are satisfied with their job, 2006–2009[d]	Y	N
Percentage of population who are satisfied with their personal health, 2006–2009[d]	Y	N
Percentage who are satisfied with their standard of living, 2006–2009[d]	Y	N
Poverty		
Multidimensional poverty index value, 2000–2008[d]	N	
Percentage of population in multidimensional poverty, 2000–2008[d]	Y	N

Percentage of population at risk of multidimensional poverty, 2000–2008[d]	Y	N
Percentage of population below the national poverty line, 2000–2008[d]	N	

Literacy

Adult literacy rate (percentage of population age 15 or older), 2005–2008[d]	Y	N
Percentage of the total population age 15 and over who can read and write, 1969–2008[e]	Y	N
Percentage of the male population age 15 and over who can read and write, 1969–2008[e]	Y	N
Percentage of the female population age 15 and over who can read and write, 1969–2008[e]	Y	N

Crime and victimization

Homicide rate per 100,000 people, 2003–2008[d]	N	
Robbery rate per 100,000 people, 2003–2008[d]	Y	N
Percentage of population that reported having been a victim of an assault, 2006–2009[d]	N	
Percentage of population who say they feel safe walking alone at night, 2006–2009[d]	N	

NOTE: In addition to these measures, it is possible to combine a number of different measures into a single index. For example, the human development index combines measures of (1) life expectancy; (2) an education index that includes mean years of school and expected years of schooling; and (3) an income index. Similarly, Norris and Inglehart (2012) use a Cosmopolitan Index, which includes measures from the KOF (an acronym for the German word *Konjunkturforschungsstelle*) Globalization Index, which has measures of: (1) economic, social, and political globalization; (2) media freedom; and (3) economic development. One strength of an index is that reliability can be strengthened because multiple measures are now being used to assess a single concept (cosmopolitan or human development). However, if a number of different concepts (e.g. economic development, democracy) are being combined into a single index, it is no longer possible to ascertain which factor is causing an effect, and parsimony can be lost. For example, Norris and Inglehart's Cosmopolitan Index includes elements like media freedom, which is a factor of democracy. They also include a straightforward measure of economic development. If their Cosmopolitan Index is used, it is not possible to unravel which dimension (i.e. economic development, democracy, both, or some other factor included in the index) is affecting the outcome. One of the strengths of the research presented in this book is that I am able to show how fairly simple and straightforward measures like GDP can explain the majority of the variation in how nations view homosexuality. Moreover, as discussed in the second chapter, some popular measures—like educational attainment, which are typically highly correlated with economic development—do not necessarily shape attitudes about homosexuality in the same way as economic development. Hence, combining factors like economic development and educational attainment into a single index would be misleading since it could mask the weak effect of a particular factor, like educational attainment. Throughout the case-study chapters, I discuss the processes embedded in concepts like economic development and democracy so that readers have a fuller understanding of the multiple ways in which these forces may shape attitudes.

[a]Measure was from the 2008 U.S. State Department's International Religious Freedom Reports.

[b]Y = Yes, significant correlation (p < .05)

[c]N = No significant correlation

[d]Measure was from the 2010 United Nations Human Development Report (HDR).

[e]Measure was from the CIA World Factbook 2011.

[f]Measure was constructed from individual-level information on education included in WVS, wave 4.

Details on the Content Analysis of Newspaper Articles

Newspaper articles were analyzed for three Christian countries (the United States, South Africa, and Uganda)[1] and three Muslim nations (Indonesia, Malaysia, and Turkey). The analysis focused on all articles that were published between January 1, 2008, and December 31, 2008. This time period was selected because this is the latest period for which there was online access to all of the papers. Additionally, the fourth and fifth waves of the World Values Survey were carried out in all of these countries shortly before this period, making it possible to confirm the reliability of the findings with an additional data source. Below I present details of the newspaper analysis, beginning with a discussion of the Christian nations.

NEWSPAPER SELECTION IN UGANDA, SOUTH AFRICA, AND THE UNITED STATES

To capture the dominant view within each of these nations, five newspapers from the three Christian countries were analyzed. In Uganda, the *New Vision* and the *Daily Monitor* were selected, and in South Africa, the *Star* and the *Daily News* were chosen. The United States publishes a lot more papers than these other countries, making selection more difficult. *USA Today* was chosen because it has the third-largest circulation in the country, following the *Wall Street Journal* and the *New York Times*. *USA Today* is known as the best representation of a "national" American paper. Additionally, the *New York Times* has a liberal bent (Pan, Meng, and Zhou 2010), and the smaller number of articles in *USA Today*, compared with the *Wall Street Journal* and *New York Times*, meant that every article could be analyzed rather than only a subsample.

Two papers were analyzed from each of the African nations, in part, because they had many fewer articles than *USA Today*. Additionally, while the United States has full freedom of the press, South Africa and Uganda have only partial freedom (Freedom House 2015), and like many African papers, Uganda's *New Vision* is government owned. By analyzing two papers from each African nation, I was able to increase reliability of the findings.

In addition to having large circulations and being leading sources of news, these newspapers were selected because they are published at least five days a week and either the full content can be found online at the newspaper's website or the full text is available from LexisNexis, which is a commonly used database for newspaper analyses (e.g., Benson and Saguy 2005; Wheelock and Hartmann 2007; A. Kim, Kumanyika, Shive, et al. 2010). A number of other studies (S. Cooper, Anafi, Sun et al. 2008–9; Meintjes and Bray 2005; Strand 2012) have analyzed articles from these papers, in part, because they are accessible and considered prominent within these nations. All of the newspapers are published in English, which is the official language in the United States, Uganda, and South Africa.

NEWSPAPER SELECTION IN INDONESIA, MALAYSIA, AND TURKEY

Three English-language papers were selected for analysis in the three Muslim nations. In Indonesia the *Jakarta Post* was selected. In Malaysia the *New Strait Times* was selected, and in Turkey the *Turkish Daily News* was selected.[2] Ideally, newspapers written in the native language would have been selected and analyzed, but my research team and I did not have the diverse language abilities that would have made this sort of an analysis possible. Instead, three English-language newspapers that are geared toward residents, have relatively high circulations, were published at least five days a week, and had electronic access for the study period (i.e. 2008) were selected. There was not a particularly wide selection of papers that met these criteria, and in part, for this reason only one paper from each nation was used. Additionally, these papers were chosen because there is a history of researchers using them to better understand the construction of various social issues in these countries (Bakan 2014; Kenyon 2010; S. T. Kim 2004; S. T. Lee and Maslog 2005; Massey and Chang 2002; Vergne 2011).

Because the Christian papers are all written in English, which is the dominant language, making them accessible to all residents, and an additional two papers were selected from South Africa and Uganda, the validity of the findings for the analysis of papers in Christian nations is likely higher. However, in contrast to an analysis that relies only on public-opinion survey data, the newspapers from the Muslim-majority nations bring a more nuanced and at times more insightful understanding of how the public views homosexuality and how media elites would like their audiences to understand LGBTQ-related issues. The findings from the newspaper analysis align with both public-opinion survey data and also what is currently known through existing research about attitudes in these nations.

CODING OF NEWSPAPER ARTICLES

The sample from each paper was created by first developing a long list of homo-sexuality-related terms (e.g., *fag, queer, dyke, transgender*), which were used to search for articles. The list was then reduced to seven terms (i.e., *homosexuality, homosexual, homo, lesbian, bisexual, sodomy,* and *gay*), which appeared in at least one article. For the one-year period every newspaper was searched for every article that contained one of the terms. For the Christian sample there were 379 unique articles from the five papers, and for the Muslim sample there were 427 unique articles from three papers.

The dependent variables consist of the themes and claimsmakers that are associated with the homosexuality term. To develop these variables, several articles were initially read and a list of ideas and claimsmakers that were associated with the text immediately surrounding the homosexuality term were inductively created. Based on this preliminary list, the coding scheme was developed, and two people coded a subsample of articles into categories. Inconsistencies were then discussed, and the coding instrument was further developed. In the end, one person coded every article and a second person coded a subset of articles, so that intercoder reliability (i.e., the extent to which independent reviewers code a theme or frame the same way) could be assessed.

The findings for both sets of papers, Christian and Muslim, focus on the following themes or associations: (1) rights; (2) fictional characters, celebrities, and famous people; (3) religion; and (4) morality.[3] The findings of both also examined religious authorities as claimsmakers. The analysis of Christian newspapers also includes the theme of Western influences, and the Muslim newspaper analysis includes social-movement leaders as claimsmakers. The theme of Western influences was not included with the Muslim analysis because there were only three articles that mentioned it in any of the papers, and an analysis of it was not, therefore, feasible. The theme of claimsmakers as social-movement leaders was not included in the analysis of Christian nations because the reliability (i.e. kappa) of the coding was quite low, in part, because there were very few papers (less than 5%) that had this theme.

Intercoder reliability is assessed with a kappa statistic. As shown in table 11, the average intercoder reliability for themes in the newspapers from the Christian-majority countries was 0.75. and 0.80 for those from the Muslim-majority nations. An absolute standard for intercoder reliability does not exist (Kaid and Wadsworth 1989), but a minimum bound of 0.70 is advised (Singletary 1994). Some of the scores for individual associations fall slightly below this bound. Kappa is influenced by small cell sizes, where a more infrequent category will result in lower reliability, even if intercoder agreement is relatively high. For example, in the Christian sample the theme "West" was found in only 15% of articles, resulting in a kappa of .66, even though there was 99% agreement between the coders. Additionally, when coders are asked to make more-complicated assessments (Kaid and Wadsworth 1989), which occurred in this study, lower reliability scores are more common.

A set of dummy variables for each country is used as the key independent predictor. Because different countries and newspapers may vary in the extent to

TABLE 11 INTERCODER RELIABILITY AND THEMES/ASSOCIATIONS AND
CLAIMSMAKERS USED IN ANALYSIS BY NEWSPAPERS COMING FROM CHRISTIAN
AND MUSLIM NATIONS

	Christian nations (N=379)		Muslim nations (N=427)	
	Kappa	Agreement (%)	Kappa	Agreement (%)
Themes/associations				
Rights: Including human rights, women's rights, civil rights, legislation regarding pro–gay rights, same-sex marriage etc.	0.95	98.65	0.87	96.47
West or Western influences, including European or American influences	0.66	98.65	Not used	
Fictional character, celebrities, famous people, including writers, politicians, characters in a movie or play, actors, etc.	0.67	85.14	0.77	94.12
Religion: discussed in the context of religious terms, against religion, Catholic, etc.	0.85	95.95	0.87	96.47
Morality: using terms like *immoral* or *moral* and grouping or association with other so-called moral or immoral issues (e.g. abortion, terrorism, pornography)	0.61	90.54	0.69	89.41
Average:	0.75	93.78	0.80	94.12
Claimsmakers				
Religious official: archbishop, clergy	0.89	97.30	0.82	97.65
Social movement leader: nongovernment, not religious	Not used		0.69	95.29

which they publish various types (i.e., news, opinion, etc.) of articles, a control for article type was created. It had five exclusive categories: opinion pieces; reviews (i.e., book, movie, theater); interviews of someone (i.e., politician, congressman, entertainer, archbishop, etc.); and other, where news story (including serious or entertainment news) was the comparison. Additionally, in smaller and poorer nations, whether the newspaper information is originating from outside or inside the country could shape the portrayal of homosexuality. Hence, a variable assessing where the information originates, whether inside or outside the nation, is also included. Finally, since the number of days on which the papers are published could influence the content, a control is included for this. All newspapers published articles at least five days a week.

TABLE 12 LOGISTIC REGRESSION OF DIFFERENCES BETWEEN UGANDA, SOUTH AFRICA, AND THE UNITED STATES ON ASSOCIATIONS AND CLAIMSMAKERS IN ARTICLES THAT MENTIONED HOMOSEXUALITY DURING 2008

	Model 1 Character association	Model 2 Rights association	Model 3 Religious association	Model 4 Religious official claimsmaker	Model 5 Morality association	Model 6 Western association[a]
Uganda[b]	0.367*	0.200***	2.659*	3.411**	2.564*	7.673*
South Africa	0.881	0.204***	0.659	0.680	0.409+	
Opinion piece[c]	1.040	1.315	1.694	1.623	4.471***	
Review (movie, book, theater)	5.085***	0.126***	0.363+	0.088*	1.240	
Interview	3.544**	0.200*	0.250	0.232	1.006	
Focus of information is outside	2.118*	2.518*	1.136	0.863	0.328+	1.115
Published on the weekend and weekdays[d]	0.607	1.130	0.801	0.742	1.043	0.965
Constant	0.313***	0.690	0.152***	0.162***	0.104***	0.011***
Pseudo R-squared	0.14	0.14	0.10	0.17	0.17	0.10
Observations	379	379	379	379	379	245

+ = < 0.10, * = < 0.05, ** = < 0.01, *** = < 0.001

[a] The United States is not included in this analysis since it would be considered a Western nation. Article type is not included because few articles had a Western association and hence there were several article types where no Western association was mentioned. South Africa is the reference.

[b] The United States is the reference, unless otherwise indicated. For differences between South Africa and Uganda, see figure 14 in chapter 3.

[c] The reference group is "news article."

[d] The reference group is "published only during the week."

TABLE 13 LOGISTIC REGRESSION OF DIFFERENCES BETWEEN INDONESIA, MALAYSIA, AND TURKEY ON ASSOCIATIONS AND CLAIMSMAKERS IN ARTICLES THAT MENTIONED HOMOSEXUALITY DURING 2008

	Model 1 Character association	Model 2 Social-movement claimsmaker	Model 3 Rights association	Model 4 Religious association	Model 5 Religious official claimsmaker	Model 6 Morality association
Indonesia[a]	0.212**	1.333	0.618	0.693	1.473	1.713+
Malaysia	0.258**	0.032***	0.014***	0.199***	0.528	0.470**
Opinion piece[b]	2.352*	0.267**	0.610	1.325	1.375	1.318
Review (movie, book, theater)	13.428***	0.197*	0.227*	0.556	0.387	0.522
Interview	7.089+	0.938	0.263	1.217	1.899	0.592
Focus of information is outside	6.807***	0.175***	0.363**	0.471*	0.975	0.960
Published on weekend and weekdays[c]	2.422*	0.822	0.658	0.991	0.442	0.740
Constant	0.069***	0.683	1.524	0.558*	0.098***	0.570*
Pseudo R-squared	0.37	0.26	0.30	0.08	0.05	0.06
Observations	427	427	427	427	427	427

+<0.10, *<0.05, **<0.01, ***<0.001

[a] Turkey is the reference group, unless otherwise indicated. For differences between Indonesia and Malaysia, see bar chart of predicted marginal values presented in figure 20 in chapter 4.

[b] The reference group is "news article."

[c] The reference group is "published only during the week."

Logistic regression analysis techniques are used to examine how the themes and claimsmakers vary by the newspapers analyzed in each country, while accounting for control variables. Information on differences between the reference nation and the others are included in the tables. For information on how any two nations listed in tables 12 and 13 differ from each other (e.g., Uganda vs. South Africa, Indonesia vs. Malaysia), see figures 14 and 20, which present predicted percentages using information from the logistic regression analysis.

Notes

1. This book is focused on public opinion, and the primary data used in the analysis asks about "homosexuality." Throughout the book the term *homosexuality* is used to describe same-sex desire and behavior. The acronym *LGBTQ* is reserved for specific references, such as organizations where this acronym is relevant, individuals when it is appropriate to discuss this group as a whole, and the description of the newspaper content analysis where my research team and I searched for these specific terms, as well as others.

2. For additional discussion of the complications in how homosexuality has been framed in some European nations, including the Netherlands, see Kuhar 2013.

3. West and Green's 1997 edited volume *Sociolegal Control of Homosexuality* also takes a case-study approach to compare the social and legal influences in various nations on homosexuality. The authors do not, however, isolate the factors that shape attitudes across a wide range of nations.

4. There have been three ongoing survey initiatives supported with government and private funds to gather cross-national data across a wide range of economically and regionally diverse nations (i.e., over forty countries) that ask questions that extend beyond health, well-being, and demographical characteristics (see Heath, Fisher, and Smith 2005). These surveys are the World Values Survey (WVS), the International Social Survey Programme (ISSP), and Pew's Global Attitudes Project. These are the only surveys that regularly ask about feelings regarding homosexuality across many nations in several different regions of the world. The majority of the quantitative analysis in this book relies on the WVS, which includes a larger number of nations than the other surveys and for some countries has data going back to 1981.

5. Some good examples where newspapers present a lot of discussion about homosexuality, despite its being criminalized, are Malaysia and Uganda.

6. Later he said that he was misquoted. (See Reuters 2007).

1. THE IMPORTANCE OF RELIGION, AND THE ROLE OF INDIVIDUAL DIFFERENCES

1. Some of the countries in the WVS include a survey category for "Christian," and they do not provide any additional information, though other data sources suggest that they are likely Protestant. When results are reported in this chapter, Christians and Protestants are grouped in the same category, with Catholics and Orthodox Christians being kept separate.

2. The standard deviation in attitudes for Protestants (i.e. 3.28) is almost twice as large as it is for Muslims (i.e. 1.61), reflecting the much greater amount of variation in public opinion about homosexuality for Protestants versus Muslims.

3. Berger has since reversed his position on secularization (see Berger 1997).

4. The estimates presented in figure 3 are taken from a model that includes controls for religious importance. However, the model does not include measures of religious attendance or other facets of religion. As explained, many religious faiths do not encourage religious attendance to the same extent as Christians, and hence it is not included in these analyses.

5. Macro influences explain a substantial amount of the variation in tolerance for homosexuality around the world. If all of the personal characteristics, like age and gender, but also things that have not yet been measured across nations, such as positive interactions with gay and lesbian individuals or level of television exposure to gay characters, could be isolated these individual factors would account for about 60% of the difference in public opinion about homosexuality across the world. The remaining 40% of the variation would come from more-macro-level influences. Among the macro forces that can be measured, the religious environment of a nation is one of the most important.

2. THE IMPORTANCE OF DEMOCRACY AND ECONOMIC DEVELOPMENT

1. There are a lot of different ways to measure economic development. Other researchers have used more-complex measures (e.g. Human Development Index) to assess the relationship between economic development and modernization processes and public opinion and laws regarding homosexuality. Regardless of the measures used for economic development and disapproval of homosexuality, there appears to be an inverse relationship between these two factors.

2. The question states, "Please tell me whether you think [homosexuality] can always be justified, never be justified, or something in between." Respondents can choose from categories that range from "1 = never justifiable" to "10 = always justifiable." For ease in interpretation, throughout this book the scale has been reverse-coded: from 1 = always justifiable to 10 = never justifiable. See Szalma and Takács (2013) for a discussion on how this question is related to

others about homosexuality in cross-national surveys. There tends to be a very high correlation, suggesting high reliability.

3. Adamczyk and Pitt (2009) examined the influence of survival versus self-expressive cultural orientations for shaping tolerance for homosexuality. Using data from the World Values Surveys and the appropriate statistical technique, the study found a robust influence on individuals' attitudes, even after accounting for personal values related to survival and self-expression.

4. Using data from the European Social Surveys, a group of researchers (van den Akker, van der Ploeg, and Scheepers 2013) examined the influence of the dominant religious tradition, laws regulating homosexuality, and mean levels of religious belief and education for shaping public opinion about homosexuality. They found that higher overall levels of education within the nation were associated with more-tolerant attitudes. However, they did not account for economic development. Rather, education seemed to be used as an alternative measure for economic development.

5. The comparison for the dominant religious faith is Catholicism, and depending on the dominant religion being evaluated, this sometimes has as large effect. Hence, there is a big difference between Muslim and Catholic countries, but a much smaller one for comparing attitudes in Catholic versus Buddhist nations.

6. Drawing on a sample of thirty-two mostly European nations, research by Hadler (2012) found that countries with more nonprofit organizations tend to have residents with more-supportive views of homosexuality. I suspect that the reason for the effect may have to do with the sample of nations, which is much more homogenous than the sample I use, which includes eighty-seven diverse nations from across the globe.

7. See also the following research, which shows support for the influences of economic development, democracy, and the country religious context: Adamczyk and Pitt 2009; Andersen and Fetner 2008b; Gerhards 2010; Hadler 2012; van den Akker, van der Ploeg, and Scheepers 2013; Hooghe and Meeusen 2013; Štulhofer and Rimac 2009.

3. SHAPING ATTITUDES IN PROTESTANT NATIONS

1. Since the mid-2000s official religious positions have been changing rapidly, especially in the United States (see Masci and Lipka 2015).

2. Throughout the discussion of South Africa, "black South Africans" refers to the indigenous African population, while "white South African" refers to the Afrikaner and English population.

3. The United States is a very large nation, and like South Africa, it is racially diverse and has a history of racial segregation. About 12% of residents are African-American. A number of studies have found that on average African-Americans are less tolerant of gay and lesbian individuals than other residents (Hunt and Hunt 2001; Lewis 2003; Sherkat, De Vries, and Creek 2010). Given their historical denial of civil rights, this relationship is somewhat surprising. African-Americans tend to be more engaged in their religious communities than other residents, and the majority (about 67%) belong to traditional African-American churches,

which would be classified as conservative Protestant and tend to take a more conservative view of same-sex behaviors (Adamczyk, Boyd, and Hayes 2016). Several studies have found that these religious characteristics can help explain African-Americans' more-conservative attitudes (Lewis 2003; Schulte and Battle 2004; Sherkat et al. 2010). Additionally, while they may be more likely to find homosexuality morally problematic, there is some indication that they are more likely than other racial groups to support legislation curtailing homosexuality-related discrimination (Lewis 2003).

4. In a separate model I found that a variable measuring whether the nation is or is not located in Africa was not significant, indicating that differences between the dominant religion are not being driven by continental differences between Africa and the rest of the world.

5. Whereas figure 5 shows an overall attitudinal score for residents from mainline Protestant nations of 5.07, once GDP, democracy, and religious importance are included, the average disapproval score rises to 7.44. Likewise, once these country characteristics are held constant, the attitudinal score for residents from countries with mixed Protestant faiths decreases from 8.91 to 8.39. Hence, the scores are starting to converge because of differences in GDP, democracy, and religious importance.

4. UNDERSTANDING VIEWS IN MUSLIM COUNTRIES

1. Ideally, an Arab nation would be a part of this analysis, but few of them were included in the WVS, and often there was very little information on the public's views.

2. For more information on women and LGBTQ-issues in Malaysia, see Wong 2012.

3. The small number of articles in Malaysia that mention an LGBTQ character or famous person seems to validate our analysis somewhat, since we would expect newspapers to follow suit.

4. The correlation between the 2008 total democracy score and 2008 government regulation of religion measure is -0.6, and it is significant at the .001 level. Nevertheless, democracy has a greater effect on public opinion about homosexuality and works through a range of other forces, including religious freedom.

5. The general trend for both of these measures has been a decrease, but even as the percentage has declined there have been some fluctuations. Hence, in 2007 73% of Turks reported that homosexuality is never justified, but this went higher, to 79%, in 2011. Likewise, not wanting a homosexual neighbor went from 92% in 1990 to 87% in 1996, back up to 90% in 2001, down to 88% in 2007, and finally to 85% in 2011.

5. THE RELATIVELY LIBERAL VIEWS OF PEOPLE FROM CATHOLIC-MAJORITY COUNTRIES

The epigraph to this chapter is taken from Erdő 2014.

1. In their systematic review, Costa et al. (2013) make the point that research on prejudice against nonheterosexual orientation is a relatively new area in Brazil.

2. In recent years Spain has experienced an influx of immigrants (Módenes, Bayona, and López-Colás 2013). They tend to have higher levels of religious belief than other Spaniards, and they have brought some religious diversity to this historically homogenous Catholic nation (Perez-Agote 2010).

3. According to the Pew Research Center's global attitudes survey on homosexuality (Pew Research Center 2013), in Spain the percentage of residents who feel that premarital sex is unacceptable is 8%, but 28% of people living in Catholic nations feel this way. For extramarital sex, 64% of Spaniards say it is unacceptable, but 73% of residents from Catholic-majority nations feel this way. And while 6% of Spaniards say homosexuality is unacceptable, 35% of people living in Catholic nations feel this way.

4. For belief in God and life after death, the Association of Religious Data Archives (ARDA) did not present data for 2005.

5. There has been some debate about whether measures of Italians' feelings about religion and increases in belief and religious engagement are accurate. The Italian sociologist Marco Marzano (2013) described reported increases as "surprising because they are greatly at odds with my own experience, with common sense, and probably also with the perceptions of the majority of Italians" (304). One data-collection issue is that survey respondents may overestimate their level of religious engagement. Indeed, research from the United States has found that respondents tend to inflate their level of religious attendance (Hadaway, Marler, and Chaves 1993, 1998). That said, if they are exaggerating their responses, people should overestimate them to a similar degree, and over time Italians should be somewhat consistent in their exaggerations. Hence, even if the baseline is lower than the survey data suggest (i.e. people are not as religious as they say), differences over time and across nations should be consistent, especially if time-series data reveal incremental changes and estimates are consistent across a wide range of data sources, which for Italy they are (Garelli 2006, 2011; Segatti and Brunelli 2010).

6. Internal surveys have shown similar increases in acceptance (see Paiva, Aranha, and Bastos 2008).

7. The Association of Religion Data Archives provides slightly different estimates based on data from the 2000 census by the Geographic and Statistical Institute of Brazil, which indicates that approximately 74% of the population identify themselves as Roman Catholic. About 15% were categorized as Protestant, with 85% of them being Pentecostal or Evangelical.

6. INVESTIGATING PUBLIC OPINION IN CONFUCIAN NATIONS

1. The one exception to this would be my previous work (Adamczyk and Cheng 2015), which provides the basis for this chapter.

2. Since the Korean War ended in 1953, North Korea has been one of the most closed nations in the world, and the World Bank does not have information on its 2013 GDP.

3. For this analysis nations are categorized according to one of the following major religions that best represent them: Buddhism, Hinduism, Protestantism, Catholicism, Eastern Orthodoxy, and Islam. Among the Confucian countries,

Buddhism is the most representative (Association of Religious Data Archives 2011).

4. The amount is small, in part, because so few countries have a substantial Buddhist population and the effect size is not particularly large.

5. This analysis includes all of the nations from the fifth wave of the WVS that have the necessary measures. Many countries in this wave and others do not ask about homosexuality or the questions that can be used to create measures of Confucian values. If the appropriate questions were not asked, these nations had to be eliminated from the sample. Multiple imputation techniques are used to replace missing data, but these techniques are appropriate only when data are missing at random. If a question was never asked, then the data are not missing at random and these techniques should not be used. Because a substantial minority of countries from the combined fourth, fifth, and sixth waves of data, which are used in the first two chapters, were missing information on the questions needed to create the Confucian-values measures, it was not possible to use the same country sample for this analysis.

6. There are also several other questions asked in the WVS that could be seen as capturing various elements of Confucianism. These include the importance of the family, independence being important for a child, and greater respect for authority being a good thing. However, in a preliminary analysis none of these were significant. In this chapter I chose to assess the values that had the highest level of reliability and greatest likelihood of having an effect.

7. Before being combined, each item was standardized and centered, and together the items had a Cronbach's alpha of .79. I also considered including additional items in the scale, such as the extent to which the respondent agreed that being a housewife is just as fulfilling as working for pay, and whether it is ever justifiable for a man to beat his wife. These additional items lowered the alpha level, and in a factor analysis these additional items did not load on the same factor.

8. These estimates are taken from the proportion of people who report being divorced in the World Values Survey.

9. When the divorce variable is included, the coefficient for Confucian society decreases by 34% (0.65 to 0.43), suggesting that attitudes about divorce partially mediate the effect of living in a Confucian society on attitudes about homosexuality. Mediation can be said to occur when (1) the independent variable significantly affects the mediator, (2) the independent variable significantly influences the dependent variable when the mediator is absent, (3) the mediator has a significant and unique effect on the dependent variable, and (4) the effect of the independent variable on the dependent variable is reduced when the mediator is added to the model (Baron and Kenny 1986).

10. Information on the legal status of prostitution in one hundred countries around the globe can be found at ProCon.org (http://prostitution.procon.org /view.resource.php?resourceID = 000772).

11. Unfortunately, the WVS did not ask about disapproval of sex outside of marriage.

12. There were no significant differences in the proportion of people who responded affirmatively to these values in Confucian and non-Confucian societies.

13. In a separate analysis I tried Hofstede and McCrae's (2004) macro measures of: (1) collectivism versus individualism, (2) femininity versus masculinity, and (3) short-term versus long-term orientation. Although these measures are available only at the macro level, I did not find any of them to be significantly related to disapproval for homosexuality.

14. Because the data are cross-sectional, the correct causal ordering at the individual level is unclear, making it difficult to unravel whether attitudes about homosexuality shape values, or values influence attitudes about homosexuality. However, *only* individual feelings about prostitution and divorce are consistently associated with attitudes about homosexuality, and in the expected direction, for the five Confucian nations. At the country level the causal order is clearer. Through the influence of government policies, the media, informal norms, and normative family structures, societal values related to disapproval of divorce could shape micro-level feelings about same-sex behaviors. It would be a lot harder to argue that disaggregated individual or micro attitudes about homosexuality could shape societal values about divorce.

7. SHAPING ATTITUDES IN TAIWAN

1. A grant from the Chiang Ching-kuo Foundation made it possible for me to spend time in Taiwan in 2013 and 2014. Two of the interviews mentioned here included conversations with more than one person. In one case two people from a religious organization were interviewed, and in another, four people from an LGBTQ-friendly NGO were interviewed. An additional thirty hours were spent informally interacting with people from the local LGBTQ community. Some of the more formal events where these interactions occurred included university debates on the issue, as well as activities sponsored by LGBTQ-related NGOs.

2. With so few waves of data collected on attitudes about homosexuality, it is not possible to specifically test whether economic development and democracy are the driving forces in Taiwan, though the relationship is consistent with ideas I presented in chapter 2 about how these factors contribute to more-liberal attitudes.

3. Because it is the largest city in the country, many people in Taipei are quite liberal. Ideally, interviews would have been done all over the country. Some interviews were conducted outside of the city or with individuals who were traveling through Taipei. But it was not feasible to conduct interviews all over the country.

4. Part of the challenge with interviewing religious officials and people who were against homosexuality was that they could not easily be identified online or would not respond to inquiries. This challenge was also mentioned by three of the reporters who were interviewed.

5. More people requested a translator than was actually needed because they underestimated the quality of their English-language abilities.

6. Using a translator was not ideal. But by employing an interpreter who had a strong background in sexualities research and worked with Taiwanese-based LGBTQ organizations, I was able to minimize some threats to validity (Kapborg and Berterö 2002).

7. All of the interviews were transcribed by Yen-Chiao Liao, who was also the interpreter and assisted in arranging them.

8. Researching homosexuality is a challenge, in part, because what it means and implies can vary quite drastically for different people. Academics tend to carefully distinguish between different variants (i.e., identity, behavior, preference, orientation, relationships, etc.), and the WVS question asks specifically about "homosexuality," though people can interpret that to mean a range of different things. But for the most part throughout the interviews, people did not stop and make fine-grained distinctions when homosexuality was discussed. When appropriate I would try to clarify. However, it's also useful to know that discussion of the three bills loomed large in many interviews. To some extent the experts often, although not always, framed responses in the context of the possibility of same-sex marriage, as well as concerns about harassment, sometimes referencing the "sissy boy" incident.

9. While Taiwan's 2014 fertility estimate was 1.11, in Hong Kong it was 1.17, in South Korea it was 1.25, and 1.40 in Japan. In contrast, in 2014 the United States had a total fertility rate of 2.01, and the lowest for any European nation was Lithuania at 1.29 (Central Intelligence Agency, n.d., "Country Comparison").

10. For example, after Jin Tai, who is the lead singer of the Taiwanese band MissTER, publicly came out in 2014, there were reports that she was the first Taiwanese singer to do so (Wee 2014).

11. In 2016 the percentage of Taiwanese using the internet was 84%, which is higher than the percentage in Austria, Italy, Portugal and Poland. See www .internetworldstats.com/asia/tw.htm and www.internetworldstats.com/stats4 .htm#europe.

12. Stark (2003) points out that absolute monotheism is rare. But compared with Buddhism, Christianity would be seen as much more focused on a single, angry, demanding, and jealous deity.

CONCLUSION

1. If agnostics and atheists are also included in the comparison, Hinduism would be the fourth-largest group.

2. Qatar's 2008 per capita GDP was $82,990, which is higher than that of the United States, Canada, Australia, and all of Europe, except for Finland and some of the European micro states (i.e., Monaco, Lichtenstein, and Luxembourg).

3. The other countries are Egypt, Mauritania, Sudan, Afghanistan, Iran, Iraq, the Maldives, Pakistan, Qatar, Saudi Arabia, and Yemen.

4. That said, because unrelated men and women cannot easily go out together in public, many people spend a lot of time with the same gender, which can be quite conducive to same-sex romantic and sexual relationships (see Labi 2007). In chapter 4, I discuss some similar patterns found in Turkey.

5. As discussed in the second chapter, researchers have shown that economic development is associated with an increase in people's interest in democratic practices (Inglehart and Oyserman 2004; Welzel, Inglehart, and Kligemann

2003). Nevertheless, economic development and democracy appear to have separate influences on public opinion about homosexuality.

APPENDIX B

1. The WVS uses the term *society*, which is more inclusive than *nation* or *country*, since it includes some places (e.g., Taiwan) that some governing bodies (e.g., the United Nations) may not officially recognize as a country. Throughout the book all of these terms are used interchangeably.

APPENDIX D

1. Preliminary findings from these papers were published in *Sociological Forum* (see Adamczyk, Kim, and Paradis 2015).

2. In 2013, when much of the coding was being done, *Today's Zaman* had the highest circulation for English-language daily papers in Turkey. However, the scope of this analysis is limited to articles published in 2008. *Today's Zaman* was established in 2007, which was too late for this analysis, since there would not have been enough time for a substantial number of readers to know about the paper.

3. Based on the original inductive coding, the research team coded and considered analyzing several other claimsmakers, including government officials, academics, and researchers. Several additional themes, such as style, rape, family, and harmful/insulting/offensive, were also considered. However, the reliability for these additional categories was quite low, and some of the categories were found too infrequently for analysis to be feasible.

Bibliography

365Gay.com Newscenter Staff. 2003. "Indonesia Seeks to Imprison Gays." Sodomy Laws. Retrieved April 16, 2015. www.glapn.org/sodomylaws/world/indonesia/idnews003.htm.

Abrams, J. Keith, and L. Richard Della Fave. 1976. "Authoritarianism, Religiosity, and the Legalization of Victimless Crimes." *Sociology and Social Research* 61 (1): 68–82.

Adamczyk, Amy. 2008. "The Effects of Religious Contextual Norms, Structural Constraints, and Personal Religiosity on Abortion Decisions." *Social Science Research* 37 (2): 657–72.

———. 2009. "Socialization and Selection in the Link between Friends' Religiosity and the Transition to Sexual Intercourse." *Sociology of Religion* 70 (1): 5–27.

———. 2011. "The Indirect Result of Religious Norms and Practices: Explaining Islam's Role in Limiting the Spread of HIV/AIDS." In *Religion and Social Problems,* edited by T. Hjelm, 15–31. New York: Routledge.

———. 2012a. "Extracurricular Activities and Teens' Alcohol Use: The Role of Religious and Secular Sponsorship." *Social Science Research* 41 (2): 412–24.

———. 2012b. "Investigating the Role of Religion-Supported Secular Programs for Explaining Initiation into First Sex." *Journal for the Scientific Study of Religion* 51 (2): 324–42.

———. 2012c. "Understanding Delinquency with Friendship Group Religious Context." *Social Science Quarterly* 93 (2): 482–505.

———. 2013. "The Effect of Personal Religiosity on Attitudes toward Abortion, Divorce, and Gender Equality: Does Cultural Context Make a Difference?" *EurAmerica* 43 (1): 213–53.

Adamczyk, Amy, Katherine Boyd, and Brittany E. Hayes. 2016. "Place Matters: Contextualizing the Roles of Religion and Race for Understanding

Americans' Attitudes about Homosexuality." *Social Science Research* 57:1–16.

Adamczyk, Amy, and Yen-hsin Alice Cheng. 2015. "Explaining Attitudes about Homosexuality in Confucian and Non-Confucian Nations: Is There a 'Cultural' Influence?" *Social Science Research* 51:276–89.

Adamczyk, Amy, and Jacob Felson. 2006. "Friends' Religiosity and First Sex." *Social Science Research* 35 (4): 924–47.

———. 2012. "The Effect of Religion-Supported Programs on Health-Related Behaviors in Adolescence." *Review of Religious Research* 54 (4): 469–97.

Adamczyk, Amy, and Brittany E. Hayes. 2012. "Religion and Sexual Behaviors Understanding the Influence of Islamic Cultures and Religious Affiliation for Explaining Sex Outside of Marriage." *American Sociological Review* 77 (5): 723–46.

Adamczyk, Amy, Chunrye Kim, and Lauren Paradis. 2015. "Investigating Differences in How the News Media Views Homosexuality across Nations: An Analysis of the United States, South Africa, and Uganda." *Sociological Forum* 30 (4): 1038–58.

Adamczyk, Amy, and Ian Palmer. 2008. "Religion and Initiation into Marijuana Use: The Deterring Role of Religious Friends." *Journal of Drug Issues* 38 (3): 717–41.

Adamczyk, Amy, and Cassady Pitt. 2009. "Shaping Attitudes about Homosexuality: The Role of Religion and Cultural Context." *Social Science Research* 38 (2): 338–51.

Adorno, Theodor W., Else Frenkel-Brunswik, Daniel Levinson, and Nevitt Sanford. 1950. *The Authoritarian Personality.* New York: Harper & Brothers.

Agadjanian, Victor, and Cecilia Menjívar. 2008. "Talking about the 'Epidemic of the Millennium': Religion, Informal Communication, and HIV/AIDS in Sub-Saharan Africa." *Social Problems* 55 (3): 301–21.

Agence France-Presse. 2015. "Malaysian Cartoonist Zunar Arrested for Criticising Anwar Ibrahim Ruling." *Guardian.* Retrieved February 13, 2015. www.theguardian.com/world/2015/feb/11/malaysian-cartoonist-zunar-arrested-for-criticising-anwar-ibrahim-ruling.

Akers, Ronald L. 2009. *Social Learning and Social Structure: A General Theory of Crime and Deviance.* New Brunswick, NJ: Transaction Books.

Alagappar, Ponmalar N., and Karamjeet Kaur. 2009. "The Representation of Homosexuality: A Content Analysis in a Malaysian Newspaper." *Language in India* 9 (10): 9.

Allen, Jafari. 2011. *¡Venceremos?: The Erotics of Black Self-Making in Cuba.* Durham, NC: Duke University Press.

Allen, Robert. 2016. "Comparing and Contrasting Eastern Orthodox and Roman Catholics." Our Everyday Life. Retrieved August 8, 2016. http://peopleof.oureverydaylife.com/comparing-contrasting-eastern-orthodox-roman-catholics-5741.html.

Almond, Gabriel A., R. Scott Appleby, and Emmanuel Sivan. 2003. *Strong Religion: The Rise of Fundamentalisms around the World.* Chicago: University of Chicago Press.

Altemeyer, Bob. 1998. "The 'Other' Authoritarian." *Advances in Experimental Social Psychology* 30:47–92.

Alwin, Duane F., and Jon A. Krosnick. 1991. "Aging, Cohorts, and the Stability of Sociopolitical Orientations over the Life Span." *American Journal of Sociology* 97 (1): 169–95.

Aminah, Assami, and Umm Muhammad, trans. 2011. *The Noble Qur'an*. Jeddah, Saudi Arabia: Saheeh International.

Amnesty International. 2015. "Malaysia: Anwar Verdict Will Have Chilling Effect on Freedom of Expression." Amnesty International. Retrieved February 13, 2015. www.amnesty.org/en/news/malaysia-anwar-verdict-will-have-chilling-effect-freedom-expression-2015-02-10.

Anaya, Lauren A. 2014. "Policymaking in the Italian Courts: The Affermazione Civile Project and the Struggle over Recognition of Rights for Same-Sex Couples in Italy." *Anthropological Journal of European Cultures* 23 (1): 40–58.

Andersen, Robert, and Tina Fetner. 2008a. "Cohort Differences in Tolerance of Homosexuality: Attitudinal Change in Canada and the United States, 1981–2000." *Public Opinion Quarterly* 72 (2): 311–30.

————. 2008b. "Economic Inequality and Intolerance: Attitudes toward Homosexuality in 35 Democracies." *American Journal of Political Science* 52 (4): 942–58.

Anderson, Allen F., and Vincent E. Gil. 1994. "Prostitution and Public Policy in the People's Republic of China: An Analysis of the Rehabilitative Ideal." *International Criminal Justice Review* 4 (1): 23–36.

Aral, S. O., and Lieve Fransen. 1995. "STD/HIV Prevention in Turkey: Planning a Sequence of Interventions." *AIDS Education and Prevention: Official Publication of the International Society for AIDS Education* 7 (6): 544–53.

Arat, Zehra, and Charlotte Nuñez. 2014. "Violence, Tolerance and Recognition: Approaches to the LGBTI Rights in Turkey." Paper presented at the annual meeting of the American Political Science Association, Washington, DC, August 28–31. Retrieved March 4, 2015. http://papers.ssrn.com/sol3/papers.cfm?abstract_id=2453041.

Association of Religious Data Archives (ARDA). 2011. "Cross-National Socio-Economic and Religion Data." Retrieved September 21, 2014. www.thearda.com/Archive/Files/Descriptions/ECON11.asp.

————. 2013. "National Profiles, United States (General)." Retrieved September 26, 2013. www.thearda.com/internationalData/countries/Country_234_1.asp.

————. n.d. "International Religious Freedom Data, Aggregate File (2003–2008)." Retrieved April 16, 2015. www.thearda.com/Archive/Files/Descriptions/IRFAGG2.asp.

————. n.d. "Malaysia, Religion and Social Profile, National Profiles." Retrieved February 13, 2015. www.thearda.com/internationalData/countries/Country_139_1.asp.

————. n.d. "National Profile of Italy." Retrieved July 22, 2015. www.thearda.com/internationalData/countries/Country_115_5.asp.

————. n.d. "National Profile of Russia." Retrieved October 4, 2015. www.thearda.com/internationalData/countries/Country_186_5.asp.

———. n.d. "National Profiles." Retrieved January 26, 2015. www.thearda .com/internationalData/countries/Country_215_5.asp.

———. n.d. "Religion and Social Profile, National Profiles, International Data." Retrieved April 7, 2015. www.thearda.com/internationalData/index .asp.

———. n.d. "Taiwan, Religion and Social Profile, National Profiles | International Data." Retrieved June 10, 2015. www.thearda.com/internationalData /countries/Country_50_1.asp.

Asal, Victor, Udi Sommer, and Paul G. Harwood. 2013. "Original Sin: A Cross-National Study of the Legality of Homosexual Acts." *Comparative Political Studies* 46 (3): 320–51.

Asia Sentinel. 2011. "Taiwan's Astonishing Abortion Rate." Retrieved June 10, 2015. www.asiasentinel.com/society/taiwans-astonishing-abortion-rate/.

Associated Press. 2010. "Spain OKs New Abortion Law, Angers Church." NBC News. Retrieved August 8, 2016. www.nbcnews.com/id/35565952/ns/world_news-europe/t/spain-oks-new-abortion-law-angers-church/#.VeNqntNViko.

Awondo, Patrick, Peter Geschiere, and Graeme Reid. 2012. "Homophobic Africa? Toward a More Nuanced View." *African Studies Review* 55 (3): 145–68.

Ayoub, Phillip M. 2015. "Contested Norms in New-Adopter States: International Determinants of LGBT Rights Legislation." *European Journal of International Relations* 21 (2): 293–322.

———. 2016. *When States Come Out: Europe's Sexual Minorities and the Politics of Visibility*. Cambridge: Cambridge University Press.

Baba, Ismail. 2001. "Gay and Lesbian Couples in Malaysia." *Journal of Homosexuality* 40 (3–4): 143–63.

Bahati, David. 2009. *The Anti-homosexuality Bill, 2009*. Entebbe, Uganda: Uganda Printing and Publishing. Retrieved August 26, 2016. www.publiceye .org/publications/globalizing-the-culture-wars/pdf/uganda-bill-september-09 .pdf.

Baiocco, Roberto, Lilybeth Fontanesi, Federica Santamaria, Salvatore Ioverno, Emma Baumgartner, and Fiorenzo Laghi. 2014. "Coming Out during Adolescence: Perceived Parents' Reactions and Internalized Sexual Stigma." *Journal of Health Psychology* 21 (8): 1809–13.

Bakan, Ömer. 2014. "Representations of Female Athletes in Turkish Media: A Content Analysis of Three Newspapers." *Journal of Research in Gender Studies* (1): 881–94.

Balogun, Ishola, and Ebun Sessou. 2012. "Life in Nigeria Is like Slave Camp." *Vanguard News*, February 25. Retrieved October 1, 2014. www.vanguardngr .com/2012/02/life-in-nigeria-is-like-slave-camp/.

Balzer, Carsten, and Jan Simon Hutta. 2012. *Transrespect versus Transphobia Worldwide: A Comparative Review of the Human-Rights Situation of Gender-Variant/Trans People*. Berlin: Transgender Europe (TGEU). Retrieved March 9, 2015. www.transrespect-transphobia.org/uploads/downloads /Publications/TvT_research-report.pdf.

Bandeira, Luiz Alberto Moniz. 2006. "Brazil as a Regional Power and Its Relations with the United States." *Latin American Perspectives* 33 (3): 12–27.

Bao, Huai. 2012. "Buddhism: Rethinking Sexual Misconduct." *Journal of Community Positive Practices,* no. 2, 303–21.

Barnes, Catherine. 2008. "International Isolation and Pressure for Change in South Africa." *Accord* 19:36–39.

Baron, Reuben M., and David A. Kenny. 1986. "The Moderator–Mediator Variable Distinction in Social Psychological Research: Conceptual, Strategic, and Statistical Considerations." *Journal of Personality and Social Psychology* 51 (6): 1173.

Barrick, Audrey. 2007. "Study: Majority of Protestants Say Alcohol Consumption Is Not a Sin." *Christian Post,* September 26. Retrieved October 9, 2015. www.christianpost.com/news/study-majority-of-protestants-say-alcohol-consumption-is-not-a-sin-29470/.

Barro, Robert J., and Jason Hwang. 2008. *Religious Conversion in 40 Countries.* Cambridge, MA: National Bureau of Economic Research. Retrieved September 23, 2014. www.nber.org/papers/w13689.pdf.

Barro, Robert J., and Jong-Wha Lee. 2001. "International Data on Educational Attainment: Updates and Implications." *Oxford Economic Papers* 53 (3): 541–63.

———. 2013. "A New Data Set of Educational Attainment in the World, 1950–2010." *Journal of Development Economics* 104:184–98.

Basow, Susan A., and Kelly Johnson. 2000. "Predictors of Homophobia in Female College Students." *Sex Roles* 42 (5–6): 391–404.

BBC News. 2011. "Uganda Bars Media from Outing Gays." Retrieved December 22, 2014. www.bbc.co.uk/news/world-africa-12107596.

———. 2014. "World Bank Postpones $90m Uganda Loan over Anti-Gay Law." Retrieved December 22, 2014. www.bbc.com/news/world-africa-26378230.

———. 2015. "Italy Breaches Rights over Gay Marriage—European Court." Retrieved July 24, 2015. www.bbc.com/news/world-europe-33611955.

Beer, William R., and James E. Jacob. 1985. *Language Policy and National Unity.* Totowa, NJ: Rowman and Allanheld.

Bell, Daniel. 1976. *The Cultural Contradictions of Capitalism.* New York: Basic Books.

Benson, Rodney, and Abigail C. Saguy. 2005. "Constructing Social Problems in an Age of Globalization: A French–American Comparison." *American Sociological Review* 70 (2): 233–59.

Bereket, Tarik, and Barry D. Adam. 2008. "Navigating Islam and Same-Sex Liaisons among Men in Turkey." *Journal of Homosexuality* 55 (2): 204–22.

Berger, Peter L. 1997. "Epistemological Modesty: An Interview with Peter Berger." *Christian Century* 114 (30): 974.

———. 2011. *The Sacred Canopy: Elements of a Sociological Theory of Religion.* New York: Open Road Media.

Bernini, Stefania. 2010. "Family Politics, the Catholic Church and the Transformation of Family Life in the Second Republic." *Journal of Modern Italian Studies* 13 (3): 305–24.

Berry, Lynn. 2014. "Russian President Putin Links Gays to Pedophiles." NBC News. Retrieved August 8, 2016. http://worldnews.nbcnews.com/_news/2014/01/19/22358854-russian-president-putin-links-gays-to-pedophiles.

Bevins, Vincent. 2015. "In Brazil, Homicide Rate Still High despite Increased Prosperity." *Los Angeles Times.* Retrieved August 5, 2015. www.latimes.com/world/brazil/la-fg-ff-brazil-crime-20150522-story.html.

Bialik, Carl. 2014. "Catholics Are More Progressive than the Vatican, and Almost Everyone Else." FiveThirtyEight, October 17. Retrieved August 27, 2015. http://fivethirtyeight.com/datalab/catholics-are-more-progressive-than-the-vatican-and-almost-everyone-else/.

Bibby, Reginald W. 1978. "Why Conservative Churches Really Are Growing: Kelley Revisited." *Journal for the Scientific Study of Religion* 17 (2): 129–37.

Billig, Michael, and Duncan Cramer. 1990. "Authoritarianism and Demographic Variables as Predictors of Racial Attitudes in Britain." *Journal of Ethnic and Migration Studies* 16 (2): 199–211.

Black, Phil, and Alla Eshchenko. 2014. "Russia Enacts Anti-Gay Adoption Ban." *CNN.* Retrieved October 2, 2015. www.cnn.com/2014/02/13/world/europe/russia-same-sex-marriage-adoption-ban/.

Blackwood, Evelyn. 2007. "Regulation of Sexuality in Indonesian Discourse: Normative Gender, Criminal Law and Shifting Strategies of Control." *Culture, Health & Sexuality* 9 (3): 293–307.

Boellstorff, Tom. 2004. "The Emergence of Political Homophobia in Indonesia: Masculinity and National Belonging." *Ethnos* 69 (4): 465–86.

———. 2006. "Gay and Lesbian Indonesians and the Idea of the Nation." *Social Analysis* 50 (1): 158–63.

Boesveld, Sarah. 2012. "Anderson Cooper Comes out of the Closet: Does It Even Matter Anymore?" *National Post,* July 2. Retrieved May 22, 2014. http://news.nationalpost.com/news/anderson-cooper-comes-out-of-the-closet-does-it-even-matter-anymore.

Bogner, Alexander, Beate Littig, and Wolfgang Menz. 2009. *Interviewing Experts.* Basingstoke, Hampshire, England: Palgrave Macmillan.

Bogner, Alexander, and Wolfgang Menz. 2009. "The Theory-Generating Expert Interview: Epistemological Interest, Forms of Knowledge, Interaction." In *Interviewing Experts,* edited by Alexander Bogner, Beate Littig, and Wolfgang Menz, 43–80. London: Palgrave Macmillan.

Bohan, Janis S. 1996. *Psychology and Sexual Orientation: Coming to Terms.* New York: Routledge. Retrieved June 5, 2015. https://books.google.com/books?hl = en&lr = &id = vcV5rFfehNsC&oi = fnd&pg = PP9&dq = Psychology+and+sexual+orientation:+Coming+to+terms&ots = Q8DY8bUp9y&sig = ZdHjE3uLAxPTmsDG4E-aAA9WOow.

Bohon, Dave. 2013. "200,000 Reportedly March for Traditional Marriage in Taiwan." *New American.* Retrieved May 29, 2015. www.thenewamerican.com/world-news/asia/item/17101–200-000-reportedly-march-for-traditional-marriage-in-taiwan?tmpl = component&print = 1.

Bond, Michael Harris. 1991. *Beyond the Chinese Face: Insights from Psychology.* New York: Oxford University Press.

Boserup, Ester. 1985. "Economic and Demographic Interrelationships in Sub-Saharan Africa." *Population and Development Review* 11 (3): 383–97.

Bosi, Lorenzo. 2008. "Explaining the Emergence Process of the Civil Rights Protest in Northern Ireland (1945–1968): Insights from a Relational Social Movement Approach." *Journal of Historical Sociology* 21 (2–3): 242–71.

Botha, Kevan, and Edwin Cameron. 1997. "South Africa." In *Sociolegal Control of Homosexuality: A Multi-Nation Comparison,* edited by D. J. West and R. Green, 5–42. New York: Springer.

Bowleg, Lisa. 2013. "'Once You've Blended the Cake, You Can't Take the Parts Back to the Main Ingredients': Black Gay and Bisexual Men's Descriptions and Experiences of Intersectionality." *Sex Roles* 68 (11–12): 754–67.

Bowman, Karlyn, Andrew Rugg, and Jennifer Marsico. 2013. *Polls on Attitudes on Homosexuality and Gay Marriage.* American Enterprise Institute. Retrieved August 8, 2016. www.aei.org/outlook/politics-and-public-opinion/polls/polls-on-attitudes-on-homosexuality-gay-marriage-march-2013/.

Box, Zira. 2010. *España, año cero: La construcción simbólica del franquismo* [Spain, year zero: The symbolic construction of Francoism]. Madrid: Alianza Editorial.

Brandes, Stanley. 2009. "Torophiles and Torophobes: The Politics of Bulls and Bullfights in Contemporary Spain." *Anthropological Quarterly* 82 (3): 779–94.

Branigan, Tania. 2012. "Taiwan Offers Baby Bonus to Fix Plummeting Birth Rate." *Guardian.* Retrieved June 8, 2015. www.theguardian.com/world/2012/jan/23/taiwan-low-birth-rate.

Breslow, Norman E., and David G. Clayton. 1993. "Approximate Inference in Generalized Linear Mixed Models." *Journal of the American Statistical Association* 88 (421): 9–25.

Brewer, Paul R. 2003. "The Shifting Foundations of Public Opinion about Gay Rights." *Journal of Politics* 65 (4): 1208–20.

——— 2007. *Value War: Public Opinion and the Politics of Gay Rights.* Lanham, MD: Rowman and Littlefield.

Brooke, James. 1998. "Gay Man Dies from Attack, Fanning Outrage and Debate." *New York Times,* October 13. Retrieved May 11, 2016. www.nytimes.com/1998/10/13/us/gay-man-dies-from-attack-fanning-outrage-and-debate.html.

Brooks, Clem, and Catherine Bolzendahl. 2004. "The Transformation of US Gender Role Attitudes: Cohort Replacement, Social-Structural Change, and Ideological Learning." *Social Science Research* 33 (1): 106–33.

Brown, Michael J., and Ernesto Henriquez. 2008. "Socio-Demographic Predictors of Attitudes towards Gays and Lesbians." *Individual Differences Research* 6 (3): 193–202.

Bruce, Steve. 1993. "Religion and Rational Choice: A Critique of Economic Explanations of Religious Behavior." *Sociology of Religion* 54 (2): 193–205.

———. 1999. *Choice and Religion: A Critique of Rational Choice Theory.* Oxford University Press on Demand.

Bühler, Georg, trans. 1886. *Manusmriti: The Laws of Manu.* Oxford: Oxford University Press.

Bumpass, Larry L., James A. Sweet, and Andrew Cherlin. 1991. "The Role of Cohabitation in Declining Rates of Marriage." *Journal of Marriage and Family* 53 (4): 913–27.

Burchardt, Marian. 2013. "Equals before the Law? Public Religion and Queer Activism in the Age of Judicial Politics in South Africa." *Journal of Religion in Africa* 43 (3): 237–60.

Burdette, Amy M., Christopher G. Ellison, and Terrence D. Hill. 2005. "Conservative Protestantism and Tolerance toward Homosexuals: An Examination of Potential Mechanisms." *Sociological Inquiry* 75 (2): 177–96.

Burkett, Steven R., and Mervin White. 1974. "Hellfire and Delinquency: Another Look." *Journal for the Scientific Study of Religion* 13 (4): 455–62.

Burstein, Paul. 2003. "The Impact of Public Opinion on Public Policy: A Review and an Agenda." *Political Research Quarterly* 56 (1): 29–40.

Butler, Judith. 1990. *Gender Trouble: Feminism and the Subversion of Identity.* New York: Routledge.

Cabezón, José Ignacio. 1993. "Homosexuality and Buddhism." In *Homosexuality and World Religions,* edited by A. Swidler, 81–101. Valley Forge, PA: Trinity Press International.

Calvo, Borobia Kerman. 2005. *Pursuing Membership in the Polity: The Spanish Gay and Lesbian Movement in Comparative Perspective (1970–1997).* Madrid: Instituto Juan March de Estudios e Investigaciones.

———. 2007. "Sacrifices That Pay: Polity Membership, Political Opportunities and the Recognition of Same-Sex Marriage in Spain." *South European Society & Politics* 12 (3): 295–314.

Cameron, Edwin, and Mark Gevisser. 2013. *Defiant Desire: Gay and Lesbian Lives in South Africa.* New York: Routledge.

Cao, Liqun, Lanying Huang, and Ivan Sun. 2015. "From Authoritarian Policing to Democratic Policing: A Case Study of Taiwan." *Policing and Society* 26 (6): 1–17.

Cao, Liqun, and Steven Stack. 2010. "Exploring Terra Incognita: Family Values and Prostitution Acceptance in China." *Journal of Criminal Justice* 38 (4): 531–37.

Cardoso, Fernando Luiz. 2009. "Similar Faces of Same-Sex Sexual Behavior: A Comparative Ethnographical Study in Brazil, Turkey, and Thailand." *Journal of Homosexuality* 56 (4): 457–84.

Carroll, Aengus, and Lucas Paoli Itaborahy. 2015. *State-Sponsored Homophobia 2015: A World Survey of Laws: Criminalisation, Protection and Recognition of Same-Sex Love.* Geneva: International Lesbian, Gay, Bisexual, Trans and Intersex Association. Retrieved August 10, 2016. http://old.ilga .org/Statehomophobia/ILGA_State_Sponsored_Homophobia_2015.pdf.

Central Intelligence Agency. n.d. "Country Comparison: Total Fertility Rate." In *The World Factbook.* Retrieved August 17, 2016. https://www.cia.gov /library/publications/the-world-factbook/rankorder/2127rank.html.

———. n.d. "GDP: Composition, by Sector of Origin." In *The World Factbook.* Retrieved July 26, 2015. https://www.cia.gov/library/publications/the-world-factbook/fields/2012.html.

Chan, Rachel. 2013. "ROC Gender Imbalance at Birth Falls to 25-Year Low." *Taiwan Today*. Retrieved June 11, 2015. http://taiwantoday.tw/ct.asp?xItem = 203081&ctNode = 413.

Chance, Matthew. 2014. "Why Russia Is Hung Up on Homosexuality." CNN. Retrieved September 23, 2015. www.cnn.com/2014/12/16/world/europe /chance-russia-gay-rights/.

Chauncey, George. 1994. *Gay New York: Gender, Urban Culture, and the Making of the Gay Male World, 1890–1940*. New York: Basic Books.

Cheng, K'Un. 1944. "Familism, the Foundation of Chinese Social Organization." *Social Forces* 23 (1): 50–59.

Cheng, Yan, Chaohua Lou, Ersheng Gao, Mark R. Emerson, and Laurie S. Zabin. 2012. "The Relationship between External Contact and Unmarried Adolescents' and Young Adults' Traditional Beliefs in Three East Asian Cities: A Cross-Sectional Analysis." *Journal of Adolescent Health* 50 (3): S4–11.

Cheng, Yen-hsin Alice. 2016. "More Education, Fewer Divorces? Industrialization and Shifting Education Differentials of Divorce in Taiwan from 1975 to 2010." *Demographic Research* 34 (33): 927–42. Retrieved August 26, 2016. www.demographic-research.org/volumes/vol34/33/34-33.pdf.

Cheng, Yen-hsin Alice, Fen-chieh Felice Wu, and Amy Adamczyk. 2016. "Changing Attitudes toward Homosexuality in Taiwan, 1995–2012." *Chinese Sociological Review* 48 (4): 317–45.

Chong, Dennis. 1993. "How People Think, Reason, and Feel about Rights and Liberties." *American Journal of Political Science* 37 (3): 867–99.

Chothia, Farouk. 2014. "Who Are Nigeria's Boko Haram Islamists?" BBC News, May 20. Retrieved October 1, 2014. www.bbc.com/news/world-africa-13809501.

Chuang, Ya-Chung. 2013. *Democracy on Trial: Social Movements and Cultural Politics in Postauthoritarian Taiwan*. Hong Kong: Chinese University Press.

Chung, Douglas K. 1992. "Asian Cultural Commonalities: A Comparison with Mainstream American Culture." In *Social Work Practice with Asian Americans*, vol. 20, edited by S.M. Furuto, R. Biswas, D.K. Chung, K. Murase, and F. Ross-Sheriff, 27–44. Thousand Oaks, CA: SAGE.

CIA World Factbook. 2013. *The World Factbook, 2013–14*. Washington DC: Central Intelligence Agency. https://www.cia.gov/library/publications/the-world-factbook/index.html.

CIA World Factbook. 2015. *The World Factbook, 2014–2015*. Washington DC: Central Intelligence Agency. https://www.cia.gov/library/publications /the-world-factbook/rankorder/2119rank.html.

Ciaglia, Antonio. 2013. "Politics in the Media and the Media in Politics: A Comparative Study of the Relationship between the Media and Political Systems in Three European Countries." *European Journal of Communication* 28 (5): 541–55.

Cnaan, Ram A., Jill W. Sinha, and Charlene C. McGrew. 2004. "Congregations as Social Service Providers: Services, Capacity, Culture, and Organizational Behavior." *Administration in Social Work* 28 (3–4): 47–68.

CNN. 2001. "Same-Sex Marriage Legalized in Amsterdam." CNN.com. Retrieved May 22, 2014. http://transcripts.cnn.com/TRANSCRIPTS/0104 /01/sm.10.html.

Cock, Jacklyn. 2003. "Engendering Gay and Lesbian Rights: The Equality Clause in the South African Constitution." *Women's Studies International Forum* 26 (1): 35–45.

Cohen, Jon S. 1967. "Financing Industrialization in Italy, 1894–1914: The Partial Transformation of a Late-Comer." *Journal of Economic History* 27 (3): 363–82.

Coleman, James S. 1986. "Social Theory, Social Research, and a Theory of Action." *American Journal of Sociology* 91 (6): 1309–35.

Collins, Randall. 1981. "On the Microfoundations of Macrosociology." *American Journal of Sociology* 86 (5): 984–1014.

Commission on Security and Cooperation in Europe. 2012. "Cardin, Hastings Condemn Anti-Gay Hate Speech." Retrieved March 12, 2015. https://www .csce.gov/international-impact/press-and-media/press-releases/cardin-hastings-condemn-anti-gay-hate-speech.

Conway, Daniel. 2009. "Queering Apartheid: The National Party's 1987 'Gay Rights' Election Campaign in Hillbrow." *Journal of Southern African Studies* 35 (4): 849–63.

Cook, Sarah. 2013. *The Long Shadow of Chinese Censorship: How the Communist Party's Media Restrictions Affect News Outlets around the World.* Washington, DC: Center for International Media Assistance. Retrieved June 12, 2015. http://apo.org.au/research/long-shadow-chinese-censorship-how-communist-partys-media-restrictions-affect-news-outlets.

Cooper, Hellene. 2007. "Ahmadinejad, at Columbia, Parries and Puzzles." *New York Times,* November 25. Retrieved May 22, 2014. www.nytimes .com/2007/09/25/world/middleeast/25iran.html?_r = 0.

Cooper, Jonathan. 2015. "Kenya's Anti-Gay Laws Are Leaving LGBT Community at the Mercy of the Mob." *Guardian,* October 8. Retrieved April 29, 2016. /www.theguardian.com/global-development/2015/oct/08/kenya-anti-gay-laws-lgbt-community-mercy-of-mob.

Cooper, Sara, Patricia Anafi, Christina Sun, Nasheen Naidoo, Priscilla Reddy, and David Buchanan. 2008–9. "Content Analysis of Local Newspaper Coverage of the Microbicide Trials in South Africa." *International Quarterly of Community Health Education* 29 (2): 105–21.

Costa, Angelo Brandelli, Rodrigo Oliva Peroni, Denise Ruschel Bandeira, and Henrique Caetano Nard. 2013. "Homophobia or Sexism? A Systematic Review of Prejudice against Nonheterosexual Orientation in Brazil." *International Journal of Psychology* 48 (5): 900–909.

Coyne, Imelda T. 1997. "Sampling in Qualitative Research: Purposeful and Theoretical Sampling; Merging or Clear Boundaries?" *Journal of Advanced Nursing* 26 (3): 623–30.

Creswell, John W. 2004. *Research Design: Qualitative, Quantitative and Mixed Methods Approaches.* Thousand Oaks, CA: SAGE.

Creswell, John W., Vicki L. Plano Clark, Michelle L. Gutmann, and William E. Hanson. 2003. "Advanced Mixed Methods Research Designs." In *Hand-*

book of Mixed Methods in Social and Behavioral Research, edited by A. Tashakkori and C. Teddlie, 209–40. Thousand Oaks, CA: SAGE.

Crockett, Alasdair, and David Voas. 2006. "Generations of Decline: Religious Change in 20th-Century Britain." Journal for the Scientific Study of Religion 45 (4): 567–84.

Croucher, Sheila. 2002. "South Africa's Democratisation and the Politics of Gay Liberation." Journal of Southern African Studies 28 (2): 315–30.

Currier, Ashley. 2012. Out in Africa: LGBT Organizing in Namibia and South Africa. Minneapolis: University of Minnesota Press.

Dalton, Russell J. 1984. "Cognitive Mobilization and Partisan Dealignment in Advanced Industrial Democracies." Journal of Politics 46 (1): 264–84.

Dalton, Russell J., and Nhu-Ngoc T. Ong. 2005. "Authority Orientations and Democratic Attitudes: A Test of the 'Asian Values' Hypothesis." Japanese Journal of Political Science 6 (2): 211–31.

Damm, Jens. 2005. "Same Sex Desire and Society in Taiwan, 1970–1987." China Quarterly 181:67–81.

———. 2011. "Discrimination and Backlash against Homosexual Groups." In Politics of Difference in Taiwan, edited by T. Ngo and H. Wang, 152–80. London and New York: Routledge.

Dataxis. 2015. "PAY-TV / FTA Broadcasting in Uganda." Dataxis, April 22. Retrieved May 19, 2016. http://dataxis.com/pay-tv-fta-broadcasting-in-uganda/.

Davia, María A., and Nuria Legazpe. 2014. "Educational Attainment and Maternity in Spain: Not Only 'When' but Also 'How.'" Review of Economics of the Household 13 (4): 871–900.

Day, Elizabeth. 2011. "Why Was I Born Gay in Africa?" Guardian, March 26. Retrieved May 22, 2014. www.theguardian.com/world/2011/mar/27/uganda-gay-lesbian-immigration-asylum.

de Albuquerque Júnior, Durval Muniz, Rodrigo Ceballos, and Laurence Hallewell. 2002. "Urban Trails, Human Traps: The Construction of Territories of Pleasure and Pain in the Lives of Male Homosexuals in the Brazilian Northeast in the 1970s and 1980s." Latin American Perspectives 29 (2): 139–62.

De Cecco, Marcello. 2007. "Italy's Dysfunctional Political Economy." West European Politics 30 (4): 763–83.

De la Dehesa, Rafael. 2010. Queering the Public Sphere in Mexico and Brazil: Sexual Rights Movements in Emerging Democracies. Durham, NC: Duke University Press.

D'Emilio, John. 1984. Sexual Politics, Sexual Communities: The Making of a Homosexual Minority in the United States, 1940–1970. Chicago: University of Chicago Press.

Dennis, George T. 1990. "1054: The East-West Schism." Christian History. Retrieved May 26, 2016. www.christianitytoday.com/ch/1990/issue28/2820.html?start = 1.

Department of Household Registration. 2013. "Population Aged 15 and Above by Age, Sex, and Education Attainment" [in Chinese]." Retrieved January 25, 2014. www.ris.gov.tw/346.

Detenber, Benjamin H., Shirley S. Ho, Rachel L. Neo, Shelly Malik, and Mark Cenite. 2013. "Influence of Value Predispositions, Interpersonal Contact, and Mediated Exposure on Public Attitudes toward Homosexuals in Singapore: Public Attitudes toward Homosexuals." *Asian Journal of Social Psychology* 16 (3): 181–96.

DGBAS. 2014. *Statistical Database for Income and Economic Indicators* [in Chinese], vol. 2013. Taipei: Directorate General of Budget, Accounting and Statistics, Executive Yuan. www.Dgbas.Gov.Tw/Point.Asp?Index=1.

Diaz, Rafael M., George Ayala, Edward Bein, Jeff Henne, and Barbara V. Marin. 2001. "The Impact of Homophobia, Poverty, and Racism on the Mental Health of Gay and Bisexual Latino Men: Findings from 3 US Cities." *American Journal of Public Health* 91 (6): 927.

Dipartimento per le Pari Opportunità. 2013. *Linee guida per un'informazione rispettosa delle persone LGBT* [Guidelines for information respectful of LGBT people]. Governo Italiano, Presidenza del Consiglio dei Ministri. Retrieved May 26, 2016. www.pariopportunita.gov.it/images/lineeguida_informazionelgbt.pdf.

Dominguez-Folgueras, Marta, and Teresa Castro-Martin. 2013. "Cohabitation in Spain: No Longer a Marginal Path to Family Formation." *Journal of Marriage and Family* 75 (2): 422–37.

Dommaraju, Premchand, and Gavin Jones. 2011. "Divorce Trends in Asia." *Asian Journal of Social Science* 39 (6): 725–50.

Durkheim, Emile. 1912. *The Elementary Forms of Religious Life.* New York: Free Press.

———. 1951. *Suicide: A Study in Sociology.* Translated by J. A. Spaulding and G. Simpson. Glencoe, IL: Free Press. First published 1897.

———. 2014. *The Division of Labor in Society.* New York: Simon and Schuster.

Duyan, Veli, and Gülsüm Duyan. 2005. "Turkish Social Work Students' Attitudes toward Sexuality." *Sex Roles* 52 (9–10): 697–706.

Eccleston, Jennifer. 2001. "Same-Sex Marriage Legalized in Amsterdam." CNN.com.transcripts. Retrieved May 22, 2014. http://transcripts.cnn.com /TRANSCRIPTS/0104/01/sm.10.html.

Economist Intelligence Unit. 2008. "The Economist Intelligence Unit's Index of Democracy 2008." *Economist.* Retrieved May 16, 2016. http://graphics.eiu .com/PDF/Democracy%20Index%202008.pdf.

———. 2013. "Gay Rights in South-East Asia: Fifty Shades of Pink." *Economist.* Retrieved April 8, 2015. www.economist.com/news/asia/21580526-some-countries-consider-gay-marriage-elsewhere-attitudes-harden-fifty-shades-pink.

Elias, Stephen, and Clare Noone. 2011. "The Growth and Development of the Indonesian Economy." *Reserve Bank of Australia Bulletin,* December Quarter 2011, 33–43. Retrieved August 8, 2016. www.rba.gov.au/publications /bulletin/2011/dec/pdf/bu-1211-4.pdf.

Eliason, Michele J. 1997. "The Prevalence and Nature of Biphobia in Heterosexual Undergraduate Students." *Archives of Sexual Behavior* 26 (3): 317–26.

Ellison, Christopher G., Gabriel A. Acevedo, and Aida I. Ramos-Wada. 2011. "Religion and Attitudes toward Same-Sex Marriage among US Latinos." *Social Science Quarterly* 92 (1): 35–56.

Ellison, Christopher G., and Marc A. Musick. 1993. "Southern Intolerance: A Fundamentalist Effect?" *Social Forces* 72 (2): 379–98.

Ellison, Christopher G., and Darren E. Sherkat. 1995. "The 'Semi-Involuntary Institution' Revisited: Regional Variations in Church Participation among Black Americans." *Social Forces* 73 (4): 1415–37.

El Mundo. 1996. "Editorial: Orgullo Gay." *El Mundo*, June 30.

El-Tayeb, Fatima. 2011. *European Others: Queering Ethnicity in Postnational Europe.* Minneapolis: University of Minnesota Press.

Emerson, Michael O., and David Hartman. 2006. "The Rise of Religious Fundamentalism." *Annual Review of Sociology* 32 (1): 127–44.

d'Emilio, John. 2012. *Sexual Politics, Sexual Communities.* Chicago: University of Chicago Press.

Engbarth, Dennis. 2013. "Taiwan Lawmakers Push 'Marriage Equality' Bill." Inter Press Service. Retrieved June 10, 2015. www.ipsnews.net/2013/10/taiwan-lawmakers-push-marriage-equality-bill/.

Epprecht, Marc. 2013. *Sexuality and Social Justice in Africa: Rethinking Homophobia and Forging Resistance.* London: Zed Books.

Erdő, Péter. 2014. "11a Congregazione generale: 'Relatio post disceptationem' del Relatore generale." *Bollettino della Sala Stampa della Santa Sede,* November 13. Retrieved August 27, 2015. http://press.vatican.va/content/salastampa/it/bollettino/pubblico/2014/10/13/0751/03037.html.

Erofeeva, Lyubov Vladimirovna. 2013. "Traditional Christian Values and Women's Reproductive Rights in Modern Russia: Is a Consensus Ever Possible?" *American Journal of Public Health* 103 (11): 1931–34.

Esmer, Yılmaz. 2011. "2011 Türkiye değerler araştırması" [2011 Turkey values survey]. Connected VivaKi. Retrieved April 18, 2015. www.connectedvivaki.com/2011-turkiye-degerler-arastirmasi/.

Esteve, Albert, Ron Lesthaeghe, and Antonio López-Gay. 2012. "The Latin American Cohabitation Boom, 1970–2007." *Population and Development Review* 38 (1): 55–81.

Euronews. 2013. "Reflecting on 12 Years of Gay Marriage in the Netherlands." Retrieved September 15, 2015. www.euronews.com/2013/04/01/reflecting-on-12-years-of-gay-marriage-in-the-netherlands/.

European Commission. 2012. *LGBT Rights in the 2012 Accession Reports.* European Parliament's Intergroup on LGBT Rights. Retrieved May 19, 2016. www.lgbt-ep.eu/wp-content/uploads/2012/10/DOC-20121011-EU-accession-progress-reports-LGBT-Intergroup.pdf.

European Commission. n.d. "European Commission Enlargement, Turkey." Retrieved May 19, 2016. http://ec.europa.eu/enlargement/candidate-countries/turkey/eu_turkey_relations_en.htm.

European Union Election Observation Mission. 2011. *Uganda 2011 Elections: Improvements Marred by Avoidable Failures.* Kampala. Retrieved December 22, 2014. www.eueom.eu/files/pressreleases/english/preliminary_statement_uganda_2011_en.pdf.

Evans, John H. 2002. "Polarization in Abortion Attitudes in US Religious Traditions, 1972–1998." *Sociological Forum* 17 (3): 397–422.

Feng, Yongliang, Chaohua Lou, Ersheng Gao, Xiaowen Tu, Yan Cheng, Mark R. Emerson, and Laurie S. Zabin. 2012. "Adolescents' and Young Adults' Perception of Homosexuality and Related Factors in Three Asian Cities." *Journal of Adolescent Health* 50 (3): S52–60.

Festy, Patrick. 2007. "Legal Recognition of Same-Sex Couples in Europe." *Population* (English edition) 61 (4): 417–53.

Fetner, Tina. 2008. *How the Religious Right Shaped Lesbian and Gay Activism.* Minneapolis: University of Minnesota Press.

File, Thom. 2013. "Computer and Internet Use in the United States: Population Characteristics." U.S. Census Bureau. Retrieved January 27, 2015. https://www.survata.com/docs/Census_Internet.pdf.

Finke, Roger, and Amy Adamczyk. 2008. "Cross-National Moral Beliefs: The Influence of National Religious Context." *Sociological Quarterly* 49 (4): 617–52.

Finke, Roger, Avery M. Guest, and Rodney Stark. 1996. "Mobilizing Local Religious Markets: Religious Pluralism in the Empire State, 1855 to 1865." *American Sociological Review* 61 (2): 203–18.

Finke, Roger, and Rodney Stark. 2005. *The Churching of America, 1776–2005: Winners and Losers in Our Religious Economy.* New Brunswick, NJ: Rutgers University Press.

Finlay, Barbara, and Carol S. Walther. 2003. "The Relation of Religious Affiliation, Service Attendance, and Other Factors to Homophobic Attitudes among University Students." *Review of Religious Research* 44 (4): 370–93.

de Fluviá, A. 1978. "El movimiento homosexual en el estado español." In *El homosexual ante la sociedad enferma,* edited by José Ramón Enríquez, 149–67. Barcelona: Tusquets.

Forero, Juan, 2012. "Brazil's Falling Birth Rate: A 'New Way of Thinking.'" National Public Radio. Retrieved August 9, 2015. www.npr.org/2012/01/15/145133220/brazils-falling-birth-rate-a-new-way-of-thinking.

Fotheringham, Alasdair. 2011. "Spain, the World Capital of Prostitution?" *Independent,* December 4. Retrieved May 26, 2016. www.independent.co.uk/news/world/europe/spain-the-world-capital-of-prostitution-2151581.html.

Freedom House. 2015. "Freedom House." Retrieved February 27, 2015. https://freedomhouse.org/.

———. n.d. "Indonesia: Freedom of the Press, 2014." Retrieved February 27, 2015. https://freedomhouse.org/report/freedom-press/2014/indonesia#.VPC-A_nF-So.

———. n.d. "Italy: Freedom of the Press, 2014." Retrieved July 23, 2015. https://freedomhouse.org/report/freedom-press/2014/italy#.VbCoL_mqoSU.

Freedom to Marry. 2015. "The Freedom to Marry Internationally." Retrieved August 6, 2015. www.freedomtomarry.org/landscape/entry/c/international.

French, John, and Alexandre Fortes. 2012. "Nurturing Hope, Deepening Democracy, and Combating Inequalities in Brazil: Lula, the Workers' Party, and Dilma Rousseff's 2010 Election as President." *Critical Sociology* 38 (6): 777–87.

Froese, Paul. 2004a. "After Atheism: An Analysis of Religious Monopolies in the Post-Communist World." *Sociology of Religion* 65 (1): 57–75.

———. 2004b. "Forced Secularization in Soviet Russia: Why an Atheistic Monopoly Failed." *Journal for the Scientific Study of Religion* 43 (1): 35–50.

Fulton, Aubyn S., Richard L. Gorsuch, and Elizabeth A. Maynard. 1999. "Religious Orientation, Antihomosexual Sentiment, and Fundamentalism among Christians." *Journal for the Scientific Study of Religion* 38 (1): 14–22.

Gander, Kashmira. 2014. "Ugandan Newspaper *Red Pepper* Publishes 'Top 200' Homosexuals List." *Independent.* Retrieved February 12, 2015. www.independent.co.uk/news/world/africa/ugandan-newspaper-publishes-200-top-homosexuals-list-9152442.html.

Gao, Ersheng, Xiayun Zuo, Li Wang, Chaohua Lou, Yan Cheng, and Laurie S. Zabin. 2012. "How Does Traditional Confucian Culture Influence Adolescents' Sexual Behavior in Three Asian Cities?" *Journal of Adolescent Health* 50 (3): S12–17.

Garelli, Franco. 2006. *L'Italia cattolica nell'epoca del pluralismo.* Bologna: Il Mulino.

———. 2011. *Religione all'italiana: L'anima del paese messa a nudo.* Bologna: Il Mulino.

———. 2012. "Flexible Catholicism, Religion and the Church: The Italian Case." *Religions* 4 (1): 1–13.

Garretson, Jeremiah J. 2009. "Changing Media, Changing Minds: The Lesbian and Gay Movement, Television, and Public Opinion." PhD diss., Vanderbilt University, 2009. Retrieved June 24, 2013. http://etd.library.vanderbilt.edu/available/etd-08262009-113016/unrestricted/FinalDraftDissertation.pdf.

Gaskins, Ben, Matt Golder, and David A. Siegel. 2013. "Religious Participation, Social Conservatism, and Human Development." *Journal of Politics* 75 (4): 1125–41.

Gatsiounis, Ioannis. 2011. "Deadly Crackdown on Uganda's Walk-to-Work Protests." *Time,* April 23. Retrieved March 23, 2015. http://content.time.com/time/world/article/0,8599,2067136,00.html.

Gelbal, Selahattin, and Veli Duyan. 2006. "Attitudes of University Students toward Lesbians and Gay Men in Turkey." *Sex Roles* 55 (7–8): 573–79.

GeoHive. n.d. "Urban/Rural Division of Countries for the Years 2015 and 2025." Retrieved January 12, 2015. www.geohive.com/earth/pop_urban.aspx.

George, Nirmala. 2014. "India's Gay and Lesbian Community Demands End to Discrimination at New Delhi March." *Huffpost Gay Voices.* Retrieved October 5, 2015. www.huffingtonpost.com/2014/12/01/new-delhi-gay-lesbian-march-_n_6245802.html.

Gerber, Paula. 2014. "Living a Life of Crime: The Ongoing Criminalisation of Homosexuality within the Commonwealth." *Alternative Law Journal* 39 (2): 78–83.

Gerhards, Jürgen. 2010. "Non-Discrimination towards Homosexuality: The European Union's Policy and Citizens' Attitudes towards Homosexuality in 27 European Countries." *International Sociology* 25 (1): 5–28.

Gerring, John. 2007. "The Case Study: What It Is and What It Does." In *The Oxford Handbook of Comparative Politics*, edited by C. Boix and S. C. Stokes, 90–122. New York: Oxford University Press.

Gettleman, Jeffrey. 2010. "Americans' Role Seen in Uganda Anti-Gay Push." *New York Times*, January 4. Retrieved February 9, 2010. www.nytimes .com/2010/01/04/world/africa/04uganda.html?_r = 0.

———. 2011. "Ugandan Who Spoke Up for Gays Is Beaten to Death." *New York Times*, January 27. Retrieved May 22, 2014. www.nytimes.com /2011/01/28/world/africa/28uganda.html?_r = 1&.

———. 2014. "Uganda Anti-Gay Law Struck Down by Court." *New York Times*, August 2. Retrieved December 22, 2014. www.nytimes.com/2014/08/02 /world/africa/uganda-anti-gay-law-struck-down-by-court.html.

Ghandour, Lilian A., Elie G. Karam, and Wadih E. Maalouf. 2009. "Lifetime Alcohol Use, Abuse and Dependence among University Students in Lebanon: Exploring the Role of Religiosity in Different Religious Faiths." *Addiction* 104 (6): 940–48.

Global Gayz. 2009. "Gay Qatar News & Reports." Retrieved May 26, 2016. http://archive.globalgayz.com/middle-east/qatar/gay-qatar-news-and-reports/.

Global Humanitarian Assistance. n.d. "Who received the most humanitarian assistance in 2013?" Retrieved December 22, 2014. www.globalhumanitarian assistance.org/country-profiles.

Gluck, Caroline. 2007. "Remembering Taiwan's Martial Law." BBC News. Retrieved May 29, 2015. http://news.bbc.co.uk/2/hi/asia-pacific/6294902.stm.

Goodman, J. David. 2011. "Malaysia Gay Festival Is Banned." *New York Times*, November 4. Retrieved February 12, 2015. www.nytimes.com/2011 /11/04/world/asia/malaysia-gay-festival-is-banned.html.

Goodstein, Laurie. 2008. "Conservative Anglicans Plan Rival Conference as Split over Homosexuality Grows." *New York Times*, June 20. Retrieved May 18, 2016. www.nytimes.com/2008/06/20/world/20anglican.html.

Gordon, Raymond. 2005. *Ethnologue: Languages of the World*. 15th ed. Dallas: Sil International.

Gorkemli, Serkan. 2012. "'Coming Out of the Internet': Lesbian and Gay Activism and the Internet as a 'Digital Closet' in Turkey." *Journal of Middle East Women's Studies* 8 (3): 63–88.

Government of the Netherlands. n.d. "LGBT Rights Worldwide." Retrieved May 11, 2014. www.government.nl/issues/gay-rights/lgbt-rights-worldwide.

Greeley, Andrew. 1994. "A Religious Revival in Russia?" *Journal for the Scientific Study of Religion* 33 (3): 253–72.

Grim, Brian J., and Roger Finke. 2010. *The Price of Freedom Denied: Religious Persecution and Conflict in the Twenty-First Century*. New York: Cambridge University Press.

Gronewold, Sue. 1982. *Beautiful Merchandise: Prostitution in China, 1860–1936*. New York: Harrington Park Press. Retrieved November 19, 2013. www.getcited.org/pub/102447472.

Grossman, Guy. 2013. "Renewalist Christianity, Political Competition and the Political Saliency of LGBTs in Sub-Saharan Africa." Retrieved August 8,

2015. http://cega.berkeley.edu/assets/cega_events/53/WGAPE_Sp13_Grossman.pdf.

Guardian. 2009. "Anti-Gay Bigots Plunge Africa into New Era of Hate Crimes." *Guardian,* December 13. Retrieved September 9, 2015. www.theguardian.com/world/2009/dec/13/death-penalty-uganda-homosexuals.

Guasch, Oscar. 2011. "Social Stereotypes and Masculine Homosexualities: The Spanish Case." *Sexualities* 14 (5): 526–43.

Guérin, Daniel, Francois Petry, and Jean Crête. 2004. "Tolerance, Protest and Democratic Transition: Survey Evidence from 13 Post-Communist Countries." *European Journal of Political Research* 43 (3): 371–95.

Hadaway, C. Kirk, Kirk W. Elifson, and David M. Petersen. 1984. "Religious Involvement and Drug Use among Urban Adolescents." *Journal for the Scientific Study of Religion* 23 (2): 109–28.

Hadaway, C. Kirk, Penny Long Marler, and Mark Chaves. 1993. "What the Polls Don't Show: A Closer Look at US Church Attendance." *American Sociological Review* 58 (6): 741–52.

———. 1998. "Overreporting Church Attendance in America." *American Sociological Review* 63 (1): 122–30.

Haddad, Yvonne Yazbeck. 2007. "The Post-9/11 Hijab as Icon*." *Sociology of Religion* 68 (3): 253–67.

Haddock, Geoffrey, and Mark P. Zanna. 1998. "Authoritarianism, Values, and the Favorability and Structure of Antigay Attitudes." In *Stigma and Sexual Orientation: Understanding Prejudice against Lesbians, Gay Men, and Bisexuals,* edited by G.M. Harek, 82–107. Thousand Oaks, CA: SAGE.

Hadler, Markus. 2012. "The Influence of World Societal Forces on Social Tolerance: A Time Comparative Study of Prejudices in 32 Countries." *Sociological Quarterly* 53 (2): 211–37.

Haggerty, George E. 2000. *Gay Histories and Cultures: An Encyclopedia.* New York: Taylor & Francis.

Hague, Gill, and Ravi Thiara. 2009. *Bride-Price, Poverty and Domestic Violence in Uganda.* London: MIFUMI.

Hangen, Tona J. 2002. *Redeeming the Dial: Radio, Religion, & Popular Culture in America.* Chapel Hill: University of North Carolina Press.

Hausmann, Ricardo, Laura D. Tyson, and Saadia Zahidi. 2012. *The Global Gender Gap Report 2012.* Geneva: World Economic Forum. Retrieved February 16, 2015. www3.weforum.org/docs/WEF_GenderGap_Report_2012.pdf.

Hayes, Bernadette C., Ian McAllister, and Donley T. Studlar. 2000. "Gender, Postmaterialism, and Feminism in Comparative Perspective." *International Political Science Review* 21 (4): 425–39.

Hayes, Michelle Heffner. 2009. *Flamenco: Conflicting Histories of the Dance.* Jefferson, NC: McFarland.

Hazelrigg, Lawrence. 1991. "The Problem of Micro-Macro Linkage: Rethinking Questions of the Individual, Social Structure, and Autonomy of Action." *Current Perspectives in Social Theory* 11:229–54.

Heath, Anthony, Stephen Fisher, and Shawna Smith. 2005. "The Globalization of Public Opinion Research." *Annual Review of Political Science* 8: 297–333.

Heather, Saul. 2014. "Uganda Anti-Gay Bill Author David Bahati Says Western Aid Cuts Are a Small Price to Pay." *Independent,* March 4. www.independent .co.uk/news/world/africa/uganda-anti-gay-bill-author-david-bahati-says-western-aid-cuts-are-a-small-price-to-pay-9165421.html.

Heatherington, Laurie, and Justin A. Lavner. 2008. "Coming to Terms with Coming out: Review and Recommendations for Family Systems-Focused Research." *Journal of Family Psychology* 22 (3): 329.

Heaton, Tim B., Mark Cammack, and Larry Young. 2001. "Why Is the Divorce Rate Declining in Indonesia?" *Journal of Marriage and Family* 63 (2): 480–90.

Heinze, Justin E., and Stacey S. Horn. 2009. "Intergroup Contact and Beliefs about Homosexuality in Adolescence." *Journal of Youth and Adolescence* 38 (7): 937–51.

Herek, Gregory M. 1988. "Heterosexuals' Attitudes toward Lesbians and Gay Men: Correlates and Gender Differences." *Journal of Sex Research* 25 (4): 451–77.

———. 1991. "Psychological Heterosexism and Anti-Gay Violence: The Social Psychology of Bigotry and Bashing." In *Hate Crimes: Confronting Violence against Lesbians and Gay Men,* edited by G.M. Herek and K.T. Berrill. California: SAGE.

———. 2000. "Sexual Prejudice and Gender: Do Heterosexuals' Attitudes toward Lesbians and Gay Men Differ?" *Journal of Social Issues* 56 (2): 251–66.

Herek, Gregory M., and John P. Capitanio. 1995. "Black Heterosexuals' Attitudes toward Lesbians and Gay Men in the United States." *Journal of Sex Research* 32 (2): 95–105.

———. 1996. "'Some of My Best Friends': Intergroup Contact, Concealable Stigma, and Heterosexuals' Attitudes toward Gay Men and Lesbians." *Personality and Social Psychology Bulletin* 22 (4): 412–24.

Herek, Gregory M., and Kevin A. McLemore. 2013. "Sexual Prejudice." *Annual Review of Psychology* 64 (1): 309–33.

Herzog, Dagmar. 2011. *Sexuality in Europe: A Twentieth-Century History.* New York: Cambridge University Press.

Hessini, Leila. 1994. "Wearing the Hijab in Contemporary Morocco: Choice and Identity." In *Reconstructing Gender in the Middle East: Tradition, Identity, and Power,* edited by F.M. Gocek and S. Balaghi., 40–56. New York: Columbia University Press.

Hicks, Gary R., and Tien-Tsung Lee. 2006. "Public Attitudes toward Gays and Lesbians." *Journal of Homosexuality* 51 (2): 57–77.

Hill, Michael. 2000. "'Asian Values' as Reverse Orientalism: Singapore." *Asia Pacific Viewpoint* 41 (2): 177–90.

Hill, Terrence D., Benjamin E. Moulton, and Amy M. Burdette. 2004. "Conservative Protestantism and Attitudes toward Homosexuality: Does Political Orientation Mediate This Relationship?" *Sociological Focus* 37 (1): 59–70.

Hilmes, Michele. 2013. *Only Connect: A Cultural History of Broadcasting in the United States.* Boston: Cengage Learning.

Hinrichs, Donald W., and Pamela J. Rosenberg. 2002. "Attitudes toward Gay, Lesbian, and Bisexual Persons among Heterosexual Liberal Arts College Students." *Journal of Homosexuality* 43 (1): 61–84.

Hirschi, Travis. 2009. *Causes of Delinquency.* Piscataway, NJ: Transaction.

Ho, Vivian. 1998. "Malaysian Group Launches Antigay Movement." Sodomy Laws. Retrieved February 12, 2015. www.glapn.org/sodomylaws/world /malaysia/mynews001.htm.

Hoare, Liam. 2013. "Israel Won't Legalize Gay Marriage: Here's Why." *Slate.* Retrieved August 10, 2016. www.slate.com/blogs/outward/2013/11/21 /israel_won_t_legalize_gay_marriage_here_s_why.html.

Hofstede, Geert. 2001. *Culture's Consequences: Comparing Values, Behaviors, Institutions and Organizations across Nations.* Thousand Oaks, CA: SAGE.

Hofstede, Geert, and Michael H. Bond. 1988. "Confucius and Economic Growth: New Trends in Culture's Consequences." *Organizational Dynamics* 16 (4): 4–21.

Hofstede, Geert, and Robert R. McCrae. 2004. "Personality and Culture Revisited: Linking Traits and Dimensions of Culture." *Cross-Cultural Research* 38 (1): 52–88.

Holifield, Brooks. 2014. "Understanding Why Americans Seem More Religious than Other Western Powers." *Huffington Post,* February 15. Retrieved September 4, 2015 www.huffingtonpost.com/2014/02/15/americans-more-religious_n_4780594.html.

Holzhacker, Ronald. 2012. "National and Transnational Strategies of LGBT Civil Society Organizations in Different Political Environments: Modes of Interaction in Western and Eastern Europe for Equality." *Comparative European Politics* 10 (1): 23–47.

Hooghe, Marc, and Cecil Meeusen. 2013. "Is Same-Sex Marriage Legislation Related to Attitudes toward Homosexuality? Trends in Tolerance of Homosexuality in European Countries between 2002 and 2010." *Sexuality Research and Social Policy* 10 (4): 258–68.

Hookway, James. 2015. "Anwar Sodomy Verdict Leaves Malaysian Opposition Adrift." *Wall Street Journal,* February 10. Retrieved February 13, 2015. www.wsj.com/articles/anwar-sodomy-verdict-leaves-malaysian-opposition-adrift-1423576136.

Hooper, John. 2014. "In Vatican and Rome Alike, Slow Progress on Gay Rights." *Guardian,* October 12. Retrieved July 23, 2015. www.theguardian .com/world/2014/oct/19/vatican-italy-gay-rights-marriage-civil-unions.

Howard, Adam. 2014. "UN Passes Resolution on Behalf of LGBT Citizens around the Globe." MSNBC. Retrieved June 12, 2015. www.msnbc.com /msnbc/un-passes-resolution-behalf-lgbt-citizens-around-the-globe.

Hsieh, Yu-Chieh. 2012. "Shaping Young People's Gender and Sexual Identities: Can Teaching Practices Produce Diverse Subjects?" In *Educational Diversity: The Subject of Difference and Different Subjects,* edited by Y. Taylor, 75–96. London: Palgrave Macmillan. Retrieved September 15, 2015. https://books. google.com/books?hl = en&lr = &id = Wk1FVwBtc1UC&oi = fnd&pg = PA75&dq = Shaping+young+people%E2%80%99s+gender+and+sexual +identities:+can+teaching+practices+produce+diverse+subjects%3F+In+Tayl or,+Y+(Ed.)+Educational+diversity:+The+subjects+of+difference+and+differ ent+subjects.+Basingstoke:+Palgrave+Macmillan&ots = Snt92VczMi&sig = CIGBknscWxHmbbJz_rGca4gvqtU.

Hsu, Francis L.K. 1981. *Americans and Chinese: Passages to Differences.* Honolulu: University of Hawaii Press.

Hu, Anning, and Reid J. Leamaster. 2013. "Longitudinal Trends of Religious Groups in Deregulated Taiwan: 1990 to 2009." *Sociological Quarterly* 54 (2): 254–77.

Huang, Annie. 2007. "Taiwan Today: Age, Sexual Orientation Clauses Added to Employment Act." *Taiwan Today.* Retrieved May 29, 2015. http:// taiwantoday.tw/ct.asp?xItem = 24281&CtNode = 450.

Hudson, David. 2015. "Italy: Poll Reveals Majority Opposed to Gay Adoption and Same-Sex Marriage." *Gay Star News.* Retrieved July 24, 2015. www .gaystarnews.com/article/italy-poll-reveals-majority-opposed-gay-adoption-and-same-sex-marriage02021 5/.

Huebner, David M., Gregory M. Rebchook, and Susan M. Kegeles. 2004. "Experiences of Harassment, Discrimination, and Physical Violence among Young Gay and Bisexual Men." *American Journal of Public Health* 94 (7): 1200–1203.

Human Rights Campaign. n.d. "Stances of Faiths on LGBT Issues: Episcopal Church." Human Rights Campaign. Retrieved October 15, 2014. www.hrc .org/resources/entry/stances-of-faiths-on-lgbt-issues-episcopal-church.

Human Rights Watch. 2012. "Uganda: 'Walk to Work' Group Declared Illegal." Retrieved December 22, 2014. www.hrw.org/news/2012/04/04/uganda-walk-work-group-declared-illegal.

———. n.d. "World Report 2013: Turkey." Retrieved March 12, 2015. www .hrw.org/world-report/2013/country-chapters/turkey.

———. n.d. "World Report 2014: China." Retrieved June 12, 2015. www.hrw .org/world-report/2014/country-chapters/china.

Humana, Charles. 1992. *World Human Rights Guide.* New York: Oxford University Press.

Hunt, Larry L., and Matthew O. Hunt. 2001. "Race, Region, and Religious Involvement: A Comparative Study of Whites and African Americans." *Social Forces* 80 (2): 605–31.

Hunter, James Davison. 1987. *Evangelicalism: The Coming Generation.* Chicago: University of Chicago Press.

Hunter-Gault, Charlayne. 2012. "Violated Hopes: A Nation Confronts a Tide of Sexual Violence." *New Yorker.* Retrieved January 6, 2015. www .newyorker.com/magazine/2012/05/28/violated-hopes.

Hyun, Kyoung Ja. 2001. "Sociocultural Change and Traditional Values: Confucian Values among Koreans and Korean Americans." *International Journal of Intercultural Relations* 25 (2): 203–29.

Iannaccone, Laurence R. 1991. "The Consequences of Religious Market Structure Adam Smith and the Economics of Religion." *Rationality and Society* 3 (2): 156–77.

———. 1994. "Why Strict Churches Are Strong." *American Journal of Sociology* 99 (5): 1180–1211.

———. 1995. "Risk, Rationality, and Religious Portfolios." *Economic Inquiry* 33 (2): 285–95.

Iannaccone, Laurence R., Roger Finke, and Rodney Stark. 1997. "Deregulating Religion: The Economics of Church and State." *Economic Inquiry* 35 (2): 350–64.

Ignazi, Piero, and E. Spencer Wellhofer. 2013. "Votes and Votive Candles Modernization, Secularization, Vatican II, and the Decline of Religious Voting in Italy: 1953–1992." *Comparative Political Studies* 46 (1): 31–62.

Index Mundi. n.d. "GDP—per Capita (PPP)—Country Comparison." Retrieved September 15, 2015. www.indexmundi.com/g/r.aspx?c = tw&v = 67.

———. n.d. "Turkey—Urban Population." Retrieved April 14, 2015. www.indexmundi.com/facts/turkey/urban-population.

Inglehart, Ronald. 1971. "The Silent Revolution in Europe: Intergenerational Change in Post-Industrial Societies." *American Political Science Review* 65 (4): 991–1017.

———. 1990. *Culture Shift in Advanced Industrial Society.* Princeton, NJ: Princeton University Press.

———. 1997. *Modernization and Postmodernization: Cultural, Economic, and Political Change in 43 Societies.* Cambridge: Cambridge University Press.

———. 2006. "Mapping Global Values." *Comparative Sociology* 5 (2): 115–36.

Inglehart, Ronald, and Wayne E. Baker. 2000. "Modernization, Cultural Change, and the Persistence of Traditional Values." *American Sociological Review* 65 (1): 19–51.

Inglehart, Ronald, Pippa Norris, and Christian Welzel. 2002. "Gender Equality and Democracy." *Comparative Sociology* 1 (3): 321–45.

Inglehart, Ronald, and Daphna Oyserman. 2004. "Individualism, Autonomy, Self-Expression: The Human Development Syndrome." *International Studies in Sociology and Social Anthropology* 93:74–96.

Inman, Phillip. 2012. "Brazil's Economy Overtakes UK to Become World's Sixth Largest Business." *Guardian.* Retrieved August 9, 2015. www.theguardian.com/business/2012/mar/06/brazil-economy-worlds-sixth-largest.

Internet World Stats. n.d. "Uganda Internet Usage and Telecommunications Reports." Retrieved May 19, 2016. www.internetworldstats.com/af/ug.htm.

Introvigne, Massimo, and Rodney Stark. 2005. "Religious Competition and Revival in Italy: Exploring European Exceptionalism." *Interdisciplinary Journal of Research on Religion* 1, no. 1. Retrieved July 18, 2015. www.cesnur.org/mi_com/ijrr.pdf.

Itaborahy, Lucas Paoli. 2012. "State-Sponsored Homophobia." International Lesbian, Gay, Bisexual, Trans and Intersex Association. Retrieved June 24, 2013. http://aids-freeworld.org/PlanetAIDS/~/media/796515F2D74A4158A C599504E042F4A8.pdf.

Itaborahy, Lucas, and Jingshu Zhu. 2014. *State-Sponsored Homophobia: A World Survey of Laws: Criminalisation, Protection and Recognition of Same-Sex Love.* International Lesbian Gay Bisexual Trans and Intersex Association (ILGA). Retrieved October 13, 2014. http://old.ilga.org/Statehomophobia/ILGA_SSHR_2014_Eng.pdf.

Jackman, Mary R., and Michael J. Muha. 1984. "Education and Intergroup Attitudes: Moral Enlightenment, Superficial Democratic Commitment, or Ideological Refinement?" *American Sociological Review* 49 (6): 751–69.

Jennings, Ralph. 2011. "Taiwan Birth Rate Falls to World's Lowest." Voice of America. Retrieved May 22, 2015. www.voanews.com/content/taiwan-birth-rate-falls-to-worlds-lowest-challenging-productivity-127933153/167887.html.

Johnston, Hank, and Jozef Figa. 1988. "The Church and Political Opposition: Comparative Perspectives on Mobilization against Authoritarian Regimes." *Journal for the Scientific Study of Religion* 27 (1): 32–47.

Jones, Gavin W. 1981. "Malay Marriage and Divorce in Peninsular Malaysia: Three Decades of Change." *Population and Development Review* 7 (2): 255.

———. 2007. "Delayed Marriage and Very Low Fertility in Pacific Asia." *Population and Development Review* 33 (3): 453–78.

Jones, Gavin W., and Kamalini Ramdas. 2004. "Not 'When to Marry' but 'Whether to Marry': The Changing Context of Marriage Decisions in East and Southeast Asia." In *(Un)tying the Knot: Ideal and Reality in Asian Marriage,* edited by G. Jones and K. Ramdas, 3–56. Singapore: Asia Research Institute, National University of Singapore.

Jones, Gavin W., Paulin Straughan, and Angelique Chan. 2008. "Very Low Fertility in Pacific Asian Countries." In *Ultra-Low Fertility in Pacific Asia: Trends, Causes and Policy Issues,* edited by G. Jones, P. Straughan, and A. Chan, 1–22. London: Routledge. Retrieved June 8, 2015. https://books.google.com/books?hl = en&lr = &id = L_Z8AgAAQBAJ&oi = fnd&pg = PA1&dq = ultra+low+fertility+in+pacific+asia&ots = AFk-kmB-JH&sig = YcPsXWPo5I6FPok4u6QzbPBIcUM.

Jones, Jeffrey M. 2014. "Record-High 42% of Americans Identify as Independents." Gallup. Retrieved January 26, 2015. www.gallup.com/poll/166763/record-high-americans-identify-independents.aspx.

Ju, Sam. 2012. "Adoption: Finding That 'Forever Family.'" *Taiwan Panorama Magazine.* Retrieved September 15, 2015. www.taiwan-panorama.com/en/show_issue.php?id = 201210101072e.txt&table = 2&cur_page = 1&distype = text.

Jung, Kim Dae. 1994. "Is Culture Destiny? The Myth of Asia's Anti-Democratic Values." *Foreign Affairs* 73 (6): 189–94.

Juster, Robert-Paul, Nathan Grant Smith, Émilie Ouellet, Shireen Sindi, and Sonia J. Lupien. 2013. "Sexual Orientation and Disclosure in Relation to Psychiatric Symptoms, Diurnal Cortisol, and Allostatic Load." *Psychosomatic Medicine* 75 (2): 103–16.

Kagitçibasi, Çigdem, and Diane Sunar. 1992. "Family and Socialization in Turkey." In *Annual Advances in Applied Developmental Psychology,* edited by Irving E. Sigel, vol. 5, *Parent-Child Relations in Diverse Cultures,* edited by J. P. Roopnarine and D. B. Carter, 75–88. Norwood, NJ: Ablex.

Kahn, Marla J. 1991. "Factors Affecting the Coming Out Process for Lesbians." *Journal of Homosexuality* 21 (3): 47–70.

Kaid, Lynda Lee, and Anne Johnston Wadsworth. 1989. "Content Analysis." In *Measurement of Communication Behavior,* edited by P. Emmert and L. L. Barker, 197–217. New York: Longman.

Kangas, Olli, and Joakim Palme. 2009. "Making Social Policy Work for Economic Development: The Nordic Experience." *International Journal of Social Welfare* 18 (s1): S62–72.

Kan, R. W. M., K. P. Au, W. K. Chan, L. W. M. Cheung, C. Y. Y. Lam, H. H. W. Liu, L. Y. Ng, M. Y. Wong, and W. C. Wong. 2009. "Homophobia in Medical Students of the University of Hong Kong." *Sex Education* 9 (1): 65–80.

Kaoma, Kapya. 2009. *Globalizing the Culture Wars: US Conservatives, African Churches, and Homophobia.* Political Research Associates. Retrieved March 23, 2015. www.politicalresearch.org/resources/reports/full-reports /globalizing-the-culture-wars/#.

Kao, M. Bob. 2014. "The Same-Sex Marriage Battle in Its Historical Context." *Thinking Taiwan.* Retrieved May 29, 2015. thinking-taiwan.com/the-same-sex-marriage-battle-in-its-historical-context/.

Kapborg, Inez, and Carina Berterö. 2002. "Using an Interpreter in Qualitative Interviews: Does It Threaten Validity?" *Nursing Inquiry* 9 (1): 52–56.

Kassam, Ashifa. 2014. "Spain Abandons Plan to Introduce Tough New Abortion Laws." *Guardian,* September 23. Retrieved May 26, 2016. www.theguardian .com/world/2014/sep/23/spain-abandons-plan-introduce-tough-new-abortion-laws.

Keating, Joshua. 2014. "Russian LGBT Activists on the Effects of Gay Propaganda Law." *Slate.* Retrieved October 2, 2015. www.slate.com/blogs /outward/2014/10/09/russian_lgbt_activists_on_the_effects_of_gay_ propaganda_law.html.

Kelley, Dean M. 1977. *Why Conservative Churches Are Growing: A Study in Sociology of Religion with a New Preface for the Rose Edition.* Macon, Georgia: Mercer University Press.

———. 1978. "Why Conservative Churches Are Still Growing." *Journal for the Scientific Study of Religion* 17 (2): 165–72.

Kelley, Kathryn, Donn Byrne, Virginia Greendlinger, and Sarah K. Murnen. 1997. "Content, Sex of Viewer, and Dispositional Variables as Predictors of Affective and Evaluative Responses to Sexually Explicit Films." *Journal of Psychology & Human Sexuality* 9 (2): 53–71.

Kelman, Herbert C. 2006. "Interests, Relationships, Identities: Three Central Issues for Individuals and Groups in Negotiating Their Social Environment." *Annual Review of Psychology* 57:1–26.

Kennedy, M. Alexis, and Boris B. Gorzalka. 2002. "Asian and Non-Asian Attitudes toward Rape, Sexual Harassment, and Sexuality." *Sex Roles* 46 (7–8): 227–38.

Kenyon, Andrew T. 2010. "Investigating Chilling Effects: News Media and Public Speech in Malaysia, Singapore and Australia." *International Journal of Communication* 4:440–67.

Kerns, John G., and Mark A. Fine. 1994. "The Relation between Gender and Negative Attitudes toward Gay Men and Lesbians: Do Gender Role Attitudes Mediate This Relation?" *Sex Roles* 31 (5–6): 297–307.

Khazan, Olga. 2013. "Why Is Russia So Homophobic?" *Atlantic,* June 12. Retrieved September 28, 2015. www.theatlantic.com/international/archive /2013/06/why-is-russia-so-homophobic/276817/.

Khoo, Boo Teik. 1995. *Paradoxes of Mahathirism: An Intellectual Biography of Mahathir Mohamad*. Kuala Lumpur and New York: Oxford University Press. Retrieved February 16, 2015. http://repository.tufs.ac.jp/handle/10108/2955.

Kielwasser, Alfred P., and Michelle A. Wolf. 1992. "Mainstream Television, Adolescent Homosexuality, and Significant Silence." *Critical Studies in Media Communication* 9 (4): 350–73.

Kim, Annice E., Shiriki Kumanyika, Daniel Shive, Uzy Igweatu, and Son-Ho Kim. 2010. "Coverage and Framing of Racial and Ethnic Disparities in US Newspapers, 1996–2005." *American Journal of Public Health* 100 (1): S224–S231.

Kim, Bryan S. K., Donald R. Atkinson, and Peggy H. Yang. 1999. "The Asian Values Scale: Development, Factor Analysis, Validation, and Reliability." *Journal of Counseling Psychology* 46 (3): 342–52.

Kim, So Young. 2010. "Do Asian Values Exist? Empirical Tests of the Four Dimensions of Asian Values." *Journal of East Asian Studies* 10 (2): 315–44.

Kim, Sung Tae. 2004. "Mapping an Economic 'Globalization' News Paradigm: A Multi-National Comparative Analysis." *Journalism & Mass Communication Quarterly* 81 (3): 601–21.

Kim, Yung-Myung. 1997. "'Asian-Style Democracy': A Critique from East Asia." *Asian Survey* 37 (12): 1119–34.

Kollman, Kelly. 2013. *The Same-Sex Unions Revolution in Western Democracies: International Norms and Domestic Policy Change*. Manchester, UK: Manchester University Press.

Kuang, Me-Fun, and Kazuhiko Nojima. 2005. "The Mental Health and Sexual Orientation of Females: A Comparative Study of Japan and Taiwan." *Kyushu University Psychological Research* 6:141–48.

Kuhar, Roman. 2013. "Introduction to the Issue: 'In the Name of Hate: Homophobia as a Value.'" *Southeastern Europe* 37 (1): 1–16.

Kunovich, Robert M. 2004. "Social Structural Position and Prejudice: An Exploration of Cross-National Differences in Regression Slopes." *Social Science Research* 33 (1): 20–44.

Kurtz, Lester. 2016. "The Anti-Apartheid Struggle in South Africa (1912–1992)." International Center on Nonviolent Conflict. Retrieved May 18, 2016. https://www.nonviolent-conflict.org/the-anti-apartheid-struggle-in-south-africa-1912-1992/.

Kuyper, Lisette, J. Iedema, and Saskia Keuzenkamp. 2013. "Towards Tolerance: Exploring Changes and Explaining Differences in Attitudes towards Homosexuality in Europe." Netherlands Institute for Social Research. Retrieved January 31, 2014. http://dare2.ubvu.vu.nl/handle/1871/49778.

Labi, Nadya. 2007. "The Kingdom in the Closet." *Atlantic,* May. Retrieved September 26, 2015. www.theatlantic.com/magazine/archive/2007/05/the-kingdom-in-the-closet/305774/.

Lakeland, Paul. 2006. "The Laity." In *From Trent to Vatican II: Historical and Theological Investigations,* edited by Raymond F. Bulman and Frederick J. Parrella, 193–208. Oxford and New York: Oxford University Press.

La Pastina, Antonio C. 2002. "The Sexual Other in Brazilian Television Public and Institutional Reception of Sexual Difference." *International Journal of Cultural Studies* 5 (1): 83–99.

Laurent, Erick. 2005. "Sexuality and Human Rights: An Asian Perspective." *Journal of Homosexuality* 48 (3–4): 163–225.

Lavers, Michael K. 2013. "Report Documents Anti-Transgender Violence, Discrimination in Brazil." *Washington Blade*. Retrieved August 5, 2015. www .washingtonblade.com/2013/11/25/report-documents-anti-transgender-violence-discrimination-brazil/.

———. 2015. "European Court: Italy Violates Rights of Same-Sex Couples." *Washington Blade*. Retrieved August 27, 2015. www.washingtonblade .com/2015/07/21/european-court-italy-violates-rights-of-same-sex-couples/.

Leahy, Joe. 2015. "Brazil Economy to Contract Nearly One-Quarter This Year in Dollar Terms." *Financial Times*. Retrieved August 9, 2015. www.ft .com/intl/cms/s/0/702d7640–022c-11e5–92ce-00144feabdco.html#axzz3s WJqs4Md.

Lee, Mei-Lin, and Te-Hsiung Sun. 1995. "The Family and Demography in Contemporary Taiwan." *Journal of Comparative Family Studies* 26 (1): 101–15.

Lee, Seow Ting, and Crispin C. Maslog. 2005. "War or Peace Journalism? Asian Newspaper Coverage of Conflicts." *Journal of Communication* 55 (2): 311–29.

Legal Beer. n.d. "Liquor Laws by State." Retrieved September 4, 2015. www .legalbeer.com/liquor-laws-by-state.

Lehohla, Pali. 2012. *Census 2011: Census in Brief*. Pretoria: Statistics South Africa. Retrieved August 8, 2016. www.statssa.gov.za/census/census_2011 /census_products/Census_2011_Census_in_brief.pdf.

Lesthaeghe, Ron. 2010. "The Unfolding Story of the Second Demographic Transition." *Population and Development Review* 36 (2): 211–51.

Lewis, Gregory B. 2003. "Black-White Differences in Attitudes toward Homosexuality and Gay Rights." *Public Opinion Quarterly* 67 (1): 59–78.

———. 2009. "Does Believing Homosexuality Is Innate Increase Support for Gay Rights?" *Policy Studies Journal* 37 (4): 669–93.

Lewis, Gregory B., and Charles W. Gossett. 2008. "Changing Public Opinion on Same-Sex Marriage: The Case of California." *Politics & Policy* 36 (1): 4–30.

Lewis, Michele K., and Isiah Marshall. 2012. "Indigenous and Intersecting: People of African Descent in LGBT Psychology." In *LGBT Psychology: Research Perspectives and People of African Descent*, edited by Michele K. Lewis and Isiah Marshall, 1–19. New York: Springer.

Lim, Eng-Beng. 2013. *Brown Boys and Rice Queens: Spellbinding Performance in the Asias*. New York: New York University Press.

Lim, Song Hwee. 2008. "How to Be Queer in Taiwan: Translation, Appropriation, and the Construction of a Queer Identity in Taiwan." In *AsiaPacifiQueer: Rethinking Genders and Sexualities*, edited by Fran Martin, Peter A. Jackson, Mark McLelland, and Audrey Yue, 235–48. Urbana and Chicago: University of Illinois Press.

Lim, V.K.G. 2002. "Gender Differences and Attitudes towards Homosexuality." *Journal of Homosexuality* 43 (1): 85–97.

Lincoln, C. Eric, and Lawrence H. Mamiya. 1990. *The Black Church in the African American Experience*. Durham, NC: Duke University Press.

Lin, Eric. 1998. "Between Us: A Friendly Focus for Lesbian Activity." *Taiwan Panorama Magazine*. Retrieved September 15, 2015. www.taiwan-panorama.com/en/show_issue.php?id = 199888708105E.TXT&table = 2&cur_page = 1&distype =.

Lin, Yu-Ting. 2013. "The Legalization of Same-Sex Marriage Has Passed the First Reading in Taiwan." *Hong Kong Law Blog*. Retrieved May 29, 2015. http://hklawblog.com/2013/11/13/the-legalization-of-same-sex-marriage-has-passed-the-first-reading-in-taiwan/.

Lingiardi, Vittorio, Simona Falanga, and Anthony R. D'Augelli. 2005. "The Evaluation of Homophobia in an Italian Sample." *Archives of Sexual Behavior* 34 (1): 81–93.

Linz, Juan J., and José Ramón Montero. 1999. *The Party Systems of Spain: Old Cleavages and New Challenges*. Madrid: Instituto Juan March de Estudios e Investigaciones.

Loa, Iok-sin. 2009. "Activists March against Upcoming Gay Parade." *Taipei Times*. Retrieved May 28, 2015. www.taipeitimes.com/News/taiwan/archives/2009/10/25/2003456842.

———. 2013. "Rally against Same-Sex Marriage Held." *Taipei Times*. Retrieved May 29, 2015. www.taipeitimes.com/News/front/print/2013/12/01/2003578041.

Loftus, Jeni. 2001. "America's Liberalization in Attitudes toward Homosexuality, 1973 to 1998." *American Sociological Review* 66 (5): 762–82.

Lor, Peter Johan. 2016. *International and Comparative Librarianship: A Thematic Approach*. Munich: K. G. Saur.

Lottes, Ilsa L., and Tapani Alkula. 2011. "An Investigation of Sexuality-Related Attitudinal Patterns and Characteristics Related to Those Patterns for 32 European Countries." *Sexuality Research and Social Policy* 8 (2): 77–92.

Luirink, Bart. 2000. *Moffies: Gay Life in Southern Africa*. Havertown, PA: New Africa Books.

Lumina Foundation. 2014. *A Stronger Nation through Higher Education*. Retrieved August 12, 2016. www.luminafoundation.org/files/resources/a-stronger-nation-through-higher-education-2014.pdf.

Mackey, Michael. 2012. "Malaysian Government Bans Gay TV Characters." *Hollywood Reporter*. Retrieved April 14, 2015. www.hollywoodreporter.com/news/malaysian-government-gay-characters-ban-313774.

Mahari, Madam Zarinah. 2011. "Demographic Transition in Malaysia: The Changing Roles of Women." New Delhi. Retrieved February 16, 2015. http://cwsc2011.gov.in/papers/demographic_transitions/Paper_1.pdf.

Malaysia. 1997. "Laws of Malaysia, Act 559, Syariah Criminal Offenses (Federal Territories) Act 1997." *Yearbook of Islamic and Middle Eastern Law Online* 4:571–80.

Manchin, Robert. 2004. "Religion in Europe: Trust Not Filling the Pews." Gallup. Retrieved September 4, 2015. www.gallup.com/poll/13117/religion-europe-trust-filling-pews.aspx.

Marsiaj, Juan P. 2006. "Social Movements and Political Parties: Gays, Lesbians, and *Travestis* and the Struggle for Inclusion in Brazil." *Canadian Journal of Latin American and Caribbean Studies* 31 (62): 167–96.

Marszal, Andrew, and Harriet Alexander. 2015. "Mapped: One-in-Five Murder Victims in World Is Brazilian, Colombian or Venezuelan." Retrieved August 5, 2015. *Telegraph.* www.telegraph.co.uk/news/worldnews/southamerica/brazil /11588886/Mapped-One-in-five-murder-victims-in-world-is-Brazilian-Colombian-or-Venezuelan.html.

Martina, Egbert Alejandro. 2013. "Wanted for Love, But Not Here: The Travelling Rights of African LGBT Activists." Critical Legal Thinking. Retrieved September 10, 2015. http://criticallegalthinking.com/2013/08/12/wanted-for-love-but-not-here-the-travelling-rights-of-african-lgbt-activists/.

Marx, Karl. 1867. *Capital.* Harmondsworth, England: Penguin/New Left Review.

Marzano, Marco. 2013. "The 'Sectarian' Church: Catholicism in Italy since John Paul II." *Social Compass* 60 (3): 302–14.

Masci, David, and Michael Lipka. 2015. "Where Christian Churches, Other Religions Stand on Gay Marriage." Pew Research Center. Retrieved September 7, 2015. www.pewresearch.org/fact-tank/2015/07/02/where-christian-churches-stand-on-gay-marriage/.

Massey, Brian L., and Li-jing Arthur Chang. 2002. "Locating Asian Values in Asian Journalism: A Content Analysis of Web Newspapers." *Journal of Communication* 52 (4): 987–1003.

Massoud, Mark F. 2003. "The Evolution of Gay Rights in South Africa." *Peace Review* 15 (3): 301–7.

McCarthy, Margaret H. 2012. "Vatican II and the Church's 'Openness to the World.'" *Communio* 39 (1): 227–68.

McKinley, James C., Jr. 1998. "A New Model for Africa: Good Leaders above All." *New York Times,* March 25. Retrieved May 26, 2016. www.nytimes.com/1998/03/25/world/clinton-in-africa-the-region-a-new-model-for-africa-good-leaders-above-all.html.

McLean, Renwick. 2005. "Spain Legalizes Gay Marriage; Law Is Among the Most Liberal." *New York Times,* July 1. Retrieved August 27, 2015.www.nytimes.com/2005/07/01/world/europe/spain-legalizes-gay-marriage-law-is-among-the-most-liberal.html.

McVeigh, Rory, and D. Diaz Maria-Elena. 2009. "Voting to Ban Same-Sex Marriage: Interests, Values, and Communities." *American Sociological Review* 74 (6): 891–915.

Meaney, Glenn J., and Barbara J. Rye. 2010. "Gendered Egos: Attitude Functions and Gender as Predictors of Homonegativity." *Journal of Homosexuality* 57 (10): 1274–1302.

Meintjes, Helen, and Rachel Bray. 2005. "'But Where Are Our Moral Heroes?': An Analysis of South African Press Reporting on Children Affected by HIV/AIDS." *African Journal of AIDS Research* 4 (3): 147–59.

Messner, Francis. 2015. *Public Funding of Religions in Europe.* Burlington, VT: Ashgate.

Meyer, Holly. 2013. "Truck Driver Calls Billboard Ministry a Sign from Above." *USA Today,* September 23. Retrieved September 4, 2015. www.usatoday.com/story/news/nation/2013/09/23/jesus-billboard-ministry /2858243/.

Miceli, Melinda S. 2005. "Morality Politics vs. Identity Politics: Framing Processes and Competition among Christian Right and Gay Social Movement Organizations." *Sociological Forum* 20 (4): 589–612.

Middleton, Russell, and Snell Putney. 1962. "Religion, Normative Standards, and Behavior." *Sociometry* 25 (2): 141–52.

Mira, Alberto. 2000. "Laws of Silence: Homosexual Identity and Visibility in Contemporary Spanish Culture." In *Contemporary Spanish Cultural Studies*, edited by B. Jordan and R. Morgan-Tamosunas, 241–50. London: Arnold.

Módenes, Juan A., Jordi Bayona, and Julián López-Colás. 2013. "Immigration and Residential Change in Spain." *Population, Space and Place* 19 (3): 294–310.

Monkhouse, Lien Le, Bradley R. Barnes, and Thi Song Hanh Pham. 2013. "Measuring Confucian Values among East Asian Consumers: A Four Country Study." *Asia Pacific Business Review* 19 (3): 320–36.

Moo, Douglas, trans. 1973. *Bible, the New International Version.* Grand Rapids, MI: Zondervan.

Moolman, Benita. 2013. "Rethinking 'Masculinities in Transition' in South Africa: Considering the 'Intersectionality' of Race, Class, and Sexuality with Gender." *African Identities* 11 (1): 93–105.

Moscati, Maria Federica. 2010. "Trajectory of Reform: Catholicism, the State and the Civil Society in the Developments of LGBT Rights." *Liverpool Law Review* 31 (1): 51–68.

Mudu, Pierpaolo. 2002. "Repressive Tolerance: The Gay Movement and the Vatican in Rome." *GeoJournal* 58 (2–3): 189–96.

Muhame, Giles. 2010. "Hang Them." *Rolling Stone*, October 19.

Mukwaya, Paul, Yazidhi Bamutaze, Samuel Mugarura, and Todd Benson. 2011. *Rural-Urban Transformation in Uganda.* Accra, Ghana: Citeseer. Retrieved May 26, 2016. www.ifpri.org/sites/defa

Munro, Brenna M. 2012. *South Africa and the Dream of Love to Come: Queer Sexuality and the Struggle for Freedom.* Minneapolis: University of Minnesota Press.

Murray, Stephen O. 1992. "The 'Underdevelopment' of Modern/Gay Homosexuality in Mesoamerica." In *Modern Homosexualities: Fragments of Lesbian and Gay Experiences,* edited by Ken Plummer, 29–38. London: Routledge.

Muslim Women's League. 1999. "An Islamic Perspective on Sexuality." Retrieved January 23, 2011. www.mwlusa.org/topics/sexuality/sexuality_pos.html.

Myers, Scott M. 1996. "An Interactive Model of Religiosity Inheritance: The Importance of Family Context." *American Sociological Review* 61 (5): 858–66.

Nannestad, Peter. 2008. "What Have We Learned about Generalized Trust, If Anything?" *Annual Review of Political Science* 11 (1): 413–36.

Necef, Mehmet Ümit. 1999. "The Transformation of the Culture and Language of Intimacy." *Psyke & Logos* 3:435–55.

Nel, Juan A., and Melanie Judge. 2008. "Exploring Homophobic Victimisation in Gauteng, South Africa: Issues, Impacts and Responses." *Acta Criminologica* 21 (3): 19–36.

Nelson, Thomas E., Rosalee A. Clawson, and Zoe M. Oxley. 1997. "Media Framing of a Civil Liberties Conflict and Its Effect on Tolerance." *American Political Science Review* 91 (3): 567–83.

Newport, Frank. 2015. "Frequent Church Attendance Highest in Utah, Lowest in Vermont." Gallup. Retrieved September 4, 2015. www.gallup.com/poll /181601/frequent-church-attendance-highest-utah-lowest-vermont.aspx.

New Vision. 2008. "New Vision Tops Circulation Figures." *New Vision*, September 17. Retrieved May 18, 2011. www.newvision.co.ug/new_vision/news /1180988/vision-tops-circulation-figures.

New York Times. 1999. "Execution by Taliban: Crushed under Wall." *New York Times*, January 16. Retrieved August 28, 2015. www.nytimes.com/1999/01/16 /world/execution-by-taliban-crushed-under-wall.html.

Niehof, Anke, and Firman Lubis, eds. 2003. *Two Is Enough: Family Planning in Indonesia under the New Order, 1968–1998.* Leiden: KITLV Press.

Norris, Pippa, and Ronald Inglehart. 2012. "Do Cosmopolitan Communications Threaten Traditional Moral Values." In *The Sage Handbook of Political Communication,* edited by H. A. Semetko and M. Scammell, 22–35. London: SAGE.

O'Dwyer, Conor, and Katrina Z. S. Schwartz. 2010. "Minority Rights after EU Enlargement: A Comparison of Antigay Politics in Poland and Latvia." *Comparative European Politics* 8 (2): 220–43.

OECD. 2012. *Education at a Glance 2012: OECD Indicators.* OECD Publishing. Retrieved July 26, 2015. www.oecd-ilibrary.org/education/education-at-a-glance-2012_eag-2012-en.

Oetomo, Dede. 2001. *Giving Voice to Those Who Cannot Speak.* Yogyakarta, Indonesia: Galang Press.

Offord, Baden. 2003. *Homosexual Rights as Human Rights: Activism in Indonesia, Singapore, and Australia.* New York: Peter Lang. Retrieved February 27, 2015. www.michaelkirby.com.au/images/stories/speeches/2000s/vol50 /2002/1817-FOREWORD,_HOMOSEXUAL_RIGHTS.doc.

———. 2011. "Singapore, Indonesia and Malaysia: Arrested Development!" In *The Lesbian and Gay Movement and the State: Comparative Insights into a Transformed Relationship,* edited by M. Tremblay, D. Paternotte, and C. Johnson, 135–52. Farnham, UK, and Burlington, MA: Ashgate.

———. 2013. "Queer Activist Intersections in Southeast Asia: Human Rights and Cultural Studies." *Asian Studies Review* 37 (3): 335–49.

Offord, Baden, and Leon Cantrell. 2001. "Homosexual Rights as Human Rights in Indonesia and Australia." *Journal of Homosexuality* 40 (3–4): 233–52.

Ogland, Curtis P., and Ana P. Verona. 2014. "Religion and the Rainbow Struggle: Does Religion Factor into Attitudes toward Homosexuality and Same-Sex Civil Unions in Brazil?" *Journal of Homosexuality* 61:1334–49.

Oguli Oumo, Margret. 2004. "Bride Price and Violence against Women: The Case of Uganda." Paper presented at the International Conference on Bride Price, February 2004, Kampala, Uganda.

Ohlander, Julianne, Jeanne Batalova, and Judith Treas. 2005. "Explaining Educational Influences on Attitudes toward Homosexual Relations." *Social Science Research* 34 (4): 781–99.

Okazaki, Sumie. 2002. "Influences of Culture on Asian Americans' Sexuality." *Journal of Sex Research* 39 (1): 34–41.

Oksal, Aynur. 2008. "Turkish Family Members' Attitudes toward Lesbians and Gay Men." *Sex Roles* 58 (7–8): 514–25.

Oliver, Marcia. 2012. "Transnational Sex Politics, Conservative Christianity, and Antigay Activism in Uganda." *Studies in Social Justice* 7 (1): 83–105.

Olson, Laura R., Wendy Cadge, and James T. Harrison. 2006. "Religion and Public Opinion about Same-Sex Marriage." *Social Science Quarterly* 87 (2): 340–60.

Ortiz-Gómez, Teresa, and Agata Ignaciuk. 2010. "The Family Planning Movement in Spain during the Democratic Transition." Paper presented at the Health Activism Symposium, Yale University, New Haven, CT, October 22–23. Retrieved September 5, 2015. http://wdb.ugr.es/~proyectopf/admin/wp-content/uploads/2013/02/Yale_OrtizIgnaciuk_para-web.pdf.

Outtraveler. 2013. "15 Pride Celebrations You Can't Miss." OUTTraveler.com. Retrieved August 5, 2015. www.outtraveler.com/pride/2013/04/11/15-pride-celebrations-you-cant-miss.

Ozorak, Elizabeth Weiss. 1989. "Social and Cognitive Influences on the Development of Religious Beliefs and Commitment in Adolescence." *Journal for the Scientific Study of Religion* 28 (4): 448–63.

Paiva, Vera, Francisco Aranha, and Francisco I. Bastos. 2008. "Opinions and Attitudes regarding Sexuality: Brazilian National Research, 2005." *Revista de saúde pública* 42 (1): 54–64.

Pak, Jennifer. 2014. "What Is Malaysia's Sedition Law?" BBC News. Retrieved March 20, 2015. www.bbc.com/news/world-asia-29373164.

Pan, Po-Lin, Juan Meng, and Shuhua Zhou. 2010. "Morality or Equality? Ideological Framing in News Coverage of Gay Marriage Legitimization." *Social Science Journal* 47 (3): 630–45.

Pappas, Stephanie. 2014. "Why Russia Is So Anti-Gay." LivesScience. Retrieved September 28, 2015. www.livescience.com/43273-why-russia-is-anti-gay.html.

Parent, Mike C., Cirleen DeBlaere, and Bonnie Moradi. 2013. "Approaches to Research on Intersectionality: Perspectives on Gender, LGBT, and Racial/Ethnic Identities." *Sex Roles* 68 (11–12): 639–45.

Peffley, Mark, and Robert Rohrschneider. 2003. "Democratization and Political Tolerance in Seventeen Countries: A Multi-Level Model of Democratic Learning." *Political Research Quarterly* 56 (3): 243–57.

Perez-Agote, Alfonso. 2010. "Religious Change in Spain." *Social Compass* 57 (2): 224–34.

Permanent Mission of Brazil to the United Nations Office in Geneva. 2015. "Brazil's Update of Report A/HRC/19/41." Retrieved August 9, 2015. https://www.google.com/url?sa = t&rct = j&q = &esrc = s&source = web&cd = 2&cad = rja&uact = 8&ved = 0CCAQFjABahUKEwizw_CdnpzHAh WE1x4KHevJAZw&url = http%3A%2F%2Fwww.ohchr.org%2FDocume nts%2FIssues%2FDiscrimination%2FLGBT%2FRes_27_32%2FBrazil. pdf&ei = BWfHVfOsIISve-uTh-AJ&usg = AFQjCNF1EzIP6V8xAUGmtxzu NqeTt4Z3hA&sig2 = hBYa-fz0Anq-0_ago3Jjvw.

Peters, Gerhard, and John T. Woolley. 1984. "Republican Party Platforms: Republican Party Platform of 1984." American Presidency Project. Retrieved January 23, 2015. www.presidency.ucsb.edu/ws/?pid = 25845.

———. 1988. "Republican Party Platforms: Republican Party Platform of 1988." American Presidency Project. Retrieved January 23, 2015. www .presidency.ucsb.edu/ws/?pid = 25846.

———. 1992. "Republican Party Platforms: Republican Party Platform of 1992." American Presidency Project. Retrieved January 23, 2015. www .presidency.ucsb.edu/ws/?pid = 25847.

Peterson, Dana, and Vanessa R. Panfil. 2013. *Handbook of LGBT Communities, Crime, and Justice.* New York: Springer. Retrieved March 19, 2015. http://link.springer.com/content/pdf/10.1007/978–1–4614–9188–0.pdf.

Pew Research Center. 2008. "U.S. Religious Landscape Survey; Religious Affiliation: Diverse and Dynamic." Retrieved September 21, 2014. http:// religions.pewforum.org/pdf/report-religious-landscape-study-full.pdf.

———. 2009. "Generational Differences in Online Activities." Retrieved June 12, 2015. www.pewinternet.org/2009/01/28/generational-differences-in-online-activities/.

———. 2011a. "Global Christianity: A Report on the Size and Distribution of the World's Christian Population." Retrieved May 26, 2016. www.pewforum .org/files/2011/12/Christianity-fullreport-web.pdf.

———. 2011b. "Table: Christian Population as Percentages of Total Population by Country." Retrieved August 14, 2016. www.pewforum.org/2011/12 /19/table-christian-population-as-percentages-of-total-population-by-country/.

———. 2012a. "The American–Western European Values Gap." Retrieved September 4, 2015. www.pewglobal.org/2011/11/17/the-american-western-european-values-gap/.

———. 2012b. "The Global Religious Landscape: A Report on the Size and Distribution of the World's Major Religious Groups as of 2010. Washington, DC. Retrieved October 5, 2015. www.pewforum.org/2012/12/18/global-religious-landscape-hindu/.

———. 2012c. "Religious Groups' Official Positions on Same-Sex Marriage." Retrieved September 7, 2015. www.pewforum.org/2012/12/07/religious-groups-official-positions-on-same-sex-marriage/.

———. 2012d. "The World's Muslims: Unity and Diversity." Retrieved September 4, 2015. www.pewforum.org/2012/08/09/the-worlds-muslims-unity-and-diversity-2-religious-commitment/.

———. 2013. "The Global Divide on Homosexuality: Greater Acceptance in More Secular and Affluent Countries." Retrieved August 14, 2016. www .pewglobal.org/2013/06/04/the-global-divide-on-homosexuality/.Pew Research Center, Religion & Public Life. 2013. "A Portrait of Jewish Americans." Retrieved October 5, 2015. //www.pewforum.org/2013/10/01 /jewish-american-beliefs-attitudes-culture-survey/.

———. 2015a. "America's Changing Religious Landscape." Retrieved January 26, 2015. http://religions.pewforum.org/reports.

———. 2015b. "Gay Marriage around the World." Retrieved September 7, 2015, www.pewforum.org/2015/06/26/gay-marriage-around-the-world-2013/#countries-that-allow-gay-marriage.

———. 2015c. "Support for Same-Sex Marriage at Record High, but Key Segments Remain Opposed." Retrieved October 12, 2015. www.people-press.org/2015/06/08/support-for-same-sex-marriage-at-record-high-but-key-segments-remain-opposed/.

———. 2016. "Israel's Religiously Divided Society." Retrieved May 26, 2016. www.pewforum.org/2016/03/08/israels-religiously-divided-society/.

Philpott, Daniel. 2004. "The Catholic Wave." *Journal of Democracy* 15 (2): 32–46.

Pierucci, Antônio Flávio, and Reginaldo Prandi. 2000. "Religious Diversity in Brazil: Numbers and Perspectives in a Sociological Evaluation." *International Sociology* 15 (4): 629–39.

Platero, Raquel. 2007. "Love and the State: Gay Marriage in Spain: Spanish Law no. 13/2005, 1 July 2005, concerning, through a Change in the Civil Code, the Access of Lesbians and Gay Men to the Institution of Marriage." *Feminist Legal Studies* 15 (3): 329–40.

Plaut, Martin. 2014. "Uganda Donors Cut Aid after President Passes Anti-Gay Law." *Guardian.* Retrieved December 22, 2014. www.theguardian.com/global-development/2014/feb/25/uganda-donors-cut-aid-anti-gay-law.

Polaski, Adam. 2012. "Brazil's São Paolo Extends the Freedom to Marry to Same-Sex Couples." Freedom to Marry. Retrieved August 9, 2015. freedomtomarry.org/blog/entry/brazils-sao-paolo-extends-the-freedom-to-marry-to-same-sex-couples.

Polimeni, Anne-Maree, Elizabeth Hardie, and Simone Buzwell. 2000. "Homophobia among Australian Heterosexuals: The Role of Sex, Gender Role Ideology, and Gender Role Traits." *Current Research in Social Psychology* 5 (4): 47–62.

Pope, John. 2012. "Vatican II Changed the Catholic Church—and the World." *Huffington Post,* October 11. Retrieved September 5, 2015. www.huffingtonpost.com/2012/10/11/vatican-ii-catholic-church-changes_n_1956641.html.

Povoledo, Elisabetta, and Laurie Goodstein. 2014. "At the Vatican, a Shift in Tone toward Gays and Divorce." *New York Times,* October 14. Retrieved August 27, 2015. www.nytimes.com/2014/10/14/world/europe/vatican-signals-more-tolerance-toward-gays-and-remarriage.html.

Puar, Jasbir. 2007. *Terrorist Assemblages: Homonationalism in Queer Times.* Durham, NC: Duke University Press.

Pullella, Philip. 2012. "Gay Marriage a Threat to Humanity's Future: Pope." Reuters. Retrieved April 9, 2015. www.reuters.com/article/2012/01/09/us-pope-gay-idUSTRE8081RM20120109.

Qureshi, Imran. 2014. "Indian Man Arrested in Bangalore for Being Gay." BBC News. Retrieved October 5, 2015. www.bbc.com/news/world-asia-india-29822149.

Ragin, Charles C. 2014. *The Comparative Method: Moving beyond Qualitative and Quantitative Strategies.* Berkeley: University of California Press.

Ramakrishnan, Mageswary. 2000. "'Homosexuality Is a Crime Worse than Murder.'" *Time*, September 26. Retrieved February 9, 2015. http://content.time.com/time/world/article/0,8599,2040451,00.html.

Rape Crisis Cape Town Trust. n.d. "Rape in South Africa." Retrieved February 12, 2015. http://rapecrisis.org.za/rape-in-south-africa/.

Raphael, Joy. 2009. *Matawas: Saudi Arabia's Dreaded Religious Police*. Mumbai, India: Turtle Books.

Raymo, James M., and Hiromi Ono. 2007. "Coresidence with Parents, Women's Economic Resources, and the Transition to Marriage in Japan." *Journal of Family Issues* 28 (5): 653–81.

Reddy, Chandan. 2011. *Freedom with Violence: Race, Sexuality, and the US State*. Durham, NC: Duke University Press. Retrieved May 26, 2016. https://www.dukeupress.edu/Freedom-with-Violence/index-viewby = reading+list&categoryid = 436&sort = title.html.

Regnerus, Mark D. 2002. "Friends' Influence on Adolescent Theft and Minor Delinquency: A Developmental Test of Peer-Reported Effects." *Social Science Research* 31 (4): 681–705.

———. 2003. "Moral Communities and Adolescent Delinquency." *Sociological Quarterly* 44 (4): 523–54.

Reid, Graeme. 2010. "The Canary of the Constitution: Same-Sex Equality in the Public Sphere." *Social Dynamics* 36 (1): 38–51.

Reid, Graeme, and Teresa Dirsuweit. 2002. "Understanding Systemic Violence: Homophobic Attacks in Johannesburg and Its Surrounds." *Urban Forum* 13 (3): 99–126. Retrieved December 4, 2014. www.springerlink.com.ez.lib.jjay.cuny.edu/index/885488LJF2TVH7KY.pdf.

Reisig, Michael D., Scott E. Wolfe, and Travis C. Pratt. 2012. "Low Self-Control and the Religiosity–Crime Relationship." *Criminal Justice and Behavior* 39 (9): 1172–91.

Requena, Miguel. 2005. "The Secularization of Spanish Society: Change in Religious Practice." *South European Society and Politics* 10 (3): 369–90.

Requena, Miguel, and Leire Salazar. 2014. "Education, Marriage, and Fertility: The Spanish Case." *Journal of Family History* 39 (3): 283–302.

Requena, Miguel, and Mikolaj Stanek. 2014. "Religiosity and Politics in Spain and Poland: A Period Effect Analysis." *Social Compass* 61 (3): 348–67.

Resource Information Center. 2001. "Qatar: Information on Homosexuals." U.S. Bureau of Citizenship and Immigration Services. Retrieved May 26, 2016. www.refworld.org/docid/3deceae24.html.

Reuters. 2007. "President Misquoted over Gays in Iran: Aide." Reuters. Retrieved March 20, 2015. www.reuters.com/article/2007/10/10/us-iran-gays-idUSBLA05294620071010.

Rhodebeck, Laurie A. 2015. "Another Issue Comes Out: Gay Rights Policy Voting in Recent US Presidential Elections." *Journal of Homosexuality* 62 (6): 701–34.

Rindfuss, Ronald R., Karin L. Brewster, and Andrew L. Kavee. 1996. "Women, Work, and Children: Behavioral and Attitudinal Change in the United States." *Population and Development Review* 22 (3): 457–82.

Robertson, Christopher J., and James J. Hoffman. 2000. "How Different Are We? An Investigation of Confucian Values in the United States." *Journal of Managerial Issues* 12 (1): 34–47.

Rodgers, Matthew. 2013. "Brazil Has Highest LGBT Murder Rate in the World." *FourTwoNine,* March 11. Retrieved August 5, 2015. http://dot429 .com/articles/1641-brazil-retains-highest-lgbt-murder-rate-in-the-world.

Rubin, Jeffrey W. 2010. "The Roots of Brazil's Success." *World Post.* Retrieved August 7, 2015. www.huffingtonpost.com/jeffrey-w-rubin/the-roots-of-brazils-succ_b_777793.html.

Rubinstein, Murray A. 1990. *The Protestant Community on Modern Taiwan: Mission, Seminary, and Church.* London: Routledge.

Ruiter, Stijn, and Frank Van Tubergen. 2009. "Religious Attendance in Cross-National Perspective: A Multilevel Analysis of 60 Countries1." *American Journal of Sociology* 115 (3): 863–95.

Rural Poverty Portal. 2014. "Rural Poverty in Nigeria." Retrieved September 23, 2014. www.ruralpovertyportal.org/country/home/tags/nigeria#.

Ryder, Norman B. 1965. "The Cohort as a Concept in the Study of Social Change." *American Sociological Review* 30 (6): 843–61.

Rydström, Jens. 2000. *The Ombudsman for Gays and Lesbians: The Swedish Welfare State and Its Tolerance of Deviation.* New York: Swedish Information Service.

Rydström, Jens, and Kati Mustola, eds. 2007. *Criminally Queer: Homosexuality and Criminal Law in Scandinavia, 1842–1999.* Amsterdam: Aksant Academic Publishers.

Sacirbey, Omar. 2015. "Sharia Law in the USA 101: A Guide to What It Is and Why States Want to Ban It." *Huffington Post,* September 26. Retrieved September 26, 2015. www.huffingtonpost.com/2013/07/29/sharia-law-usa-states-ban_n_3660813.html.

Sadgrove, Joanna, Robert M. Vanderbeck, Johan Andersson, Gill Valentine, and Kevin Ward. 2012. "Morality Plays and Money Matters: Towards a Situated Understanding of the Politics of Homosexuality in Uganda." *Journal of Modern African Studies* 50 (1): 103–29.

Sakalh, Nuray. 2003. "Pictures of Male Homosexuals in the Heads of Turkish College Students: The Effects of Sex Difference and Social Contact on Stereotyping." *Journal of Homosexuality* 43 (2): 111–26.

Scappucci, Gioia. 2001. "Italy Walking a Tight Rope between Stockholm and the Vatican: Will Legal Recognition of Same-Sex Partnerships Ever Occur?" In *Legal Recognition of Same-Sex Partnerships: A Study of National, European and International Law,* edited by R. Wintemute and M. T. Andenæs, 519–30. Oxford: Hart.

Scheepers, Peer, Manfred Te Grotenhuis, and Frans Van Der Slik. 2002. "Education, Religiosity and Moral Attitudes: Explaining Cross-National Effect Differences." *Sociology of Religion* 63 (2): 157–76.

Scheitle, Christopher P., and Amy Adamczyk. 2009. "It Takes Two: The Interplay of Individual and Group Theology on Social Embeddedness." *Journal for the Scientific Study of Religion* 48 (1): 16–29.

———. 2010. "High-Cost Religion, Religious Switching, and Health." *Journal of Health and Social Behavior* 51 (3): 325–42.

Scheitle, Christopher P., and Bryanna B. Hahn. 2011. "From the Pews to Policy: Specifying Evangelical Protestantism's Influence on States' Sexual Orientation Policies." *Social Forces* 89 (3): 913–33.

Schiappa, Edward, Peter B. Gregg, and Dean E. Hewes. 2006. "Can One TV Show Make a Difference? *Will & Grace* and the Parasocial Contact Hypothesis." *Journal of Homosexuality* 51 (4): 15–37.

Schlueter, Elmar, and Peer Scheepers. 2010. "The Relationship between Outgroup Size and Anti-Outgroup Attitudes: A Theoretical Synthesis and Empirical Test of Group Threat-and Intergroup Contact Theory." *Social Science Research* 39 (2): 285–95.

Schmalz, Jeffrey. 1993. "Poll Finds an Even Split on Homosexuality's Cause." *New York Times*, March 5. Retrieved June 8, 2015. www.nytimes.com/1993 /03/05/us/poll-finds-an-even-split-on-homosexuality-s-cause.html.

Schmitt, Sophie, Eva-Maria Euchner, and Caroline Preidel. 2013. "Regulating Prostitution and Same-Sex Marriage in Italy and Spain: The Interplay of Political and Societal Veto Players in Two Catholic Societies." *Journal of European Public Policy* 20 (3): 425–41.

Schmitz, David F. 1999. *Thank God They're on Our Side: The United States and Right-Wing Dictatorships, 1921–1965*. Chapel Hill: University of North Carolina Press.

Schnabel, Landon. 2016. "Gender and Homosexuality Attitudes across Religious Groups from the 1970s to 2014: Similarity, Distinction, and Adaptation." *Social Science Research* 55:31–47.

Schulte, Lisa J., and Juan Battle. 2004. "The Relative Importance of Ethnicity and Religion in Predicting Attitudes towards Gays and Lesbians." *Journal of Homosexuality* 47 (2): 127–42.

Schwadel, Philip. 2005. "Individual, Congregational, and Denominational Effects on Church Members' Civic Participation." *Journal for the Scientific Study of Religion* 44 (2): 159–71.

Schwartz, Shalom H. 1999. "A Theory of Cultural Values and Some Implications for Work." *Applied Psychology* 48 (1): 23–47.

———. 2006. "A Theory of Cultural Value Orientations: Explication and Applications." *Comparative Sociology* 5 (2): 136–82.

———. 2014. "National Culture as Value Orientations: Consequences of Value Differences and Cultural Distance." In *Handbook of the Economics of Art and Culture*, vol. 2, edited by V. A. Ginsburgh and D. Throsby, 547–86. Oxford: Elsevier.

Sebaggala, Richard. 2008. "Wage Determination and Gender Discrimination in Uganda." Kampala, Uganda: Makerere University. Retrieved December 18, 2014. http://hdl.handle.net/10570/2522.

Segatti, P., and G. Brunelli. 2010. "L'Italia religiosa: Da cattolica a genericamente cristiana." *Il regno* 10:337–51.

Serbin, Kenneth P. 1999. *The Catholic Church, Religious Pluralism, and Democracy in Brazil*. Notre Dame, IN: Helen Kellogg Institute for International

Studies. Retrieved August 5, 2015. http://kellogg.nd.edu/publications/workingpapers/WPS/263.pdf.

Shah, Shanon. 2013. "The Malaysian Dilemma: Negotiating Sexual Diversity in a Muslim-Majority Commonwealth State." In *Human Rights, Sexual Orientation and Gender Identity in the Commonwealth: Struggles for Decriminalisation and Change,* edited by C. Lennox and M. Waites, 261–86. London: Human Rights Consortium, Institute of Commonwealth Studies. Retrieved February 9, 2015. http://core.kmi.open.ac.uk/download/pdf/13120160.pdf.

Sharot, Stephen. 2002. "Beyond Christianity: A Critique of the Rational Choice Theory of Religion from a Weberian and Comparative Religions Perspective." *Sociology of Religion* 63 (4): 427–54.

Sheng-en, Chang. 2013. "US Lead in Gay Rights Should Be Emulated." *Taipei Times,* July 2. Retrieved September 15, 2015. www.taipeitimes.com/News/editorials/archives/2013/07/02/2003566123.

Sherkat, Darren E., Kylan Mattias de Vries, and Stacia Creek. 2010. "Race, Religion, and Opposition to Same-Sex Marriage." *Social Science Quarterly* 91 (1): 80–98.

Sherkat, Darren E., and Christopher G. Ellison. 1997. "The Cognitive Structure of a Moral Crusade: Conservative Protestantism and Opposition to Pornography." *Social Forces* 75 (3): 957–80.

Sherkat, Darren E., Melissa Powell-Williams, Gregory Maddox, and Kylan Mattias de Vries. 2011. "Religion, Politics, and Support for Same-Sex Marriage in the United States, 1988–2008." *Social Science Research* 40 (1): 167–80.

Sherwood, Harriet. 2016. "Anglican Church Risks Global Schism over Homosexuality." *Guardian,* January 12. Retrieved May 18, 2016. www.theguardian.com/world/2016/jan/12/anglican-church-england-global-schism-homosexuality-gay-rights.

Shin, Doh Chull, and Russell J. Dalton, eds. 2006. *Citizens, Democracy, and Markets around the Pacific Rim: Congruence Theory and Political Culture.* Oxford: Oxford University Press.

Signorile, Michelangelo. 2003. *Queer in America: Sex, the Media, and the Closets of Power.* Madison: University of Wisconsin Press.

Singletary, Michael W. 1994. *Mass Communication Research: Contemporary Methods and Applications.* New York and London: Longman.

Skupas, Danielle P. 2007. *Contesting Francoist Domestic Ideology: Carmen de Icaza's Mothers and Daughters.* Ann Arbor, MI: ProQuest.

Smith, Christian. 1991. *The Emergence of Liberation Theology: Radical Religion and Social Movement Theory.* Chicago: University of Chicago Press.

Smuts, Letitia. 2011. "Coming Out as a Lesbian in Johannesburg, South Africa: Considering Intersecting Identities and Social Spaces." *South African Review of Sociology* 42 (3): 23–40.

Sniderman, Paul M., Barbara Kaye Wolfinger, Diana C. Mutz, E. James, and Phillip E. Tetlock. 1991. "Values under Pressure: AIDS and Civil Liberties." In *Reasoning and Choice: Explorations in Political Psychology,* edited by P. M. Sniderman and R. A. Brody, 31–57. Cambridge, MA: Cambridge University Press.

Sodomy Laws. n.d. "Sodomy Laws, Malaysia." Retrieved February 12, 2015. www.glapn.org/sodomylaws/world/malaysia/malaysia.htm.

Solsten, Eric, and Sandra W. Meditz, eds. 1990. *Spain: A Country Study.* Area Handbook Series. Washington, DC: Federal Research Division, Library of Congress. Retrieved August 27, 2015. http://oai.dtic.mil/oai/oai?verb = getRecord&metadataPrefix = html&identifier = ADA231407.

Spencer, Robert. 2008. "Complicity in Iran's Anti-Gay Jihad." FrontPageMag.com. Retrieved March 19, 2015. http://archive.frontpagemag.com/readArticle.aspx?ARTID = 30264.

Sprig, Peter. n.d. "Questions and Answers: What's Wrong with Letting Same-Sex Couples 'Marry?'" Family Research Council. Retrieved April 9, 2015. www.frc.org/whats-wrong-with-letting-same-sex-couples-marry.

Stack, Steven, Amy Adamczyk, and Liqun Cao. 2010. "Survivalism and Public Opinion on Criminality: A Cross-National Analysis of Prostitution." *Social Forces* 88 (4): 1703–26.

Stan, Lavinia, and Lucian Turcescu. 2000. "The Romanian Orthodox Church and Post-Communist Democratisation." *Europe-Asia Studies* 52 (8): 1467–88.

Stark, Rodney. 1996a. "Religion as Context: Hellfire and Delinquency One More Time." *Sociology of Religion* 57 (2): 163–73.

———. 1996b. "Why Religious Movements Succeed or Fail: A Revised General Model." *Journal of Contemporary Religion* 11 (2): 133–46.

———. 2003. *One True God: Historical Consequences of Monotheism.* Princeton, NJ: Princeton University Press.

Stark, Rodney, and Roger Finke. 2000. *Acts of Faith: Explaining the Human Side of Religion.* Berkeley: University of California Press.

Stark, Rodney, and Laurence R. Iannaccone. 1994. "A Supply-Side Reinterpretation of the 'Secularization' of Europe." *Journal for the Scientific Study of Religion* 33 (3): 230–52.

———. 1996. "Response to Lechner: Recent Religious Declines in Quebec, Poland, and the Netherlands; A Theory Vindicated." *Journal for the Scientific Study of Religion* 35 (3): 265–71.

———. 1997. "Why the Jehovah's Witnesses Grow So Rapidly: A Theoretical Application." *Journal of Contemporary Religion* 12 (2): 133–57.

Stark, Rodney, Lori Kent, and Daniel P. Doyle. 1982. "Religion and Delinquency: The Ecology of a 'Lost' Relationship." *Journal of Research in Crime and Delinquency* 19 (1): 4–24.

Statista. n.d. "U.S. Higher Education Enrollment Rates from 1970–2012, by Age Group." *Statista.* Retrieved January 26, 2015. www.statista.com/statistics/236093/higher-education-enrollment-rates-by-age-group-us/.

Statistics South Africa. 2004. *Census 2001: Primary Tables South Africa; Census '96 and 2001 Compared.* Pretoria. Retrieved February 16, 2015. www.statssa.gov.za/censuso1/html/RSAPrimary.pdf.

Steel, G., and I. Kabashima. 2008. "Cross-Regional Support for Gender Equality." *International Political Science Review* 29 (2): 133–56.

Steensland, Brian, Jerry Z. Park, Mark D. Regnerus, Lynn D. Robinson, W. Bradford Wilcox, and Robert D. Woodberry. 2000. "The Measure of American

Religion: Toward Improving the State of the Art." *Social Forces* 79 (1): 291–318.

Steiner, Linda, Fred Fejes, and Kevin Petrich. 1993. "Invisibility, Homophobia and Heterosexism: Lesbians, Gays and the Media." *Critical Studies in Mass Communication* 10 (4): 396–422.

Strand, Cecilia. 2012. "Homophobia as a Barrier to Comprehensive Media Coverage of the Ugandan Anti-Homosexual Bill." *Journal of Homosexuality* 59 (4): 564–79.

Štulhofer, Aleksandar, and Ivan Rimac. 2009. "Determinants of Homonegativity in Europe." *Journal of Sex Research* 46 (1): 24–32.

Stycer, Mauricio. 2015. "SBT: Do beijo entre mulheres de 'Amor e Revolução' à 'novela para família.'" UOL. Retrieved May 26, 2016. http://mauriciostycer .blogosfera.uol.com.br/2015/03/22/sbt-do-beijo-entre-mulheres-de-amor-e-revolucao-a-novela-para-familia/.

Suroyo, Gayatri, and Charlotte Greenfield. 2014. "Strict Sharia Forces Gays into Hiding in Indonesia's Aceh." Reuters. Retrieved February 27, 2015. www.reuters.com/article/2014/12/28/us-indonesia-religion-gay-idUSKBN0 K600W20141228.

Sustainable Demographic Dividend. 2011. *Global Family Structure*. Social Trends Institute. Retrieved June 28, 2015. http://sustaindemographicdividend.org /articles/international-family-indicators/global-family-structure.

Sutherland, Edwin H. 1947. *Principles of Criminology*. Chicago: J. B. Lippincott.

Svonkin, Stuart. 1997. *Jews against Prejudice: American Jews and the Fight for Civil Liberties*. New York: Columbia University Press.

Swarr, Amanda Lock, and Richa Nagar. 2004. "Dismantling Assumptions: Interrogating 'Lesbian' Struggles for Identity and Survival in India and South Africa." *Signs* 29 (2): 491–516.

Szalma, Ivett, and Judit Takács. 2013. "How to Measure Homophobia in an International Comparison?" *Družboslovne razprave* (73): 11–42.

Szostkiewicz, Adam. 1999. "Religion after Communism." *Commonweal* 126 (16): 17–19.

Takács, Judit. 2006. *Social Exclusion of Young Lesbian, Gay, Bisexual and Transgender (LGBT) People in Europe*. Brussels: ILGA Europe. Retrieved September 15, 2015. www.presidencia.ccoo.es/comunes/recursos/99922 /doc21162_Report_Social_Excluson.pdf.

Taiwan Alliance to Promote Civil Partnership Rights. 2014. "Draft Bill of the Diverse Family Formation Act" [in Chinese]. Retrieved January 15, 2014. http://tapcpr.wordpress.com/%E4%BC%B4%E4%BE%B6%E7%9B%9F %E8%8D%89%E6%A1%88/%E8%8D%89%E6%A1%88%E7%B0% A1%E4%BB%8B/.

Tallantyre, Steve. 2014. "Spain Rated World's Most Gay-Friendly Country." The Local. Retrieved August 10, 2015. www.thelocal.es/20140422/spain-rated-worlds-most-gay-friendly-country.

Tamale, Sylvia. 2003. "Out of the Closet: Unveiling Sexuality Discourses in Uganda." *Feminist Africa*, no. 2: 42–49.

Tang, Zongli. 1995. "Confucianism, Chinese Culture, and Reproductive Behavior." *Population and Environment* 16 (3): 269–84.

Tanturri, Maria Letizia, and Letizia Mencarini. 2008. "Childless or Childfree? Paths to Voluntary Childlessness in Italy." *Population and Development Review* 34 (1): 51–77.

Tapinc, Huseyin. 1992. "Masculinity, Femininity, and Turkish Male Homosexuality." In *Modern Homosexualities: Fragments of Lesbian and Gay Experience,* edited by Ken Plummer, 39–49. New York: Routledge.

Tatchell, Peter. 1987. "ANC Rejects Gay Rights." *Labour Briefing* 49:14–27.

———. 2005. "The Moment the ANC Embraced Gay Rights." In *Sex & Politics in South Africa,* edited by N. Hoad, K. Martin, and G. Reid, 140–47. Cape Town: Double Storey Books.

Tejeda, Armando G. 1998. "Miles de homosexuales se manifiestan en España por el derecho al matrimonio civil." *El País,* June 28.

Tereškinas, Artūras. 2002. "On the Margins: Representations of Sexual Minorities in Lithuanian Press (2000–01)." *Sociology: Thought and Action* 9 (1): 34–40.

Thomas, Jeremy N., and Daniel V. A. Olson. 2012. "Evangelical Elites' Changing Responses to Homosexuality, 1960–2009." *Sociology of Religion* 73 (3): 239–72.

Thomas, Oliver. 2008. "Yearning for the Truth." *USA Today,* September 22.

Thompson, Dennis F. 1970. *The Democratic Citizen: Social Science and Democratic Theory in the Twentieth Century.* Cambridge: Cambridge University Press.

Thoreson, Ryan Richard. 2008. "Somewhere over the Rainbow Nation: Gay, Lesbian and Bisexual Activism in South Africa." *Journal of Southern African Studies* 34 (3): 679–97.

Thornhill, Ted. 2013. "Gulf States to Introduce Medical Testing on Travellers to 'Detect' Gay People and Stop Them from Entering the Country." Daily Mail Online. Retrieved September 30, 2015. www.dailymail.co.uk/news /article-2449051/Gulf-states-introduce-medical-testing-travellers-detect-gay-people-stop-entering-country.html.

Tiezzi, Shannon. 2013. "Why Taiwan's Allies Are Flocking to Beijing." *Diplomat,* November 19. Retrieved September 15, 2015. http://thediplomat.com /2013/11/why-taiwans-allies-are-flocking-to-beijing/.

Tittle, Charles R., and Michael R. Welch. 1983. "Religiosity and Deviance: Toward a Contingency Theory of Constraining Effects." *Social Forces* 61 (3): 653–82.

Tommasoli, Massimo, Andrea Cornwall, and Andrea Lynch. 2013. *Democracy and Gender Equality: The Role of the UN.* Stockholm: International IDEA; New York: Office of the Permanent Observer for International IDEA to the United Nations. Retrieved May 12, 2014. www.idea.int/publications /democracy-and-gender-equality/loader.cfm?csModule=security/getfile& pageid=59108.

Tong, Goh Chok. 1994. "Social Values, Singapore Style." *Current History* 93 (587): 417–22.

Toumi, Habib. 2013. "Gays 'to Be Barred from Entering Gulf.'" *Gulfnews.* Retrieved September 30, 2015. http://gulfnews.com/news/gulf/kuwait/gays-to-be-barred-from-entering-gulf-1.1240199.

Towns, Ann E. 2012. "Norms and Social Hierarchies: Understanding International Policy Diffusion 'from Below.'" *International Organization* 66 (02): 179–209.

Trading Economics. n.d. "Rural Population in Malaysia." Retrieved February 25, 2015. www.tradingeconomics.com/malaysia/rural-population-wb-data.html.

———. n.d. "Rural Population (% of Total Population) in Indonesia." Retrieved February 25, 2015. www.tradingeconomics.com/indonesia/rural-population-percent-of-total-population-wb-data.html.

Treas, Judith. 2002. "How Cohorts, Education, and Ideology Shaped a New Sexual Revolution on American Attitudes toward Nonmarital Sex, 1972–1998." *Sociological Perspectives* 45 (3): 267–83.

Trent, Katherine, and Scott J. South. 1989. "Structural Determinants of the Divorce Rate: A Cross-Societal Analysis." *Journal of Marriage and Family* 51 (2): 391–404.

Tu, Wei-Ming. 1988. "A Confucian Perspective on the Rise of Industrial East Asia." *Bulletin of the American Academy of Arts and Sciences* 42 (1): 32–50.

Turcescu, Lucian, and Lavinia Stan. 2005. "Religion, Politics and Sexuality in Romania." *Europe-Asia Studies* 57 (2): 291–310.

Turkish Daily News. 2008. "Gay Associations Calls Turkey to Sign Declaration." *Turkish Daily News,* December 22.

Twombly, Eric C. 2002. "Religious versus Secular Human Service Organizations: Implications for Public Policy." *Social Science Quarterly* 83 (4): 947–61.

Uganda Bureau of Statistics. 2012. *Uganda: Demographic and Health Survey, 2011.* Kampala, Uganda. Retrieved May 26, 2016. http://dhsprogram.com/pubs/pdf/FR264/FR264.pdf.

UNESCO Institute for Statistics. n.d. "Education." Retrieved February 28, 2015. http://data.uis.unesco.org/Index.aspx?DataSetCode=EDULIT_DS&popupcustomise=true&lang=en.

United Nations. 2011. *Discriminatory Laws and Practices and Acts of Violence against Individuals Based on Their Sexual Orientation and Gender Identity.* Geneva, Switzerland: Office of the United Nations High Commissioner for Human Rights.

———. 2013. "World Population Prospects: The 2012 Revision; Highlights and Advanced Tables." Department of Economic and Social Affairs, Population Division. Retrieved February 18, 2015. https://esa.un.org/unpd/wpp/publications/Files/WPP2012_HIGHLIGHTS.pdf.

———. 2015. "World Urbanization Prospects: The 2014 Revision." Department of Economic and Social Affairs, Population Division. Retrieved May 26, 2016. http://esa.un.org/unpd/wup/Publications/Files/WUP2014-Report.pdf.

United Nations Development Programme. 2014. "Work for Human Development: Briefing Note for Countries on the 2015 Human Development Report; Brazil." Retrieved May 26, 2016. http://hdr.undp.org/sites/all/themes/hdr_theme/country-notes/BRA.pdf.

———. n.d. "Table 5: Gender Inequality Index." Retrieved January 12, 2015. www.hdr.undp.org/en/content/table-4-gender-inequality-index.

United Nations Population Division. 2009. "World Marriage Data 2008." Retrieved August 30, 2016. www.un.org/en/development/desa/population /publications/dataset/marriage/data.shtml.

U.S. Department of State. 2011. *Indonesia 2010 International Religious Freedom Report.* Retrieved February 27, 2015. www.state.gov/j/drl/rls/irf /2010_5/168356.htm.

U.S. Department of State, Bureau of Democracy, Human Rights and Labor. 2013. *Nigeria 2013 Human Rights Report.* Retrieved May 26, 2016. www .state.gov/documents/organization/220358.pdf.

———. 2014. *Taiwan 2013 Human Rights Report.* Retrieved June 12, 2015. http://ait.org.tw/en/officialtext-ot1402.html.

U.S. Department of State, Bureau of Public Affairs. 2012. "Arrest and Harassment of Gay, Lesbian, and Transgender Activists in Zimbabwe." Retrieved April 29, 2016. www.state.gov/r/pa/prs/ps/2012/08/196864.htm.

Uslaner, Eric M., and Mitchell Brown. 2005. "Inequality, Trust, and Civic Engagement." *American Politics Research* 33 (6): 868–94.

Valiente, C. 2002. "An Overview of Research on Gender in Spanish Society." *Gender & Society* 16 (6): 767–92.

van den Akker, Hanneke, Rozemarijn van der Ploeg, and Peer Scheepers. 2013. "Disapproval of Homosexuality: Comparative Research on Individual and National Determinants of Disapproval of Homosexuality in 20 European Countries." *International Journal of Public Opinion Research* 25 (1): 64–86.

Vatican II—Voice of the Church. n.d. "The Need for Vatican II." Retrieved August 27, 2015. www.vatican2voice.org/2need/need.htm#fn2.

Vergne, J.P. 2011. "Toward a New Measure of Organizational Legitimacy: Method, Validation, and Illustration." *Organizational Research Methods* 14 (3): 484–502.

Vezzoni, Cristiano, and Ferruccio Biolcati-Rinaldi. 2015. "Church Attendance and Religious Change in Italy, 1968–2010: A Multilevel Analysis of Pooled Datasets." *Journal for the Scientific Study of Religion* 54 (1): 100–118.

Vianna, Adriana, and Sérgio Carrara. 2007. "Sexual Politics and Sexual Rights in Brazil: A Case Study." In *SexPolitics: Reports from the Front Lines,* edited by R. Parker, R. Petchesky, and R. Sember, 27–51. Sexual Policy Watch. Retrieved August 26, 2016. www.sxpolitics.org/frontlines/book/pdf/sexpolitics.pdf.

Vicario, Brett A., Becky J. Liddle, and Darrell Anthony Luzzo. 2005. "The Role of Values in Understanding Attitudes toward Lesbians and Gay Men." *Journal of Homosexuality* 49 (1): 145–59.

Villagrasa Alcaide, Carlos. 2005. "Las parejas de hecho: Una realidad con distinto tratamiento." *Cuadernos de derecho judicial* 24:15–66.

Voas, David. 2009. "The Rise and Fall of Fuzzy Fidelity in Europe." *European Sociological Review* 25 (2): 155–68.

Voas, David, and Mark Chaves. 2016. "Is the United States a Counterexample to the Secularization Thesis?" *American Journal of Sociology* 121 (5): 1517–56.

Voas, David, and Alasdair Crockett. 2005. "Religion in Britain: Neither Believing nor Belonging." *Sociology* 39 (1): 11–28.

Vogt, Andrea. 2015. "'We're Next' Says Italy after Irish Gay Marriage Vote." *Telegraph*. Retrieved July 16, 2015. www.telegraph.co.uk/news/worldnews /europe/italy/11627693/Were-next-says-Italy-after-Irish-gay-marriage-vote .html.

Voyé, Liliane, and Karel Dobbelaere. 1994. "Roman Catholicism: Universalism at Stake." In *Religions sans Frontières? Present and Future Trends of Migration, Culture, and Communication*, edited by Roberto Cipriani, 83–113. Rome: Presidenza del Consiglio dei Ministri.

Wang, Frank T. Y., Herng-Dar Bih, and David J. Brennan. 2009. "Have They Really Come Out: Gay Men and Their Parents in Taiwan." *Culture, Health & Sexuality* 11 (3): 285–96.

Ware, Helen Ruth Elizabeth. 1978. *Economic Value of Children in Asia and Africa: Comparative Perspectives*. Honolulu: East-West Center. Retrieved May 19, 2016. http://scholarspace.manoa.hawaii.edu/handle/10125/22646.

Warner, Carolyn M. 2013. "Christian Democracy in Italy: An Alternative Path to Religious Party Moderation." *Party Politics* 19 (2): 256–76.

Warner, R. Stephen. 1993. "Work in Progress toward a New Paradigm for the Sociological Study of Religion in the United States." *American Journal of Sociology* 98 (5): 1044–93.

Wee, Darren. 2014. "First Taiwan Singer Comes Out as Gay." *Gay Star News*. Retrieved June 12, 2015. www.gaystarnews.com/article/first-taiwan-singer-comes-out-gay211114.

Wells, Helen, and Louise Polders. 2006. "Anti-Gay Hate Crimes in South Africa: Prevalence, Reporting Practices, and Experiences of the Police." *Agenda* 20 (67): 20–28.

Welzel, Christian, Ronald Inglehart, and Hans-Dieter Kligemann. 2003. "The Theory of Human Development: A Cross-Cultural Analysis." *European Journal of Political Research* 42 (3): 341–79.

Wen-ting, Tsai. 2002. "The Mixed-Up World of Gender Identity Disorders." *Taiwan Panorama Magazine*. Retrieved September 15, 2015. www.taiwan-panorama.com/en/show_issue.php?id = 2002119111062e.txt&table = 2&cur_ page = 1&distype =.

West, Donald J., and Richard Green, eds. 1997. *Sociolegal Control of Homosexuality: A Multi-Nation Comparison*. New York: Springer Science & Business Media.

Westley, Sidney B. 1995. "Evidence Mounts for Sex-Selective Abortion in Asia." *Asia-Pacific Population & Policy* 34 (May/June): 1–4.

Wheelock, Darren, and Douglas Hartmann. 2007. "Midnight Basketball and the 1994 Crime Bill Debates: The Operation of a Racial Code." *Sociological Quarterly* 48 (2): 315–42.

Whitley, Bernard E., Jr. 2001. "Gender-Role Variables and Attitudes toward Homosexuality." *Sex Roles* 45 (11–12): 691–721.

Whitley, Bernard E., Jr., and Sarah E. Lee. 2000. "The Relationship of Authoritarianism and Related Constructs to Attitudes toward Homosexuality." *Journal of Applied Social Psychology* 30 (1): 144–70.

Wike, Richard A. 2014. "Europeans Hold More Liberal Views on Moral Issues." Pew Research Center. Retrieved April 27, 2016. www.pewresearch

.org/fact-tank/2014/04/16/europeans-hold-more-liberal-views-on-moral-issues/.

Wilkinson, Cai. 2014. "Putting 'Traditional Values' into Practice: The Rise and Contestation of Anti-Homopropaganda Laws in Russia." *Journal of Human Rights* 13 (3): 363–79.

Williams, Walter L. 2009. "Strategies for Challenging Homophobia in Islamic Malaysia and Secular China." *Nebula* 6 (1): 1–20.

Wilson, Bryan. 1968. "Religion and the Churches in Contemporary America." *Religion in America* 62 (6): 771–88.

Wilson, Thomas C. 1985. "Urbanism and Tolerance: A Test of Some Hypotheses Drawn from Wirth and Stouffer." *American Sociological Review* 50 (1): 117–23.

Winter, Sam, Beverley Webster, and Pui Kei Eleanor Cheung. 2008. "Measuring Hong Kong Undergraduate Students' Attitudes towards Transpeople." *Sex Roles* 59 (9): 670–83.

Wiseman, Paul. 2004. "In Taiwan, Not Much Ado over Gays Saying 'I Do.'" USAToday.com. Retrieved June 4, 2015. http://usatoday30.usatoday.com/news/world/2004-02-04-taiwan-gay-marriage_x.htm.

Wong, Yuenmei. 2012. "Islam, Sexuality, and the Marginal Positioning of Pengkids and Their Girlfriends in Malaysia." *Journal of Lesbian Studies* 16 (4): 435–48.

World Bank. 2013a. "GDP per Capita, PPP (Current International $)." Retrieved February 12, 2015. http://data.worldbank.org/indicator/NY.GDP.PCAP.PP.CD.

———. 2013b. "World Development Indicators." Retrieved February 12, 2015. http://data.worldbank.org/data-catalog/world-development-indicators.

———. n.d. "GDP per Capita (current US$) 2011–2015." Retrieved April 8, 2015. http://data.worldbank.org/indicator/NY.GDP.PCAP.CD.

World Bank Development Indicators. 2016. "GDP Growth (Annual %)." Retrieved August 26, 2016. http://data.worldbank.org/indicator/NY.GDP.MKTP.KD.ZG.

World Divorce Statistics. n.d. "World Divorce Statistics: Comparisons among Countries." DIVORCESCIENCE: The Scientific Study of Divorce & Support for Families. Retrieved April 7, 2015. http://divorcescience.org/for-students/world-divorce-statistics-comparisons-among-countries/.

World Resources Institute. n.d. "Economics, Business, and the Environment—GDP: GDP per Capita, Current US Dollars." Retrieved April 17, 2015. www.wri.org/our-work/project/earthtrends-environmental-informationtext/economics-business/variable-638.html.

World Values Survey (WVS). 2015. "World Values Survey Official Aggregate File: 1981–2014." World Values Survey Association. Retrieved August 26, 2016. www.worldvaluessurvey.org/WVSContents.jsp?CMSID=intinfo.

Worthen, Meredith G. F. 2013. "An Argument for Separate Analyses of Attitudes toward Lesbian, Gay, Bisexual Men, Bisexual Women, MtF and FtM Transgender Individuals." *Sex Roles* 68 (11–12): 703–23.

Wright, Teresa. 1999. "Student Mobilization in Taiwan: Civil Society and Its Discontents." *Asian Survey* 39 (6): 986–1008.

Wu, Jing. 2003. "From 'Long Yang' and 'Dui Shi' to Tongzhi: Homosexuality in China." *Journal of Gay & Lesbian Psychotherapy* 7 (1–2): 117–43.

Xu, Xiaohe, and Shu-Chuan Lai. 2004. "Gender Ideologies, Marital Roles, and Marital Quality in Taiwan." *Journal of Family Issues* 25 (3): 318–55.

Yan-chih, Mo. 2005. "Adoption Becoming More Open." *Taipei Times*, August 15. Retrieved September 15, 2015. www.taipeitimes.com/News/taiwan/archives/2005/08/15/2003267800.

Yang, Chung-Chuan. 2000. "The Use of the Internet among Academic Gay Communities in Taiwan: An Exploratory Study." *Information, Communication & Society* 3 (2): 153–72.

Yang, Wen-Shan, and Pei-Chih Yen. 2011. "A Comparative Study of Marital Dissolution in East Asian Societies: Gender Attitudes and Social Expectations towards Marriage in Taiwan, Korea and Japan." *Asian Journal of Social Science* 39 (6): 751–75.

Yen, Cheng-Fang, Shung-Mei Pan, Shu-Ying Hou, Hsiu-Chin Liu, Shu-Jung Wu, Wen-Chiung Yang, and Hsing-Hu Yang. 2007. "Attitudes toward Gay Men and Lesbians and Related Factors among Nurses in Southern Taiwan." *Public Health* 121 (1): 73–79.

Zaharom, Nain. 2014. "The Structure of the Media Industry: Implications for Democracy." In *Democracy in Malaysia: Discourses and Practices*, edited by K. B. T. Khoo and F. Loh, 111–37. New York: Routledge.

Zakaria, Fareed, and Lee Kuan Yew. 1994. "Culture Is Destiny: A Conversation with Lee Kuan Yew." *Foreign Affairs* 73 (2): 109–26.

Index

Printed in Great Britain
by Amazon